A
SINGLE
DOOR

A
SINGLE
DOOR

Social Work with the Families of Disabled Children

Caroline Glendinning

Social Policy Research Unit, University of York

London
ALLEN & UNWIN

Boston   Sydney

Allen & Unwin (Publishers) Ltd,
40 Museum Street, London WC1A 1LU, UK

Allen & Unwin (Publishers) Ltd,
Park Lane, Hemel Hempstead, Herts HP2 4TE, UK

Allen & Unwin, Inc.,
8 Winchester Place, Winchester, Mass. 01890, USA

Allen & Unwin (Australia) Ltd,
8 Napier Street, North Sydney, NSW 2060, Australia

First published in 1986

British Library Cataloguing in Publication Data

Glendinning, Caroline
    A single door: Social work with the families of disabled children.
1. Family social work   2. Handicapped children – Services for
3. Sick children – Services for
I. Title
362.853   HV697
ISBN 0–04–361060–9
ISBN 0–04–361061–7 Pbk

HV
888
·G47
1986

Library of Congress Cataloging-in-Publication Data

Glendinning, Caroline, 1950–
    A single door.
Bibliography: p.
Includes index.
1. Handicapped children – Services for.   2. Family social work.
3. Social work with handicapped children.
I. Title.
HV88.G47   1986   362.44726   85–15740
ISBN 0–04–361060–9 (alk. paper)
ISBN 0–04–361061–7 (pbk. : alk. paper)

Set in 10 on 11 point Imprint by Computape (Pickering) Ltd
and printed in Great Britain by Billing and Sons Ltd,
London and Worcester

To Alison, Janet, Kathleen, Lynne and Ruth

Contents

List of Tables   *page* xiii

List of Figures   xv

Acknowledgements   xvii

**Chapter 1 'Community Care', Specialization and
Evaluation: Current Issues in Social Services and
Social Work**   1
'Community care': the growing demand   1
The debate about specialization   5
Evaluation and effectiveness   7
The resource worker project   10

**Chapter 2 'Community Care': The Case of Severely
Disabled Children**   12
Research background   12
Disabled children and their families: the policy context   14
The resource worker project   18

Chapter 3 Setting up the Project   22
The resource workers and the intervention   22
The research design and methods   25
Meeting the families   31

Chapter 4 Inputs: the Role of a Specialist Social Worker   37
Establishing working relationships   37
The intervention of the resource workers   41
The resource workers' perspectives on the intervention   64
Immediate outcomes   68

Chapter 5 Outcomes: the Parents' Views   71
'Consumer' opinion in social work research   71
The help received from the resource workers   72
Parents' voices   81
Retrospective reflections   86

**Chapter 6 Outcome Measures 1: Disability and
Day to Day Practical Care**   89
Disability, handicap and health care   90
The personal care of the disabled child   95

Giving extra attention and supervision 105
Practical problems at home 108
Getting about outside the home 114

Chapter 7 Outcome Measures 2: Homes and Gardens 123
Moving house 125
Adaptations to the home 127
Outside the house 132
Conclusions 132
Appendix   George Jackson 133
                    Caroline Barton 138

**Chapter 8 Outcome Measures 3: Education, Leisure
and Respite Care** 142
Educational issues 142
Leaving school and after 148
Educational equipment and toys 151
Leisure 152
Respite care 158

**Chapter 9 Outcome Measures 4: Financial Problems,
Welfare Benefits and the Family Fund** 161
Disability benefits 162
Supplementary benefit 166
Help from the Family Fund 169
The alleviation of financial worries 170

**Chapter 10 Outcome Measures 5: The Impact on
Families and Carers** 172
Relationships within the family 172
Who cares? 176
The impact on carers 178

Chapter 11 Conclusions: Issues for Evaluation 185
The intervention and its outcomes 185
Interpretation: the research context 192
The development of evaluative research 196

Chapter 12 Implementation: Issues for Policy 199
Recent policy developments 199
The resource worker project and policy: the development
of the key worker role 201
The key worker role and future policy 204

Appendix A   Briefing the resource workers   207

Appendix B   A note on
statistical testing   210

References   211

Index   216

List of Tables

		page
3.1	Summary of changes in the samples	29
3.2	Principal handicapping conditions of the children	32
3.3	Social class of head of household	33
3.4	Economic activity of mothers	34
3.5	Parents' knowledge of social services	35
4.1	Resource worker group families' contacts with other welfare professionals at the start of the project	38
4.2	Resource workers' contacts with health services personnel	57
4.3	Resource workers' contacts with welfare and personal social services	58
4.4	Resource workers' contacts with education, training and employment services	59
4.5	Resource workers' contacts with housing and planning services	60
4.6	Resource workers' contacts with sources of financial help	60
4.7	Resource workers' contacts with specialist voluntary organizations	61
5.1	The most important feature of the resource workers' intervention	81
7.1	Moving house as a solution to earlier housing problems or anticipated problems	127
9.1	Help received from Family Fund before and during the project	169

List of Figures

page

4.1 Intervention connected with child's disability, handicap and medical health care 44

4.2 Intervention connected with education, short-term and residential care facilities 46

4.3 Intervention connected with recreation and leisure opportunities 48

4.4 Intervention connected with practical problems of daily care 50

4.5 Intervention to resolve housing problems and to obtain adaptations and equipment for the home 53

4.6 Intervention in connection with family finances 55

4.7 Total amount of time spent by resource workers on different types of problem 63

5.1 Help received from resource workers in connection with child's disability and medical care 73

5.2 Help received from resource workers in connection with child's day to day care and development 74

5.3 Help received from resource workers in obtaining aids, equipment, or suitable housing 75

5.4 Help received from resource workers in dealing with financial problems and benefits 76

5.5 Help received from resource workers with liaison and advocacy, family problems and personal counselling 77

5.6 Proportions of families who received a little, a fair amount and a great deal of help of different kinds 78

5.7 Overall score of total amounts of help received from the resource workers 79

6.1 Use of incontinence equipment and its supply from the authorities 104

6.2 Help received from authorities with clothing, bedding and footwear 112

6.3 Ownership of telephones among families needing a telephone because of their child's disability 113

7.1 Current and anticipated housing problems at the start of the project 124

7.2 Adaptations carried out or planned during the project 131

10.1 Practical help and moral support received from relatives and friends 178

10.2 Number of people to whom mothers could turn to discuss problems 181

Acknowledgements

The completion of all great works, and even more the lesser ones, depends upon the labour, help and goodwill of very many more people than the conventional system of formal authorship actually recognizes. The following acknowledgements can only hint at the depth of my gratitude to those who helped me write this book.

The research described in this book was commissioned by the Department of Health and Social Security, and was jointly funded by the DHSS and the Joseph Rowntree Memorial Trust. Within the DHSS the encouragement of Gerard Bebb helped the project to be established, while Jeremy Metters, Phoebe Hall and the late Jean Browning showed a continuing interest in its progress and outcomes. Lewis Waddilove, then Director of the Joseph Rowntree Memorial Trust, Eleanor Barnes and other staff at the Family Fund gave much encouragement and practical help.

Crucial to the success of the project were the expertise and commitment of the five resource workers Janet Bower, Lynne Hutchinson, Kathleen Morgan, Alison Robertson and Ruth Truett. Their conscientiousness, determination and enthusiasm for the project never flagged during the long fieldwork period. Derek Spicer, Beryl Davies, Rita Hartigan and Ian Booth of the Yorkshire Divisional Office of Dr Barnardo's gave encouragement to the research team, practical help and support to the resource workers, and hospitality to everyone at the bi-monthly project meetings. Thanks must go as well to the very many people in the local authorities, health services and voluntary organizations whose co-operation and support helped to make the resource workers' job pleasant and rewarding.

The evaluation of the project also involved many people. Evelyn Fernando and Jean Morton Williams at Social and Community Planning Research assisted in the design of the interview schedules. The two sets of interviews, before and after the intervention, were carried out by interviewers from SCPR. Clerical assistance with selecting the samples for the study, and with editing and coding the interview schedules, was given by Jill Freeman, Edwina Goodwin, Pamela Horsfield and Lesley Bradshaw.

The help of colleagues in the Social Policy Research Unit has been invaluable. Thanks must go to Jonathan Bradshaw, to Michael Hirst for statistical advice and to Sally Baldwin for reading and commenting on an earlier draft of this book. Very special words of thanks must go to Dot Lawton, who was closely involved in every stage of the research and who, with unfailing patience and good humour, carried out all the computation and statistical analysis of the results. Her contribution has been immense and, quite literally, irreplaceable.

Special thanks must also go to Beverley Searle, Anne Jackson and, in particular, Su Wompra, who made the preparation of the manuscript a far less tedious and nerve-racking business than it could have been. Thanks are also due to Woof Clarke for doing more than his share of child care, and to Amy for tolerating my absence, during this book's preparation.

Above all, very grateful thanks must go to all the families who took part in the project. For some of them it is hoped that their contact with one of the resource workers was some recompense for agreeing to take part in two lengthy interviews; but to all of them I am deeply indebted.

CHAPTER 1

'Community Care', Specialization and Evaluation: Current Issues in Social Services and Social Work

This book has three major themes. First, it is about the provision of care in 'the community' for a group of children who, because of physical or mental disablement, are more than normally dependent on others for physical and social care. Specifically it describes an experiment to try to improve the level, quality and delivery of care to those children and to their parents who look after them from day to day.

Secondly, the book arises from, and forms part of, a continuing debate about the relative degrees of genericism and specialization which are appropriate or desirable within social work practice and the organization of social services. Thirdly – and underscoring these first two themes – it is concerned with evaluation. Innovative developments in social services delivery or practice need systematic evaluation of their effectiveness – the more so nowadays if the deployment of additional resources is to be justified. But the criteria by which that effectiveness can be judged may not easily be agreed on. For example, 'success' can mean different things to different people: professionals, clients and resource-allocating politicians may take it to signify very different kinds of outcome. Furthermore, the criteria used to evaluate the effectiveness of one kind of social work intervention may prove inappropriate for other interventions which have different goals or use different methods.

These three themes converge in the subject of this book, which is an account of the establishment, implementation and evaluation of an experimental specialist support service for families caring at home for a severely disabled child. However, before this account begins, these three interweaving themes are discussed in more detail; first of all, in general terms, and then, in Chapter 2, with specific reference to recent policies and current provision for children with severe physical or mental disabilities.

'Community Care': the Growing Demand

The Changing Meaning of 'Community Care'

There is nothing particularly new about 'community care'. There have

1

always been groups of people who, because of age, physical impairment, or mental handicap, are dependent to some degree on others for help with domestic, self-care, or other personal tasks; and the provision of that help outside the context of large-scale formal institutions is by no means a recent development. For people with mental handicaps, for example, a policy of 'community' care (as an alternative to care in large segregated institutions) appears to have originated around the turn of the century (Jones, 1960). The emphasis on this goal was strengthened in successive policy statements and legislation: by 1957 the Royal Commission on the Law Relating to Mental Illness and Mental Deficiency was recommending a firm shift from hospital to 'community'-based care. The commission also recommended the specific use of the term 'community care' to replace 'supervision' (Jones, Brown and Bradshaw, 1978). In contrast, the 'community care' of children unable for social reasons to live with their own families appears to have emerged somewhat later, following the Curtis Committee Report of 1946 and the subsequent 1948 Children's Act (Walker, 1982).

As the term 'community care' has come to be used in an increasing number of contexts it has taken on a variety of different meanings. Indeed it has been suggested that both the durability and the attractiveness of the phrase owe much to 'its manipulation to encompass the widest possible range of institutions – it is all things to all politicians and policy makers' (ibid., p. 19). In the context of policies for people with mental handicaps, for example, 'community care' has generally described the transfer of those not in need of medical treatment from large, isolated hospitals to smaller units of accommodation – hostels, group homes and 'core and cluster' schemes. Various joint finance initiatives between health authorities, local authority social services departments and voluntary organizations have been developed to encourage and facilitate these moves. For children in local authority care, 'community care' has meant the growing use of small-scale, family group sized homes and, increasingly, fostering and adoption schemes to provide care with private families. In contrast, 'community care' for elderly people typically denotes a policy of encouraging them to remain in their *own* homes for as long as possible; or if that is impracticable, in the home of a child or other close relative.

Despite the varying contexts in which the term 'community care' has been used and the different policies to which it has been applied, there has been, at least until recently, a widespread consensus of opinion underpinning the promotion of 'community care' as a policy goal. 'Care in the community' is desirable because long-term residence in a large segregated institution is universally held to be detrimental to the social, emotional, psychological and sometimes even physical interests of a dependent elderly or disabled person. It is therefore far more beneficial to remain at home, or in the home of close family members. For example, the 1954–7 Royal Commission on the Law Relating to Mental Illness and Mental Deficiency asserted that 'the sense of belonging may be of great importance to the patient. It is not always in his best interests to remove him from a not entirely satisfactory home to even the best run foster home or public institution'. Later research into the quality of accommodation and treatment in institutional settings (Townsend, 1962; Morris, 1969; Oswin, 1971; Goffman, 1974), and a series of public outcries over conditions in long-stay hospitals (DHSS, 1969; 1971), all reinforced this consensus view. By 1971 a White Paper on services for people with mental handicaps stated categorically that 'Each handicapped person should live with his own family as long as this does not impose an undue burden on them or him' (HMSO, 1971, para. 40).

More recently, however, another justification for the promotion of 'community care' has emerged: that of financial expediency. Since the mid-1970s policy statements and politicians have argued that the welfare state is no longer able to bear the costs not only of expensive institutional care but also of a comprehensive network of supportive welfare services for the many dependent people who live outside formal institutional settings. The rapidly growing numbers of elderly and very elderly people in the population have increased the strength of the financial arguments. There are at present about 3 million people aged 75 and over, and this number is likely to increase by another 0·5 million by 1990 (CSO, 1980). Increases are also expected by the end of the century in the numbers of people of all ages who have appreciable or severe handicaps, although the largest increases will again be among the elderly and very elderly (EOC, 1982).

Popular beliefs about the breakdown of traditional family responsibilities (see, for instance, Moroney, 1976) have added moral overtones to these fiscal imperatives. For example, a 1981 White Paper on policies for elderly people asserted that 'Providing adequate support and care for elderly people in all their varying circumstances is a matter which concerns – and should involve – the whole community ... Public authorities simply will not command the resources to deal with it alone' (HMSO, 1981, paras 9–11). 'Community care' has thus come to mean more than just the movement of former hospital patients to smaller local units; or the provision of domiciliary services for elderly people living alone. Increasingly 'community care' is also about the care of growing numbers of elderly and disabled people for whom institutional provision or comprehensive domiciliary services are simply not available on any comparable scale. This has led to an increasingly explicit reliance upon relatives, friends and neighbours to provide most or all of the help needed by physically or socially dependent people.

Of course, it has been pointed out that families, neighbours and friends have always provided the vast proportion of such care (Goldberg and Connelly, 1982; Family Policy Studies Centre, 1984). The only change has been the official acknowledgement of this fact by politicians, policy-makers and service providers, with the further acknowledgement that these 'informal' carers will be relied upon increasingly in the future.

The changing meaning of 'community care' has had implications for the provision and delivery of personal social services and for the focus of social work intervention, and these are now discussed in turn.

The Implementation of 'Community Care': Developments in Social Work

As the meaning of 'community care' has altered, so have the measures designed to *implement* that policy. Throughout the 1950s and 1960s the planning of social care provision was principally concerned with the levels of domiciliary and other welfare services needed by elderly or dependent people living outside formal institutional settings (see, for example, HMSO, 1966; 1971). As Walker (1982, p. 8) points out, both social policy and social services, because of their preoccupation with professional social work, largely ignored 'those who actually carry out practical caring tasks . . . particularly . . . the role of kin in providing care'.

However, as noted above, the role of 'informal' carers – those relatives, friends and neighbours who are increasingly being called upon to carry responsibility for the provision of day to day care – has begun to attract attention. This has led to some debate about the appropriate relationship between informal carers and the formally organized statutory and voluntary services. On the one hand, there are explicit assertions that social services provision should be secondary to (and, implicitly, less important than) the help given by informal carers: 'It is the role of public authorities to sustain and, where necessary, develop – but never to displace – such support and care' (HMSO, 1981, para. 1.9). This line of argument was developed by the Barclay Committee of Inquiry into the role and functions of social workers (NISW, 1982).

The Barclay Working Party took as its starting-point the assumption that the major proportion of social care is provided not by the formally organized statutory or voluntary social services, but 'by ordinary people . . . who may be linked into informal caring networks in their communities' (ibid., pp. 199–200). But the demands and stresses of providing care can render those 'informal caring networks' vulnerable and fragile. The Barclay Working Party therefore argued that 'If social work policy and practice were directed more to the support and strengthening of informal networks, to caring for the carers . . . it is likely that the need for . . . referrals would be reduced' (ibid., p. 200). The focus of social work intervention and the role of social workers should therefore be 'to enable, empower, support and encourage, but not usually to take over from, social networks' (ibid., p. 209).

On the other hand, the stresses and strains which can be experienced by informal carers are increasingly being recognized. In the light of these sometimes substantial personal costs of 'community care' it is argued that formal welfare organizations have a crucially important role to play. Far from undermining or displacing networks of informal care, direct intervention and the provision of services such as day care, overnight respite care, domiciliary help and practical equipment can actually help to prevent the breakdown of informal care arrangements. For example, Levin, Sinclair and Gorbach (1986) found that the services received by a sample of supporters of confused elderly people reduced the supporters' levels of stress, enabled them to continue caring and lowered the chances of the elderly person being admitted to hospital.

The same broad approach seems to be reflected in a current Department of Health and Social Security Social Work Service Development Group initiative, begun during 1982. The Development Group began from the premiss that 'most care in the community is provided not by formal services but by family and to a lesser extent friends and neighbours' (DHSS, 1983a, p. 5). The group has, however, recognized that direct intervention and practical help from voluntary and statutory sources is essential if informal carers are to be prevented from carrying an excessive – and ultimately crippling – burden of care. It has therefore tried to promote an awareness of the needs of carers, disseminated information about local statutory and voluntary services and promoted models of 'good practice', albeit without the addition of any extra financial resources (DHSS, 1983b, 1983c, 1984).

The Debate about Specialization

Running parallel to the changing profile of informal carers in the provision of 'community care', there has been a continuing debate about specialization in social services organization and, particularly, in social work practice. The recommendations of the Seebohm Committee (1968) on the organization of the personal social services led to the unification, in a single organization, of three formerly separate welfare departments: those responsible for child care, mental welfare and old people's welfare. While this resulted in a broad family and community-oriented organizational framework, rather than a fragmented and problem-oriented one, the reorganization of the personal social services had other consequences which have been more problematic. One of these was that many former specialist workers in the fields of child care, mental health and welfare work with elderly or chronically ill people became generic workers, with caseloads containing a wide diversity of clients and problems. As Hall (1976, p. 129) has observed, 'this element of the Seebohm Committee's recommendations was perhaps the most misunderstood part of the report and the section most open to subsequent misquotation. The Committee suggested that ... one social worker should take primary responsibility for each case, not that every social worker should be able to deal with any eventuality.' The loss of specialist skills and experience was, however, not just a temporary transitional phenomenon; generic caseloads underpinned by generic social work training still form the foundations of most contemporary social work practice.

Nevertheless, there have been some moves to reintroduce specialization, to various degrees and in different forms; according to tasks, methods of working, or 'client' groups. Sometimes this reflects formal management policy, with the establishment of special administrative and practitioner posts; more frequently it just reflects the particular interests of individual social workers who have managed to develop an informal specialization or 'bias' in their caseloads (Stevenson, Parsloe and Hill, 1978; Hill, 1980).

Initially the reintroduction of some specialized social work practice, particularly when this was done as a matter of formal policy, was prompted by the low morale reported among generic workers. Increasingly, however, concern about the quality of the professional service given to particular groups of clients has stimulated the arguments in favour of a greater degree of specialization. In particular, considerable scepticism has been expressed about whether social workers with generic caseloads can become sufficiently knowledgeable about the relatively specialized problems experienced by adults and children with disabilities, and hence whether they are able to provide appropriate and useful information, advice and support (CCETSW, 1974; Snowdon Working Party, 1976).

A particularly trenchant argument for increased specialization in the organization and delivery of the personal social services was made by Pinker in a dissenting statement on the Barclay Working Party Report (NISW, 1982, appendix B). Pinker argued that one of the most serious flaws in the report was its neglect of specialized skills and knowledge and their role in social work practice; such expertise was effectively relegated to a residual one. On the contrary, Pinker argued, there are major features of social services departments' activities whose effectiveness depends upon specialization of some kind. As far as individual social workers are concerned the development of expertise depends upon continuous experience 'on a basis of specialization'. Secondly, the organization of social services' activities as a whole needs both 'an orderly internal division of labour' and liaison with external services to be 'based on specialized expertise' (ibid., pp. 249–52). Pinker cited in support of his argument the recurrent complaints from people with disabilities, among others, that most social workers lacked sufficient specialized knowledge and experience. Furthermore, the consensus of evidence to the Barclay Working Party from the courts, the medical services and voluntary organizations all, according to Pinker, pointed to the need for a greater degree of specialization within social services.

Research into the organization of work within social services teams confirmed that, while informal specialization (or 'bias' towards working with a particular client group) within the framework of a generic caseload was relatively common, formal specialization by client group was rare. As a result, the researchers concluded that 'those specialists who do exist seem, quite frankly, to be muddling through without a clear idea of their role and function' (Stevenson, Parsloe and Hill, 1978, p. 189). The specific implications of this relative lack of specialization for the levels and quality of the services received by disabled children and their families will be discussed further in Chapter 2. But the degree of specialization or genericism in the organization and delivery of social services may also have implications for their effectiveness. The evaluation of that effectiveness is the third major theme of this book, to which the discussion now turns.

Evaluation and Effectiveness

One common factor has underlaid both the growing interest in 'community' and informal care and the continuing debates about specialization, and furthermore has exerted a clear influence on the direction of both concerns. This factor is the restriction on public spending on the personal social services, which over the last decade has become increasingly stringent.

The recommendations of the Seebohm Committee, with its unwavering assumption of continuing economic growth, reflected the expansionist ethos of the late 1960s when there 'was international concern to increase spending on social services in a more positive, promotional manner' (Algie, 1980, p. 181). The implementation of these recommendations, together with other contemporary legislation such as the 1970 Chronically Sick and Disabled Persons Act, required a sudden massive expansion in the operations of the personal social services. In addition, the publicity surrounding the post-Seebohm reorganization increased public knowledge of the services available, while the creation of unified social services departments helped to improve access to them (Hall, 1976). As a result of all these factors, expenditure on the personal social services increased dramatically between 1972/3 and 1974/5 (Stevenson, 1980, p. 155).

However, with the publication in 1976 of a White Paper on public expenditure (HMSO, 1976, pp. 92–3), there began a period of retrenchment which has continued – with increasing severity – ever since (Webb and Wistow, 1982). The rate of growth in public expenditure on the personal social services has been sharply reduced, and service providers have had to abandon their earlier 'uncritical faith in the effectiveness of social work' (Stevenson, 1980, p. 174). Instead there have developed on social services managers and social work practitioners increasing pressures to evaluate the effectiveness of their interventions – and to demonstrate that effectiveness to politicians and public alike.

Early attempts to evaluate the impact of social work intervention were on the whole disappointing and failed to demonstrate any unequivocally positive outcomes. However, these early studies have been criticized (Goldberg, 1984) for their lack of clear aims and hypotheses; for their failure to identify the particular needs of specific 'client' groups; and for the absence of any precise description of the social work 'input' – what social workers actually did with and on behalf of their clients.

In comparison, more recent evaluative studies, such as those reviewed by Reid and Hanrahan (1981), are characterized by far more explicit, organized intervention programmes, designed to achieve relatively specific goals with circumscribed target groups. Such studies have on the whole demonstrated that intervention carried out by social workers can be effective, especially structured intervention which is directed towards changing specific problems, behaviours, or social skills. However, Reid and Hanrahan do call into question the limited scope of some of these interventions as well as the practical significance and durability of the changes they effect.

More generally, although a social work programme may be demonstrably effective in one setting, it may be wholly inappropriate and of no value whatsoever in another: 'The indiscriminate application of one type of intervention to almost any problem situation is like dispensing aspirin for all ills' (Goldberg, 1984, p. 1). For example, the type of task-centred, behavioural-contracting intervention which apparently proved successful in the studies reviewed by Reid and Hanrahan (1981) may have only limited relevance to the long-term and relatively intractable difficulties of disabled or dependent people and their carers.

As well as questioning whether a particular type of intervention is appropriate for a specific problem, critical questions also need to be asked about the appropriateness of outcome measures and criteria of 'success'. An intervention programme which sets out to change certain deviant or unpleasant behaviours, for instance, could clearly be regarded as successful if those behaviour patterns actually did change – the more so if the changes persisted over an extended period. However, such behavioural criteria are, equally clearly, irrelevant for establishing the success of other types of intervention.

Economic constraints, as well as increasing the pressures for more systematic evaluation of social work intervention, can also lead to the adoption of inadequate or inappropriate criteria. As Goldberg and Connelly (1981, p. 314) warn, it can be tempting in times of economic stringency to equate 'effectiveness' with 'cost effectiveness'. For example, it may be possible to demonstrate that a particular service development, such as the 'community care' of severely disabled young children or adults, is cost effective because it leads to reduced public spending on expensive residential accommodation in hospitals, homes and hostels. But a comprehensive measure of effectiveness would also need to take account of any increased physical, social, emotional and financial costs being carried by those relatives, neighbours and friends now providing substantial amounts of care on an informal basis.

As far as the evaluation of informal care and the support of informal carers are concerned there have to date been few initiatives whose effectiveness has been systematically evaluated. For example, very few of the innovative schemes in either the statutory or voluntary sectors which have been publicized by the DHSS Social Work Service Development Group have been monitored or evaluated (DHSS, 1983c, 1984). One major contribution to the evaluation of this type of intervention has been that of the Kent Community Care scheme, which aims to mobilize extra help to maintain in 'the community' frail and isolated elderly people who might otherwise require costly residential care (Challis and Davies, 1980). Few of the Kent clients had relatives or friends who were already providing informal care; but the subsequent replication of the Kent project in Gateshead has included many more elderly people living near, or with, their relations. Early evaluation of the Gateshead scheme indicates that it too has succeeded in preventing the admission to residential care of frail elderly people, but that it has also succeeded in generating additional resources so as to relieve informal carers of some of their former burdens of care (Challis, Luckett and Chessum, 1983).

Attention has already been drawn to the growing numbers of people who will be dependent on others for some degree of personal or social care. In view of the continuing economic and political commitments to non-institutional, community-based 'informal' care the issue of how best to support those relatives and friends who will actually provide this care is a critical one for social policy and social services. This task is likely to absorb more and more welfare and personal social services resources in the coming decades. At the same time, other political and economic pressures are likely to subject the provision of social services and the activities of social workers to continuing critical scrutiny. Evaluation is therefore of crucial importance. What particular kinds of help are most needed by informal carers? What kinds of intervention, according to various criteria, appear to be most successful? Are some methods of providing services more or less effective or appreciated than others?

The Resource Worker Project

The resource worker project – the subject of this book – is directly linked to the three foregoing issues of 'community care', specialization and evaluation. Specifically it was designed to provide support and practical help to a group of informal carers looking after people with long-term physical and social dependencies – in this instance severely disabled children and their families. Secondly, it aimed to do this through the intervention of social workers with a specialized knowledge base, expertise and caseload. And thirdly, it subjected the intervention to rigorous evaluation in order to assess its effectiveness: partly by recording in detail and analysing the content of the intervention (the 'inputs' to the project); partly by asking parents to assess the extent and ways in which the intervention had been of help to them; and partly by comparing the circumstances of the families visited by the specialist workers with those of a matched comparison group who received no such specialist intervention. (These latter two aspects of the evaluation represent the 'outcomes' of the intervention.)

The focus of the project were specialist workers – the 'resource workers' – who aimed to provide information, advice and support to the carers of children with severe disabilities. From the carers' (more precisely, the parents') point of view the resource worker would, it was hoped, become a single, easily identifiable person to whom they could turn for help with *any* problem arising from the care of their child. From the perspective of the various statutory and voluntary health, welfare and other professional agencies the resource worker would be a kind of 'key worker', co-ordinating the activities of different organizations and, if necessary, liaising between them and the families.

In Chapters 2 and 3 the details of the project will be described: first, the policy and research contexts which focused concern on the support received by severely disabled children and their carers; and secondly, the detailed aims of the project itself. Chapter 3 goes on to describe the establishment and operation of the support service, and the research design and methods which were used to evaluate it. Chapter 4 summarizes the 'inputs' of the service – the types and range of activities which the resource workers carried out together with, and on behalf of, the disabled children and their families. Chapters 5–10 analyse the 'outcomes' of the project: first (in Chapter 5), the subjective assessments by parents of the immediate and long-term usefulness of the help given by the resource workers are presented; and subsequently (in Chapters 6–10) the impact of the resource workers' help, as indicated by a number of other criteria, is discussed. Finally, in Chapters 11 and 12 the implications of the project are discussed, both for the evaluation of this kind of social work intervention and for the development of policies to support informal carers.

CHAPTER 2

'Community Care': the Case of Severely Disabled Children

Research Background

The vast majority of children with physical or mental disabilities are cared for in 'the community' – at home, by their parents – throughout their childhood and, increasingly, into adult life. Yet until the early 1970s very little was known about their social, non-medical needs, or about the needs of their parents and other relatives who cared for them. Children under 16 had been excluded from the last government survey of handicapped and impaired people (Harris, Cox and Smith, 1971), thus impeding the collection of even rudimentary national data on their numbers and on the causes and severity of their disabilities. However, the establishment of the Family Fund in 1972 to 'ease the burden of living' in households containing very severely disabled children created an unprecedented opportunity to explore some of the problems and needs of disabled children and their families, and to assess the various contributions of the statutory and voluntary health and welfare services to relieving these problems (Bradshaw, 1980).

Applications and letters to the Family Fund, and a number of research studies of Family Fund applicants, revealed a wide range of unmet needs. Broadly many parents did not appear to be receiving either a coherent or comprehensive pattern of support from professional or informal sources. For the most part parents came to terms with the diagnosis of their child's disability with little or no skilled counselling help; they seemed to continue to cope with a minimum of practical or moral support from outside the immediate family; and they met many of their child's special needs from their own resources. If parents learned about services or cash benefits which were available, it was often accidentally or through their own efforts – and actually obtaining such help was sometimes only achieved after considerable frustration and delay (Glendinning, 1983; Baldwin, 1985). For example, one commonly used indicator of the support received by the families of children with disabilities is the frequency of their contacts with community-based professionals such as health visitors and social workers. A 1975 random sample survey of 303 Family Fund applicants found that only 11 per cent of parents reported having contact with a social worker as often as once every four months; for 75 per cent of the families, such contact was non-existent, or initiated by parents themselves only when a particular problem or crisis arose. Only 8 per cent of the parents reported seeing a health visitor at least three times a year. Even among the sixty-one parents whose disabled child was currently under 5, this proportion only rose to 20 per cent, while a further 20 per cent of parents said that they had been seen by a health visitor no more than once since their disabled child's birth (Bradshaw, Glendinning and Baldwin, 1977).

A smaller in-depth study of a number of Family Fund applicants found that parents generally felt isolated and without adequate support (Glendinning, 1983). Their contacts with service-providing agencies and professionals tended to be irregular, infrequent and lacking in continuity. Parents consistently pointed out how the onus lay with them to initiate such contacts as and when they felt they needed to. This often caused them considerable difficulty. Parents were reluctant to be seen to need help, and were unsure about how that expressed need would be judged by professionals and administrative officials. They were handicapped by their own ignorance of the range of services potentially available; and they found it stressful to have to present their needs and circumstances repeatedly to different people whom they did not know, and who sometimes had little understanding of childhood disability. As one father in this study commented:

You see mothers with children who ... don't know anything because nobody's ever bothered telling them. I think it would be a big help if we didn't have to fight and argue and demand every little service. Very often you go for something, and you don't know specifically what there is anyway, and unless you ask for a specific thing they won't tell you. (ibid., p. 235)

Other contemporary research findings supported this view that disabled children and their parents generally failed to receive adequate support, information and advice. For example, a 1970 National Children's Bureau Working Party canvassed information from parents of disabled children, and thereby revealed 'injustices, hardships and deficiencies of which the authorities may be only remotely aware' (Younghusband *et al.*, 1970, p. 31). A survey of London parents of disabled children found that most 'keenly felt the lack of a single committed professional who was able to combine effective advice over practical difficulties with some degree of insight into the social demands and emotional realities of their situation' (Fox, 1974, p. 3). A study of 255 severely mentally and physically disabled children living in the Bristol area found that 49 per cent of their mothers had not seen a social worker during the preceding year, and only 42 per cent reported having received advice or practical help from the social services department in the previous two years (Pomeroy *et al.*, 1978). A comparison of the help received by the parents of mentally handicapped children in Leeds and Sheffield revealed that less than one-half of the families in either city had had any social work contact during the previous two years; many parents said that they would like more advice and support (Armstrong, Race and Race, 1979). Finally, a study of the needs of families with mentally handicapped children in Northern Ireland found most parents totally unprepared for the tasks they faced in helping their child to maximize her or his independence, and the response of social workers and other professionals to be too routine and passive to meet families' multiple needs (Browne, 1982).

These studies were carried out by research workers from a variety of disciplinary backgrounds. They investigated children with a wide range of physical, mental and multiple disabilities, who lived with their families in a number of different health and local authority areas. Yet their findings are in broad agreement with each other, and with the findings of the Family Fund research. Why were the services for this group of informal carers and their dependants apparently so inadequate?

Disabled Children and their Families: the Policy Context

The needs of disabled children and their families in Britain have by no means been overlooked during the last fifteen years. The public debate following the thalidomide tragedy in the early 1970s succeeded in drawing widespread attention to the needs of all children with severe handicaps and resulted, *inter alia*, in the establishment of the Family Fund and a Royal Commission on Civil Liability and Compensation for Personal Injury (Bradshaw, 1980). Within the health services there was a rapid growth of multi-disciplinary child development and assessment centres. The entire spectrum of health services for children, including those for children with disabilities, was the subject of an extensive inquiry by the Court Committee (1976). Local projects initiated by psychologists and other therapists which aimed to involve parents in the use of behaviour modification teaching programmes with their developmentally delayed children also expanded markedly during this period (Pugh, 1981).

Within the statutory educational services special schools developed from the former junior training centres for mentally handicapped children run by local health departments. The educational needs and assessment of children with special problems were examined by the Warnock Committee of Inquiry (1978); and limited moves gradually have been made towards the educational integration of disabled children (Hegarty and Pocklington, 1981).

At the same time, the additional financial costs of childhood disability were recognized and to some extent provided for through the social security system. Children of 2 and over were included in the attendance allowance scheme, while the mobility allowance became payable to children over the age of 4. Within the personal social services children have been among those to benefit from the provisions of the 1970 Chronically Sick and Disabled Persons Act. Both statutory and voluntary welfare organizations have played an important part in the growth of a wide range of holiday and respite care facilities (DHSS, 1983c, 1984).

However, despite these important developments, significant problems clearly existed. These arose primarily from the fact that services for disabled children and their families remained widely fragmented between a number of organizations and professionals, varying according to the child's age, disability and family circumstances. During a disabled child's early years parents might, for example, come into contact with hospital and community-based medical services, health visitors, psychologists, speech therapists and physiotherapists; nursery, 'opportunity group' and special school education services; hospital and community-based social workers and occupational therapists; the Family Fund; specialist voluntary organizations; and the local and national offices of the Department of Health and Social Security for various disability-related cash benefits. Later parents and young people might add specialist careers officers, disablement resettlement officers and adult training centre and further education staff to their list of contacts.

This fragmentation had three important consequences. The first arose from the fact that the various professional and administrative workers who provided services, in person or in kind, operated from within a specific organizational framework and from the basis of a relatively specialized sphere of expertise. As a result, they tended to be less than fully prepared or able to identify and respond to any unmet needs which lay outside their own professional remit or that of their employing agency. A paediatrician might diagnose a child's need for surgery or therapy, for instance, but not remind parents to apply for the attendance allowance. An occupational therapist from the local social services department would supply the necessary bathing aids, but could omit to check whether adequate incontinence supplies were being received from the community nursing department.

Secondly, when parents themselves initiated a request for help of some kind, the fragmentation of services effectively placed additional obstacles in their way. Many parents were completely unfamiliar with the structures and operations of the various health and welfare agencies; the concepts and terminology used by the officials and professionals who provided the services; the process of applying for help; the criteria

15

which were used in assessing eligibility; and with the appeal procedures available for reviewing unsatisfactory decisions. Each of these can vary considerably between local agencies, and between different services provided by a single agency. The problems for parents were exacerbated in those agencies which exercised flexibility, discretion and professional judgement in the allocation of assistance rather than explicit formal rules and regulations. An incorrect or inappropriate request for help could therefore be discouraging for parents, who might feel their pride and independence had already been undermined by having to ask for help in the first place.

Thirdly, the fragmentation of services meant that no single agency or professional group had primary responsibility for providing information, advice and support to the carers of disabled children; for ensuring the continuity of services, or for co-ordinating multiple sources of assistance. The focus of both the health and education services was primarily on the needs of the child itself, and on the specific medical or learning problems arising from severe disablement. Furthermore, education services are age related; and both special schools and hospitals have wide catchment areas which reduce their usefulness as accessible sources of help and support for parents throughout their child's lifetime.

Local authority social services departments might be thought prima facie to offer the most appropriate professional and organizational framework for the co-ordinated provision of continuing services and support to disabled children and their families. Social workers have after all been enabled since the implementation of the Seebohm Report to adopt a perspective which is much broader than the narrow focus of former welfare intervention on specific types of problem experienced by individual people. The organization of social services departments should now facilitate a far wider concern not only with the disabled child as a whole, but also with the needs of the child's family and other informal carers:

> The scope and range of welfare and other services to be provided by local authority social services (LASS) departments have been extended ... At the same time increasing emphasis has been placed on providing more care and support services for the sick and disabled, particularly the mentally ill and retarded, in their own home or in the community rather than in hospitals. As a result LASS departments must now provide social work assistance, day care and residential services; domiciliary supportive services (including social work support for educational services), and ... social work support for the health service ... Of equal importance are the opportunities now presented for identifying neglected areas and gaps in services, and for constructive planning and deployment

of resources within one administrative entity. (CCETSW, 1974, pp. 7–8)

Furthermore, social services departments also provide many of the practical services and aids which can make the care of a severely disabled child less onerous (Keeble, 1981; Glendinning, 1983).

However, within the organizational framework of local authority social services departments, and in particular within the generic caseloads of individual social workers, disabled children and their families have on the whole been accorded low priority (Stevenson, Parsloe and Hill, 1978; Hart and Fassam, 1979; Browne, 1982). Disabled children have long-term, relatively intractable problems. A severely disabled child is unlikely to be 'cured', so the optimum outcome of any social work intervention may be little more than an amelioration of the practical and emotional stresses of this long-term dependency. The needs of their families for regular information, advice and support, for liaison with and co-ordination of other services and for occasional practical help all tend to compete poorly with social services departments' statutory obligations and with intervention in crisis or 'high-risk' situations (Algie, 1980). Research into the organization of social work practice (Stevenson, Parsloe and Hill, 1978) found that for these reasons work with physically and mentally disabled people was generally accorded low priority by social workers with generic caseloads. Although the specialist skills of social services department occupational therapists were very valuable in the supply of aids and adaptations, these skills did not necessarily extend to more general information-giving, advice and counselling. Moreover, the readiness of occupational therapists to refer clients to other social workers for these latter types of help was found to be highly variable (ibid., pp. 169–80). As we saw in Chapter 1, the issues of specialization and genericism have arisen continually over the last fifteen years, most recently in the debate following the publication of the Barclay Committee's report (NISW, 1982).

The cumulative impact of the fragmentation of services for disabled children and their families was noted with concern by both the Court and Warnock Committees of Inquiry. Although neither committee was primarily concerned with this issue, both drew attention in their final reports to the poor levels of information, advice, help and support which appeared to be available for those caring for a disabled child. For example, research carried out for the Warnock Committee found that many parents were 'in great need of someone to whom they could turn for help and advice at any time'. The committee concluded that

> there is a clear need for one person to whom the parents of children with disabilities or incipient special needs can turn for advice on the different services available to meet their child's needs. This should

be someone who is well known to and accepted by them. The principle holds whether the children are under five, of school age, or making the transition from school to adult life. (Warnock Committee, 1978, paras 5.12–5.13)

Similarly, the Court Committee of Inquiry into the organization of the child health services concluded that

> parents ... find the existing pattern of services confusing ... [They] are faced with a conglomeration of professionals, the majority working in separate unco-ordinated services with limited roles and limited communication with each other, and few of whom are specially trained to work with children. Not all are equally accessible, and parents often do not know to whom to turn for help ... So parents fail to obtain the ready help and support for which they constantly and desperately feel the need. (Court Committee, 1976, paras 4.45–4.46)

The concern expressed by the Warnock and Court Committees, and the conclusions of the various contemporary research projects, were not without some political impact. In 1976, on the initiative of the then Secretary of State for Social Services and the Minister for the Disabled, a special seminar was convened to discuss the development of policies for people with disabilities. The various representatives of voluntary organizations, professional groups people with disabilities and their carers who attended the seminar expressed concern at

> the problem facing people who had to find a way through the maze of provision and agencies which might be available to them. There was, at the moment, no single point of reference ... Even when a disabled person did identify all the agencies which could help him, he would often still find it difficult to make the appropriate contact within the agencies and secure the right help from each at the right time. (DHSS, 1976, paras 6–7)

After discussing the various roles which might be played by a local 'trouble-shooter' for people with disabilities – an information officer or local equivalents of the Minister for the Disabled – the seminar participants resolved that 'as a piece of action research, a pilot project might be set up to determine the costs of the service, its effects and efficacy, and the best way to run it' (ibid., para. 7). The resource worker project grew directly from this ministerial initiative.

The Resource Worker Project

The resource worker project created an experimental service with two primary goals. First, it was intended to overcome the problems arising from the fragmentation of services for disabled children and their families. Secondly, it aimed to alleviate the isolation and lack of support clearly expressed by so many families. Integral to this experimental service was a research programme designed to evaluate its effectiveness.

The central feature of the experimental service was a specialist worker – the 'resource worker' – whose task was to provide information, advice, practical help and support to families caring for a severely disabled child. The resource worker was to be a kind of 'single door' – an easily identifiable and accessible person to whom parents could turn for help with *any* problem arising from the care of their disabled child. The resource worker would in turn give information, offer advice and support and, where appropriate, refer families to and liaise with other professionals, agencies and services. From an organizational point of view the resource worker's role was to be that of a 'key worker' or 'case manager'. The former term denotes the complex co-ordination and liaison activities which may be required to bring the appropriate combinations of formal and informal resources to deal with a particular problem: 'when two or more social workers or other change agents are involved in one problem, often one of them is designated as the central worker, with responsibility for co-ordination' (Pincus and Minahan, 1973, pp. 244–5). Similarly, the role of a 'case manager' (although hitherto confined mainly to the provision of domiciliary care for elderly people) involves the assessment of client needs; the planning of services and the monitoring of their delivery; and the periodic reassessment of client needs (Caro, 1981; Davies and Challis, 1981).

Responsibility for initiating and maintaining contact between the resource worker and family was to lie explicitly with the resource worker, rather than the onus resting on parents to initiate contact or request help as and when they felt they needed it. Regular contact between resource worker and family would also enable future needs to be identified and, it was hoped, potential crises to be anticipated and averted. The actual frequency of contact would of course depend upon the circumstances and needs of individual families and was, in any case, expected to vary both between families and within individual families over time.

In detail the intervention was intended to achieve the following aims:

(1) To develop the role of a specialist worker (the 'resource worker'), who would provide support and help to families caring for a severely disabled child. It was anticipated that this role would include the following activities:
  (a) maintaining regular (though not necessarily frequent) visiting or other contact on the initiative of the resource worker and not solely in response to a request from parents;

19

(b) giving information – verbally and in the form of books, leaflets and pamphlets – about services, benefits, sources of professional advice, and specialist local and national organizations and facilities;

(c) offering advice on the best ways of obtaining and making use of such resources;

(d) counselling parents and other family members (including, where appropriate, disabled children themselves) about any personal or interpersonal difficulties connected with the child's disability;

(e) liaising and improving communications between family members and professional services and agencies – that is, helping parents to formulate and articulate their needs, and interpreting to parents the policies and practices of professionals and service providers;

(f) co-ordinating the delivery of services and the involvement of other professional workers;

(g) acting as an advocate on the families' behalf – for example, where difficulties occurred in establishing entitlement to benefits or substantial delays arose in the provision of a service.

(2) To document these activities in order to illustrate the skills, knowledge and expertise needed to provide support and help to the families of severely disabled children.

(3) To obtain further information on the operation of existing services in cash, kind and person, and their effectiveness in meeting the needs of those caring for a disabled child; and on the problems which could arise in the co-ordination and delivery of services.

(4) To monitor the intervention and evaluate its effectiveness.

(5) To draw conclusions about the project's replication.

The intervention was not intended to focus only on children with certain specific impairments or handicapping conditions; in particular, it was not intended to follow the distinction which is commonly made in the organization and delivery of services between children with physical handicaps and those with mental handicaps. However, it was intended that the intervention should be with the families of children whose disabilities were severe. This was based on the assumption that the most acute need for support and help was likely to arise among those caring for children with the most severe disabilities. The development of services for this group of carers was therefore assumed to be a priority for both policy and research. Children with the most severe disabilities are also likely to have multiple impairments, so the project was to include families whose children had a wide range of severe physical, mental, sensory and multiple impairments as well as those whose children suffered from seriously incapacitating or life-threatening ill-nesses.

In considering the possible role which the resource worker project might play in the future development of policies and services for disabled children, the feasibility of replicating the intervention had to be borne closely in mind. This meant that the project would not be aimed at providing a particularly intensive and, therefore, expensive service. Indeed it was desirable to avoid this if replication was to be economically feasible.

Economic constraints also limited the length of time during which the intervention could take place. Clearly, the needs of disabled children and their families are long-term ones and ideally it would have been desirable to establish a permanent intervention programme to meet those continuing needs. However, the intervention was experimental, and hence could be for a limited period only. It was decided that the project should run for two years. While this represents only a relatively brief episode in the lifetime care of a severely disabled child, it was probably the minimum length of time within which working relation-ships could be established with families and professionals, trust and rapport developed and the impact of the intervention become apparent.

As a specialist service, the focus of the resource worker's activity was to be the disabled child and the problems which were encountered by her or his carers in the course of providing that care. However, this specialist focus was not intended to preclude the resource worker's involvement in other family problems where this seemed necessary. Indeed to have made such a distinction would have been unrealistically arbitrary and rigid, particularly in the light of developments in the personal social services during the previous fifteen years.

In Chapter 3 the recruitment of the resource workers and the establishment of the intervention programme are described. This is followed by an account of the research design and methods used in the evaluation of the intervention.

CHAPTER 3

Setting up the project

The Resource Workers and the Intervention

The question of who the resource workers were to be was a critical one and, at the very beginning, open for discussion. The body of knowledge, general orientation and specific areas of expertise which workers from different professional backgrounds might bring to the intervention would clearly have a substantial impact on its subsequent direction and development. However, in view of the aims of the project and the wide-ranging scope of the intervention social work was clearly the most appropriate professional background from which to recruit the resource workers. Social work training and experience provides a basis for tackling attitudinal and emotional concerns, communication problems, material needs and practical difficulties, and the total nexus of formal and informal relationships between family members and voluntary and statutory organizations. Social workers were also more likely than other professionals to be aware of the social and emotional needs arising from severe childhood disablement; of parents' (and children's) needs for information and advice; of their potential sense of isolation and how this might be lessened; and of the vast range of physical, financial and professional resources potentially available to disabled children and their families. In addition, the absence of a specific medical or educational professional frame of reference seemed likely to offer the greatest scope for flexibility and creative innovation in the provision and delivery of services and support.

One possible strategy would have been to recruit several resource workers from a number of different professional backgrounds – a health visitor, a social worker and a teacher, for example – and perhaps even a trained volunteer with no formal professional qualifications. The evaluation of the project would then have compared their respective interventions and assessed the relative effectiveness of each. Such a strategy would, however, have been too complex for adequate evaluation. The project was based upon the premiss that a particular type and range of intervention was necessary, and it was aimed at evaluating the effectiveness of that intervention. Different professional (and non-professional) workers would be likely to focus their interventions in different ways. Evaluating the impact of these interventions would, then, have been additionally complicated by the widely variable professional inputs.

Five social workers were therefore recruited to work on a part-time basis (an average of fifteen hours each per week) as the resource workers for the project. Each was a qualified social worker who had previously worked for the Family Fund, interviewing new applicants, completing social work report forms and making any local inquiries of doctors, teachers, or social workers which were necessary to establish a child's eligibility for help from the fund.

The resource workers thus all had detailed and wide-ranging experience of the practical, social and emotional problems which may be associated with severe childhood disablement, together with a working knowledge of local statutory and voluntary services and facilities. Apart from this common background, the earlier work experience of the five resource workers was very varied. It included social work in former local authority children's, old people's and mental welfare departments; in surgical, cancer and psychiatric hospitals; and in voluntary organizations providing specialist services in the fields of adoption, fostering and child handicap. Their formal training and qualifications were in child care or general welfare work; only one of the five had undertaken any relevant specialist training (an Open University post-experience course on The Handicapped Person in the Community). However, all the resource workers firmly believed that some degree of specialization was essential in providing an effective service to disabled children and their families, as they revealed in discussions before the project began:

> You can see the sense in having one overall department, so that it is very easy to cross over the barriers from child care to elderly to handicapped ... all one set of files, and so forth. But to allow, where necessary, for specialization I think is important, very important.

> I've been fairly appalled by the fact that the specialists have been phased out. I think you need specialists. That's not to say that you can't interchange – you shouldn't get stuck in one sort of groove – but I think that the specialist is very important.

Similarly, all the resource workers were aware from their Family Fund work before the project began of the lack of practical help and emotional support often experienced by the parents of disabled children:

> Something that has cropped up very often has been families saying that there has been nobody with them ... not necessarily someone with a great deal of knowledge about disability, but just someone who was there to help and listen.

23

> I see this as being the most important thing [in the intervention] . . .
> let them talk and help them to feel that there's someone else around
> to talk to, that they're not on their own; that and the support.

> There's a need for information on the practical help available and
> putting them in touch with sources of help. Someone to talk to and
> general support, but on a deeper level a need for casework and the
> opportunity to work through some of their unresolved feelings and
> anxieties about having a handicapped child.

The goal of providing this support was, however, very clear to the
resource workers. It was to encourage and enable parents to take action
for themselves, by equipping them with the information and confidence
they needed in order to obtain help on their own behalf:

> I think that the problems arise if the family see your role as just one
> of providing material goods and of saying, 'Don't worry about
> so-and-so; I'll fix that up. I'll see so-and-so and so-and-so', instead
> of saying, 'We must try not to worry about this; let me put you in
> touch with so-and-so', and let the family do the work . . . Often one
> has to be their spokesman to begin with, or their liaison officer . . .
> Then the other thing is helping them to realize that there could be
> help available within the immediate community, that they're not on
> their own – and show them how to reach out for that help.

> You see yourself as an enabler rather than a doer, to enable them to
> go about doing it themselves. I should start off by saying, 'Well,
> social services might be able to do this; here's the phone number',
> or 'Do you know them? Will you go?', because they're going to have
> to do this eventually . . . you should only step in if they can't
> manage.

> So far as practical things are concerned, telling parents rather than
> doing it – only doing it afterwards if they can't.

The resource workers' extensive experience of interviewing and
identifying the needs of families who had applied to the Family Fund,
backed up with their professional social work training, meant that little
formal training was necessary before the project began. However, they
were given a checklist of local agencies, organizations and services, and
asked to ensure that they were familiar with the locations and functions
of each (see Appendix A).

Practical and professional support during the course of the intervention was, however, clearly necessary. This was provided by senior social
work staff in the Yorkshire Division of Dr Barnardo's, which was
beginning to expand its fieldwork services to children with disabilities

and their families at the same time as the project was being established. Information and support for the resource workers was provided by the Dr Barnardo's staff in four ways. Up-to-date information about a wide range of topics – aids, equipment, welfare benefits, voluntary organizations and local and national specialist facilities – was regularly circulated to the resource workers in the form of books, articles and pamphlets. Secondly, talks and seminars were arranged, usually on topics suggested by the resource workers themselves, in order to improve their knowledge of an unfamiliar service or facility: behaviour modification techniques, for example, and how appropriate referrals for such teaching should be made; the specialist careers service for disabled school-leavers; and the various welfare benefit review and appeals procedures. Visits were also made to local and national specialist facilities and voluntary organizations. Details of all the information supplied to the resource workers before and during the intervention are contained in Appendix A.

Thirdly, the social work staff at Dr Barnardo's were available for consultation by the resource workers about individual casework problems. Sometimes these could be lengthy consultations which gave a resource worker an opportunity to assess her intervention and develop ideas for future work with particular families. The Dr Barnardo's staff were also on occasion able to provide a backup point of contact for a family if a crisis seemed likely to arise during a resource worker's holiday (though this safety net was never actually needed). The fourth source of information and support for the resource workers came from the bi-monthly meetings which were held at the Dr Barnardo's office throughout the two-year project. As well as allowing a structured exchange of information through talks, seminars and the circulation of literature, these meetings also enabled the five resource workers to share their own problems and experiences and discuss the practical and professional issues which arose from them – an opportunity greatly valued by the resource workers.

The Research Design and Methods

A Quasi-Experimental Design

To evaluate the impact and effectiveness of the resource workers' intervention an experimental design was adopted. In Goldberg and Connelly's words, 'the essence of an experimental test ... consists in comparing the "before and after" state of two equivalent subjects or groups of subjects, one of whom has been subjected to a specified form of experience while the other has not' (Goldberg and Connelly, 1982, pp. 28–9). If it is assumed that all other factors will have had identical effects on both subjects or groups of subjects, then any differences between the two groups which are detectable at the end of the experiment may reasonably be attributed to the effects of the experimental intervention or experience. In the resource worker project the circumstances and needs of the families who received the specialist resource worker intervention were compared, before and after that intervention, with the circumstances and needs of a similar group of families who continued to receive only their usual generic community services.

Strictly controlled experimental research is of course extremely difficult to carry out in social work. The immense variability of social and emotional needs and responses means, for example, that identical inputs to two or more experimental subjects can be difficult to achieve, particularly when the affective and process dimensions of the input are taken into consideration. The varying needs and circumstances of individuals and families can also make the individual monitoring of 'experimental' and 'control' subjects highly impracticable. Modifications and qualifications therefore have to be made which, nevertheless, do not violate the scientific integrity of the research.

In the first place, because it is usually not possible to obtain identically matched pairs of experimental and control subjects, other methods of obtaining two groups of subjects from a given population may have to be devised. These two groups should, however, be broadly similar in all important respects. Interviews with both groups of subjects before the intervention begins, as well as forming part of the overall evaluation design, can provide valuable baseline data from which to check that there are no important differences between them.

This was in fact the situation in the resource worker project. The two groups of families were not matched identically on an individual basis, but were instead, overall, broadly comparable or equivalent. It is therefore probably more appropriate to call the non-intervention group of families a 'comparison' rather than a 'control' group, the latter term having more precise scientific connotations.

Secondly, it may be neither feasible nor ethically defensible actually to withhold all intervention or 'treatment' from the control group, particularly in the context of social work research where the research subjects are, by their very participation in the experiment, deemed to have some kind of unmet need. For example, it would not have been possible for the comparison group in the resource worker project to have received no social work support and help of any sort at all. In any case, that would have been inconsistent with the aim of the project, which was intended to evaluate the impact of specialist intervention in comparison with generic services, not the effects of intervention in comparison with a *withdrawal* of all support. In this respect the research design of the resource worker project resembled that of Reid and Shyne's (1969) study of the relative effectiveness of brief and extended casework, Goldberg's (1970) comparison of trained social workers and untrained welfare officers working with elderly welfare clients and the evaluation by Gibbons (1981) of the impact of special task-centred casework in comparison with routine community services for people who had attempted suicide. Like Meyer's experiment in social work with adolescent girls, the 'experimental test was not one of provision of service vs. withholding of service, but rather the known provision of service vs. unknown experiences excluding these specific services' (Meyer, Borgatta and Jones, 1965, p. 24).

A third modification to a strict experimental design had to be made to avoid the possibility of 'contamination' occurring. This term refers to the process whereby members of a control group accidentally also receive some or all of the experimental treatment. In the resource worker project it would clearly have been undesirable for a family assigned to the comparison group to have learnt of and requested the specialist intervention being provided by the resource workers to the families in the experimental group. To refuse such a request from a family in need would have been unpleasant; to have met it would have compromised the experimental design. It was therefore decided to draw the experimental and comparison groups from a similar population (families with severely disabled children) but from different geographical areas.

In view of these modifications to a basic experimental research design it was especially important to identify the social work and other supportive inputs to both the experimental and comparison groups during the project and, in particular, to obtain a precise account of the experimental service provided by the resource workers during the project. Interviews with both the experimental and comparison groups after the end of the experimental intervention were therefore partly concerned with the identification of inputs during the previous two years. Meanwhile close monitoring and analysis of the resource workers' activities during the project provided a detailed description of the experimental service whose effectiveness was being evaluated.

Selecting the Samples

As well as selecting the two groups of families from different geographical areas as described above, the families *within* each group were also drawn from across a number of local authority areas. If each group had been drawn from within a single local authority area, the project would have stood the risk of being affected by any substantial differences in socioeconomic, demographic, or service delivery patterns which may have existed between these two areas. Selecting the families in each group from a number of different areas represented an attempt to diffuse the effects of any such variations.

The resource workers were therefore each allocated to work in one of five local authority areas in the Yorkshire and north-west regions of England. These five areas were selected for purely pragmatic reasons, on the basis of their proximity to the resource workers' homes. Five further 'control' or comparison group areas were selected from within the same regions, matched to the 'experimental' group areas as far as possible in terms of need indicators (Imber, 1977) and per capita personal social service expenditure (CIPFA, 1974–5, 1975–6).

A broad sampling frame was needed in order to obtain samples of children of different ages and with different disabilities from each of the ten local authority areas. The data bank of applicants to the Family Fund (Bradshaw and Lawton, 1985) provided a fairly comprehensive sampling frame, and also facilitated the matching of the experimental and comparison groups of families. Approximately 40,000 applications had been received by the Family Fund by June 1977, when the sample for the project was being selected. For a viable final analysis an achieved sample of at least 200 families was needed – 100 each in the experimental and comparison groups. Some sample losses during the course of a two-year project were to be expected, so an initial sample of 250 families – twenty-five in each of the ten local authority areas – was drawn.

There are, however, some suspected biases in the types of applicant to the Family Fund which may correspondingly affect any samples of families with disabled children which are drawn from the fund's register of applicants. For example, it is likely that affluent families who are not in need of financial assistance are underrepresented, as are families whose disabled children are very young. The former bias may not be important for the validity and replicability of an experimental support service; the latter bias certainly would be, as the number and nature of the problems faced by individual families may be expected to vary considerably according to the age of their disabled child. Therefore, to overcome the effect of this latter bias, a stratified random sample was drawn. Within each of the ten local authority areas the total available population of families who had applied to the Family Fund was stratified according to the disabled child's age. Families were then selected at random from each of the resulting subgroups. This produced a sample where, within each of the ten areas, one-third of the twenty-five families had disabled children under 5 years old, one-third had children aged 5–10, and one-third had children aged 11–15.

As Table 3.1 shows, some families were lost from the sample before the start of the intervention because they had moved house since their application to the Family Fund, or because their children had died or gone into care; a few more were lost during the subsequent two years.

Table 3.1 *Summary of Changes in the Samples*

	Initial sample drawn	First interview completed	Loss during project	Second interview completed	Number of families per area (range)	Overall response rate (%)
Resource worker group	125	114	7	107	19–23	86
Comparison group	125	111	8	103	19–22	82
Total	250	225	15	210		84

An ultimate overall response rate of 84 per cent yielded 107 families in the experimental group and 103 in the comparison group by the end of the project, with between nineteen and twenty-three families in each of the ten local authority areas.

Sources of Data for Evaluation

A single source of data involving the use of only one method of data collection is a weak basis for evaluative research, particularly where both the inputs and outcomes of the evaluated intervention are likely to encompass attitudinal, behavioural, psychological and social dimensions. On the other hand, 'if we observe an event, examine the records which others have made . . . and talk to participants . . . we have at least some protection against the distortions that might arise if we did only one of those things' (Smith, 1980, p. 10). The evaluation of the resource workers' intervention therefore drew on a number of different, but complementary, sources of data and used different methods of data collection and analysis, as described below.

(1) The families in both the experimental and comparison groups were interviewed before and after the resource workers' intervention. The interviews were conducted with the disabled child's main carer or carers, usually the mother but often with the father or other family members taking part as well, by independent professional interviewers. The interviews with both groups of families were substantially the same, both before and after the intervention. A wide range of structured questions was asked in order to assess changes on many different dimensions. These included relatively objective topics such as the degree of dependency and amount of care needed by the disabled child; the presence and severity of a wide range of practical problems; the involvement of friends, neighbours and extended family members in the

child's care; the frequency and helpfulness of contacts with professional services; the utilization of services in kind; and the take-up of cash benefits for people with disabilities. The interviews also attempted to tap parents' subjective experience of the care of their disabled child – the extent to which the work arising from the child's dependency was felt to be onerous, for example, and their perceptions of the impact of the disability on other children in the family. Thirdly, the interviews included the malaise inventory (Rutter, Graham and Yule, 1970) and a series of questions previously used by Pomeroy *et al.* (1978), both of which were designed to detect and measure the anxiety or stress which is often experienced by parents caring for a severely disabled child (Bradshaw and Lawton, 1978b; Burden, 1978; Philp and Duckworth, 1982).

These questions formed a common core of the interviews with each group of families both before and after the intervention. By examining changes which occurred in the experimental group but not in the comparison group (assuming there were no differences between them initially), some of the outcomes of the intervention could be assessed. In addition to these common questions, the first set of interviews also obtained baseline demographic data from which the initial comparability of the two groups could be checked. The second set of interviews included additional questions on the extent and sources of help, advice and support received by all the families during the intervening two years. Families in the experimental group were asked to assess the amount of help that they had received from the resource workers in relation to specific problems and also its relative usefulness. The answers to these questions constituted additional outcome measures which complemented the structured between-group comparisons. Families in the comparison group were also asked about any similar help they had received during the same period.

(2) A second major source of data was the detailed records which were kept by the resource workers during the project, of their work with and on behalf of the families they visited. A content analysis of these records was carried out after the end of the project. In addition, the resource workers were asked at the end of the intervention to assess the amount of time they had spent in work with each family on a range of specific problems. Both the content analysis and the time analysis used a pre-coded *pro forma* from which quantitative data could be derived. These data were used to document the input of the intervention.

(3) Semi-structured, in-depth interviews were carried out with each of the resource workers at the beginning and end of the project. The first set of interviews covered their professional training and experience; their views on the needs of severely disabled children and their families and how these needs might be met by the proposed intervention; and

their knowledge of specialist local and national services. The second set of interviews concentrated on the resource workers' subjective assessments of the success of the project, and discussed in some detail the particular organizational features of the project which might have contributed to or detracted from that success.

(4) Finally, a postal questionnaire was sent to all the families in the experimental group approximately two years after the end of the resource workers' intervention. This questionnaire asked parents about the longer-term impact of the intervention, about their current sources and levels of support and their preferences for a service such as that provided by the resource workers, or its equivalent cost in the form of a cash allowance. Replies were received from over three-quarters of the experimental group.

It had been intended to monitor during the project any changes which took place in services for children with disabilities in each of the ten local authority areas from which the samples had been drawn. First, because these changes could prove to be significant intervening variables affecting the outcomes in either the resource worker or the comparison group. Secondly, the intervention of a specialist social worker might indirectly lead to a more widespread increase in demands for services from the families of disabled children; this increase would not be detected by any of the other methods of data collection. Unfortunately insufficient research resources prevented this monitoring from being carried out. In any case, it is likely that central government economic policies had a greater, and more uniform, impact on services in all areas during the period of intervention than did the resource workers.

Meeting the Families

The remainder of this chapter outlines some of the characteristics of the children and their families in the experimental ('resource worker') and comparison groups. First, some basic social and demographic characteristics are described. These are followed by an examination of the levels and sources of support and help which appeared to be available to the children and their families before the intervention began.

Characteristics of the Children and their Families

As described earlier, an initial sample of twenty-five children in each of ten local authority areas was drawn from the register of applicants to the Family Fund. The distributions of the ages and impairments of the children in each group were, however, similar. Within each of the ten

Table 3.2 *Principal Handicapping Conditions of the Children*

	Resource worker group (%)	Comparison group (%)
Disorders of central nervous system (including cerebral palsy)	33	42
Mental disorders (including Down's syndrome, autism)	26	26
Congenital malformations (including spina bifida/hydrocephalus)	22	18
Disorders of bones/organs of movement	6	6
Disorders of sense organs (blind/deaf)	7	1
Other named syndromes	3	2
Disorders of circulatory system	1	3
Metabolic/blood disorders	1	2
Disorders of digestive system	2	—
Base (= 100%)	107	103

groups approximately one-third of the twenty-five children were under 5 years old, one-third were aged 5–10 and one-third aged 11 and over. Approximately one-fifth of the children in each group had predominantly mental handicaps, two-fifths had physical impairments and two-fifths had multiple impairments (this reflected the distribution of impairments among the total population of Family Fund applicants). Table 3.2 shows the causes of these impairments, the principal handicapping conditions of the children in the resource worker and comparison groups.

The only significant difference in the handicapping conditions of the two groups of children was in the proportions of children with disorders of the sense organs. However, these children constituted a very small proportion of each group, so the overall effect on the intervention and its outcomes was not likely to be substantial.

There were no differences between the two groups of families on a number of basic socioeconomic variables. However, families in the two groups did differ in some respects from the general population of families with dependent children, as documented in the current (1977) General Household Survey (GHS). For example, 79 per cent of both the resource worker and comparison groups contained two parents and up to three children, compared with 82 per cent in the GHS; 12 per cent contained two parents and four or more children (only 6 per cent of GHS families); and between 8 and 9 per cent were headed by a single parent (11 per cent in the GHS) (OPCS, 1979, table 2.17). Similarly, there was little difference between the two groups of families in their patterns of housing tenure, but they were slightly more likely to live in local authority rented accommodation and slightly less likely to live in owner-occupied or privately rented housing than were families in the general population (ibid., 1979, table 3.9).

There were marked differences between the social class distribution of the resource worker and comparison group families, and the social class distribution of heads of households containing a child under 16 in the 1977 GHS. In both the resource worker and comparison groups significantly fewer heads of households were in non-manual occupations and more in manual occupations than in the general population, as Table 3.3 indicates.

Table 3.3 *Social Class of Head of Household*

Social class	Resource worker group (%)		Comparison group (%)		GHS, 1977* (%)	
I and II	12	} 24	13	} 24	22	} 40
III non-manual	12		11		18	
III manual	45	} 75	44	} 77	40	} 60
IV and V	30		33		20	
Base (= 100%)	106		101		4,122	

* OPCS, 1979, table 2.9

Slightly more of the heads of household in the study were unemployed at the start of the project than were fathers with dependent children in the 1977 GHS (ibid., 1979, table 4.4). However, the difference was small and there was again no difference between the resource worker and comparison group families. There was, however, a marked difference in the economic activity rates of the mothers, with significantly fewer mothers in either the resource worker or comparison group being in full-time employment than in the general population of women with dependent children (Table 3.4).

Table 3.4 *Economic Activity of Mothers*

	Resource worker group (%)		Comparison group (%)		GHS 1977* (%)	
Employed: full time	3	} 37	3	} 39	16	} 50
part time	34		36		34	
Not economically active	64		61		49	
Base (= 100%)	107		101		4,367	

* OPCS, 1979, table 4.5

While the characteristics of the resource worker and comparison groups appeared to be broadly similar on a number of socioeconomic variables, there are some indications (in particular, the size of their families, their social class and the ability of mothers to take full-time paid employment) that the families in the project may have been relatively disadvantaged in comparison with families in the general population. However, other research on the characteristics of families with disabled children (Bradshaw and Lawton, 1978a; Weale and Bradshaw, 1980) suggests that such families do differ from the general population of all families with dependent children in the ways indicated here. Therefore, as well as being similar to one another according to a number of basic demographic and socioeconomic characteristics, the families in the resource worker and comparison groups apparently resembled the wider population (of all families with disabled children) from which they were drawn.

Existing Sources of Support for the Disabled Children and their Families

Underpinning the establishment and evaluation of the specialist support service was the view that families with severely disabled children were unlikely to be in close or regular contact with a source of comprehensive information, advice and help. A number of questions in the initial interviews were designed to test this assumption.

For example, there were forty-two families (twenty-two in the resource worker group and twenty in the comparison group) whose children were under 5 years of age at the time of the first interview, and whose parents might be receiving some help from a health visitor. Certainly, the majority of these parents said that they knew how to contact a health visitor should they need to, but only about one-half (twelve in each group) reported actually having had contact with a health visitor as often as five times during the previous two years. Only six of the resource worker group parents and ten of the comparison group parents named their health visitor as someone to whom they would turn if they were having problems; and only four parents – all in the comparison group – said that they did this with any regularity. Similarly, only eight resource worker group parents and thirteen comparison group parents felt that they could turn to their general practitioner for support and help if they were having problems.

As far as support and help from their local authority social services department was concerned, the families' contacts did not appear to be either very extensive or frequent. About one-third of the parents in each group said they had been in contact with their social services department within the previous three months; but one-fifth said that their last contact had been over a year ago, and almost one-fifth reported never having been in contact, or could not recall their last contact. Not all parents appeared to know much about their local social services department and the help which could be obtained from it; only about one-half could name a social worker for whom they would ask if they contacted the department. The resource worker group parents appeared to be somewhat less familiar with their social services department than those in the comparison group; in particular, significantly fewer resource worker group parents knew either the address or telephone number of their local office (Table 3.5)

Table 3.5 *Parents' Knowledge of Social Services*

Percentage who:	Resource worker group (N = 107)	Comparison group (N = 103)
Knew their child was registered	47	54
Knew address/telephone number of office	51	72
Knew name of social worker to contact	44	54
Knew one or more types of help available from social services	63	67

When asked to name the specific types of help available from their social services department, parents most frequently cited adaptations to the home and aids to daily living. Information, advice and support formed only one-tenth of the types of help mentioned.

More generally, parents were asked whether, if things were 'getting on top of them' or they had problems, there was anyone they could talk to. Seventy-nine per cent of the parents in each group said that there was. These parents named predominantly informal sources of support – spouses, parents and other relatives, friends and neighbours. Altogether only eleven parents named a social worker as someone they could turn to, and only four identified a teacher at their child's school (there were no significant differences between the two groups of families).

Finally, what about the source of the samples for the project, the Family Fund itself? Help from the Family Fund is provided in the form of grants for specific items or services. Although the vast majority of families had received at least one such grant from the Family Fund, the fund has no commitment to provide regular support to – or even maintain contact with – the families who have applied to it. It is of course possible that those families who learn of and apply to the Family Fund are different from other families with disabled children. However, a preliminary comparison of the sociodemographic characteristics of Family Fund applicants with those of a nationally representative sample of families with disabled children drawn from the General Household Survey suggests that any such differences are small (though both groups of families with disabled children do differ in some respects from families with non-disabled children) (Weale and Bradshaw, 1980). Family Fund applicants may be atypical of all families with disabled children in other ways, which are harder to measure. They may be better informed, more articulate, better supported by professionals and services, and more able to obtain appropriate help for their disabled child. However, even if this is the case, the *effects* of these differences appear to be negligible. The research cited in Chapter 2 shows that families who had applied to the Family Fund were just as likely as other samples of families with disabled children to lack a comprehensive source of information, advice, support and practical help of the kind which the resource workers were to provide. The questions asked of families before the intervention began tended to confirm this finding. So too did the impressions of the resource workers once they had begun to meet the families and establish working relationships both with them and other professionals and organizations, as Chapter 4 will show.

CHAPTER 4

Inputs: The Role of a Specialist Social Worker

This chapter describes just what the five resource workers did during their two years' intervention with a sample of severely disabled children and their families. It draws upon three sources of data: on the content analysis of the detailed records kept by the resource workers during the intervention; on the pre-coded questionnaires which they completed after the end of the project about the amount of time they had spent working with each family on a number of specific problem areas; and on the in-depth interviews which were conducted with each resource worker after the intervention had ended. Analysis of these data provides, first, an account of the relationships which the resource workers were able to establish with parents, children and relevant professionals and agencies in their areas. Secondly, it yields summaries of the amount of contact the resource workers had with individual families during the project; the range of problems the resource workers dealt with and the amounts of time they spent in work connected with these problems; and the range of other agencies and professionals with whom they had contact during the intervention. Thirdly, the data provides a more subjective assessment from the resource workers themselves, of their inputs and achievements during the intervention.

Establishing Working Relationships

After the initial research interviews had been completed, the resource workers were able to contact each of the families in their area. During their first visit to each family the resource workers completed an initial assessment form; which included details of other professional workers with whom each family was in contact. Table 4.1, compiled from these assessment forms, documents the families' existing contacts with social or welfare workers which might have paralleled or overlapped with the resource workers' prospective intervention. (Families were of course also in contact with medical, paramedical and educational services, but these were not likely to be duplicated by the resource workers).

In one or two instances the resource workers found that another professional welfare worker was already involved with a family on a

37

Table 4.1 *Resource Worker Group Families' Contacts with Other Welfare Professionals at the Start of the Project*

Percentage of families in contact with (N = 107):	Frequency of contact	
	Regularly	Occasionally, when requested
Field social worker	7	19
Hospital social worker	—	6
Social services aids/adaptations officer	1	17
Other social services specialist worker (e.g. for blind, deaf, mental handicap)	1	3
Voluntary organization welfare officer	4	7
Education welfare officer	—	6
Health visitor	8	16
Educational psychologist	—	1

statutory basis (for example, where a child was suspected of being at risk of non-accidental injury). However, in most instances, although families may have been known to their local social services department, there was apparently little regular social work involvement. The onus was more often than not on parents to contact the department as and when a problem arose. The interviews with the resource workers after the end of the project confirmed this picture:

> At the beginning of the project I went to see the children's hospital medical social worker and she had files on three of the families in the project but admitted she didn't do anything ... With the exception of the two families who were members of ASBAH [the Association for Spina Bifida and Hydrocephalus] and had the ASBAH social worker in contact with them, none of the families had regular social work intervention ... When I started, I was very concerned not to tread on people's toes; I realized social services could give a comprehensive service but I was afraid I might upset what was already going on ... But in fact this just wasn't the case: nobody had anybody regularly giving help, and the person that most of the families turned to was the educational welfare officer with special responsibility for the ESN(S) schools.

> They were all registered with the social services but apart from [two families] none of them really had regular visits. One or two had marginal contact and did know the name of somebody to go to. There was a social worker here and there who said, 'Oh, yes, I have seen ...' – whoever it was, but the majority [of families] had nothing at all.

Even in the one local authority project area which had established teams of specialist social workers for mentally handicapped people, the situation seemed to be the same:

> There were no families that I was visiting where there was a social worker visiting ... There were some families where there was a specialist social worker in the background but they never seemed to visit ... Some of [the families] had had contact with the health visitor early on, but very few of them had had contact with social workers.

There were therefore few difficulties for the resource workers in establishing working relationships with other professional workers, and little question of the resource workers duplicating existing services. A variety of working arrangements were made, though these were most frequently based on the resource worker providing information, advice, support, liaison and advocacy to the family through regular routine visiting; and the local authority social worker providing practical services or statutory supervision as and when these were required:

> The only time social services became involved was when there was a query of non-accidental injury on David Clarke* ... Even then, they said they'd do a three-month assessment and didn't.

> They were very co-operative towards me and there was no ill feeling at all. I think they met my demands and my requests for visits, partly because often I did it direct with the occupational therapist.

> With [one family], they [social services] just kept on visiting ... We each knew what the other was doing, so we didn't duplicate it unless we thought it was necessary – sometimes we did duplicate it, if it was to push hard for something.

In total, the resource workers worked alongside social workers or probation officers, during at least part of the project, with five families who were experiencing additional problems of delinquency, domestic violence, or child neglect. Local authority social workers also maintained regular contact with three other families during the course of the project; and with two or three families, from the start of the intervention, the resource workers tried to involve a local authority social worker as well, because of the kind of help needed by the family:

> I felt they needed a social worker because they needed short-term care setting up in the holidays, and I had a social worker come in from the beginning because it had to be done through her.

* All names of children and their families have been changed to protect confidentiality.

However, as the resource workers pointed out, their intervention was not necessarily to the advantage of the local social services department:

> They were in no way grateful to me because it wouldn't have been done anyway and I was doing something extra.

> I found that the area officers without exception have been marvellous and I think it's a great tribute to them because inevitably, to some extent, what I was doing was quite an indictment on social services and what they could, and should, be doing.

It was with other agencies that the resource workers sometimes experienced difficulties in establishing working relationships:

> It wasn't social services, it was people like the architect's [department] who were hostile really.

> The difficulties occurred with agencies that you didn't have a great deal of contact with, so you couldn't build up any reputation either on a personal viability and credibility level or in terms of the work done.

As far as the families themselves were concerned, the resource workers felt that they had definitely been welcomed despite the fact that they had not come from any recognized or established agency and had had no material resources of their own to offer:

> They'd all had bad experiences. They all felt they'd been let down, so it was an advantage, I think without exception, that I was separate [from existing services] ... Certainly, the families definitely welcomed it ... I never felt I was offering less to the families. I felt sometimes I had less credibility and backing with the agencies, but in terms of the families it was an advantage.

> You weren't part of social services and that was a big advantage; they would talk to you a lot freer because a lot of it, perhaps, was against social services. But again you could point out social services' difficulties and I would hope that the ones who were very anti-social services have got a better picture of the other side.

The independent setting of the project and its implications for the project's results and replication will be discussed further at the end of this chapter. In the meantime we shall summarize just what the resource workers did during the course of their two-year intervention.

The Intervention of the Resource Workers

The Amount of Contact with the Families

The number of visits which the resource workers made to each family ranged from three to twenty-nine, with an average of thirteen visits per family over the two years – approximately one visit every two months. Thirty-six per cent of the 107 families were visited less than ten times during the project, 39 per cent had between eleven and fifteen visits and 25 per cent received more than sixteen visits. While most families were visited at fairly regular intervals throughout the two years, crises arose in some families which necessitated a series of frequent visits for a short period until the problem was resolved.

The number of visits gives only a rough indication of the scale of the resource workers' inputs to each family during the intervention. It probably underrepresents the full extent of their contacts with families because additional communications by letter and telephone often took place in between the visits. However, the visits formed the core of the home-based support service; they were most often the occasions on which needs were identified and problems discussed; and the visits were also an important element in parents' evaluation of the intervention.

The importance of the domiciliary visits became clear when, in the interviews after the end of the project, parents were asked to make a direct assessment of the overall impact which the resource workers' intervention had made on their lives. (This and other outcome measures are analysed further in Chapter 5.) Those parents who thought the intervention had made either a fair amount or a very great deal of difference to their lives had had significantly more visits on average than those who thought the intervention had made only a little or no difference. It is likely, however, that a greater number of visits from the resource workers did not simply on its own create a greater impact on families. The number and frequency of the resource workers' contacts clearly depended to some extent on the needs and problems of individual families. Parents who were coping well and whose children had no serious difficulties necessitated relatively few visits. Those families with more difficulties, on the other hand, received more frequent visits and thereby provided more opportunities for the resource workers to make some marked impact on their lives.

There were other indications that those families who were in greater need had more visits from the resource workers. For example, those families who reported having had no practical help or no moral support from friends or relations during the project had a higher average number of visits than those families who had had some informal help and support of this kind. The resource workers also made a higher average number of visits to families who reported having had additional contacts with a health visitor, social worker, or school staff during the project. The resource workers, along with other professionals, do seem therefore to have concentrated their work on families who were more isolated or who needed more help.

There were significant differences in the average number of visits received by families with children of different ages. Families whose disabled children were aged 11 and over at the start of the project received more visits than those with children aged under 5; those with children aged between 5 and 10 had fewest visits of all. This seems to reflect the particular problems – increasing difficulties with lifting and physical management, puberty and adolescence, independence and social skills training and post-school placement – of the oldest age-group, and the problems of adjustment faced by the parents of young children. Surprisingly, there were also some very small differences in the average number of visits made to families whose children had different types of impairment. Families with mentally handicapped children received more visits from the resource workers than those with physically disabled children; families with multiply disabled children received slightly fewer visits still, although it had been anticipated that their needs might be particularly extensive.

Apart from routine visiting and other contacts with the families, the resource workers also carried out a substantial amount of work with and on behalf of the 107 project families. What the resource workers did during and between those visits is described next.

The Content of the Resource Workers' Intervention with the Families

The records kept by the resource workers during the intervention documented in detail the range of issues and problems they dealt with and the various ways in which they tackled them. A content analysis of these records produced a summary of the focus, range and methods of their intervention. For example, over 90 per cent of the 107 families were given help of some kind in connection with their child's education, or provision for respite care. Over 80 per cent were given help in connection with their child's health or disability; with housing and environmental problems; or with emotional, interpersonal and family problems. The most frequent way in which the resource workers helped was by providing information and advice in general discussions or in more focused counselling; but their records show that they also often helped families to obtain help from other agencies and professionals by making formal referrals, liaising and acting as advocates.

DISABILITY, HANDICAP AND MEDICAL HEALTH CARE
The child's disability, the handicaps which resulted from the disability and the provision of clinical and paramedical health care were a focus of work with 86 per cent of the 107 families visited by the resource workers, as illustrated in Figure 4.1.

Almost all (eighty-seven) of these families were given help of some kind in connection with their child's medical condition, handicaps and general health (Figure 4.1(a)); sixty-two were helped in connection with the personal mobility problems experienced by their child (Figure 4.1(b)); and twenty-seven were helped with making or getting to hospital appointments (Figure 4.1(c)). In each instance the most frequent mode of intervention was general discussion, advice and information-giving:

Jane is sore and Mrs M. buying creams, etc. not available on prescription. I lent her Spinal Injuries Association literature which gives advice on how to obtain a special sanction for a particular item to be dispensed for a specific patient. Mrs M. will discuss this with her GP.

Mrs P. has just received new cushions for wheelchair. She repeated the order specifications for the existing (torn) cushions and has received some that will not even go in the chair. Suggested she obtain the name and telephone extension of the technical officer allocated to Margaret and only deal with him in future.

Mrs N. unaware of 'bubble' buggy cover for major buggy – gave details.

Hospital is about 15 miles from home, so Marie cannot be visited more than four times a week because of petrol costs. Suggested parents contact social worker at hospital to apply for fares grant.

This predominant information-giving role was only to be expected in view of the fact that medical and paramedical professionals had the primary responsibility for the disabled children's health care, treatment and therapy. However, the resource workers did have to take a more active role in obtaining suitable aids for personal mobility. Such intervention was necessary on behalf of thirty of the sixty-two families who were given some kind of help with this problem during the project. It consisted either of liaising with other professionals:

Asked social services occupational therapist [OT] to contact school physiotherapist to see if she could find suitable wheelchair. The OT phoned – had been in touch with school and obtained idea of

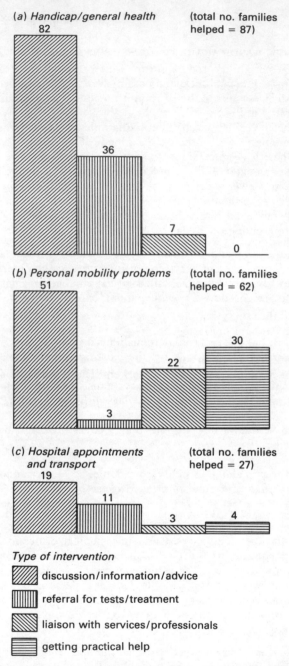

(a) *Handicap/general health*
82
(total no. families helped = 87)
36
7
0

(b) *Personal mobility problems*
51
(total no. families helped = 62)
30
22
3

(c) *Hospital appointments and transport*
19
(total no. families helped = 27)
11
3
4

Type of intervention

discussion/information/advice

referral for tests/treatment

liaison with services/professionals

getting practical help

Figure 4.1 Intervention connected with child's disability, handicap and medical health care.

suitable chair to fit in car boot. Appliance centre was arranging chair

or direct intervention and advocacy:

Phoned appliance centre for second time to inquire when wheelchair would be ready. Told it required adaptations – urgent request had been forwarded ... Chair arrived from appliance centre too big. Phoned centre and stressed urgency for chair to be collected, and right chair delivered as soon as possible.

Spoke about <u>possibility</u> of getting a powered kart – parents naturally keen. Would need doctor's letter of recommendation ... Home visit with OT and engineer from Wolfson Centre. Peter thrilled to have a go on demonstration model of kart. Hoped to expedite delivery in six weeks. Money will have to be raised locally.

EDUCATION, SHORT-TERM AND PERMANENT RESIDENTIAL CARE FACILITIES

Almost all the families in the project (95 per cent) were given some kind of help on the subject of their disabled child's education (Figures 4.2(*a*) and (*b*)), the most common focus being the child's current placement (Figure 4.2(*b*)). Here, in addition to the information and advice given to sixty-nine parents, the resource workers liaised with the schools and teachers of most of the children in the project, usually with a view to improving the quality and frequency of home–school contacts:

Rang school to make arrangements to take Mrs T. .... [Visited school with mother.] Mrs T. very much on the defensive. We put the idea that school was trying to help Graham and work with mother – if they know what he does at home, they can help. This was accepted by Mrs T. and she talked freely ... Mrs T. was delighted at results of our visit – felt it had done more good than any other time she's been.

Took Mrs J. to school. She was really afraid of seeing headteacher. At first the headteacher was volatile and quite rude. Managed to turn conversation to Mary and the way she is improving – headteacher suddenly became very nice and talked enthusiastically about Mary and how she could be helped at home ... Headteacher said she was astounded at the difference in Mrs J. .... Mrs J. said she felt headteacher much more reasonable, not so much against her.

Nineteen families needed more active assistance specifically with obtaining or keeping a suitable school place. This included one family whose

45

(a) *Educational progress and assessment*
(total no. families helped = 44)

(b) *Pre-school/school placement*
(total no. families helped = 102)

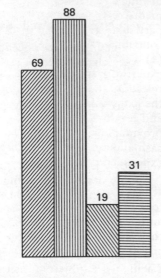

(c) *Post-school training/further education/employment*
(total no. families helped = 30)

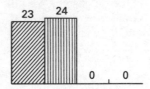

(d) *Short-term or permanent residential care*
(total no. families helped = 38)

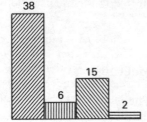

Type of intervention

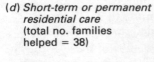 discussion/information/advice

liaison with school/professionals

getting/keeping suitable place

getting practical help: aids/grants/transport

Figure 4.2 Intervention connected with education, short-term and residential care facilities.

son's poor health had kept him at home for two years but who was admitted as a day pupil to the local hospital school after the active intervention of the resource worker:

> Rang special education centre and was told to phone headteacher of hospital school. Talked at length with head – told me who to contact in district education office for permission for Jack to come. Head would be very willing to have him.

The relatively few older children in the project meant that only thirty families were given help with finding a job, training, or other type of placement after leaving school (Figure 4.2(*c*)). Here the types of help given were the supply of information and advice and liaison with more specialized professionals such as careers officers. Thirty-eight families were given help with arranging short-term respite or eventual long-term care for their children (Figure 4.2(*d*)). As the formal bookings and admissions were usually made by hospitals or social services departments, the resource workers' intervention tended to concentrate on discussing with parents the possible alternative sources and consequences of such care:

> Asked social services if they would pay for Les to have a week at Cheshire Home. This was willingly agreed . . . Suggested to Mrs P. that she should ask social services to arrange short-term care each half-term. Mrs P. worried about payment – I contacted social services about this.

> During past week whole family have talked together about Meg's future and gradually agreed that perhaps she does need permanent [hospital] care. Mrs B. asked me if I'd start the ball rolling for her and I agreed – she felt I might be told the position as regards waiting-list, suitability, etc. more accurately than her.

RECREATION AND LEISURE OPPORTUNITIES

The resource workers helped 94 per cent of the 107 families in the project with finding and making use of recreation and leisure activities, either for the disabled child alone or for the whole family (Figure 4.3). Fifty-seven families were helped with arrangements for holidays, either for their disabled child alone or for the whole family (Figure 4.3(*a*)). Mostly this was in the form of information or advice:

> Talked of possibility of Eddie going off on holiday on his own next year and Mrs G. was very interested. Sent her names and addresses of holiday centres.

> Took parents a list of hotels and boarding-houses where meals provided, which will take a handicapped child.

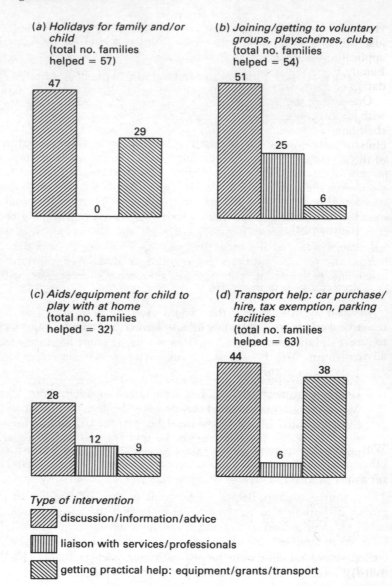

(a) *Holidays for family and/or child*
(total no. families helped = 57)

(b) *Joining/getting to voluntary groups, playschemes, clubs*
(total no. families helped = 54)

(c) *Aids/equipment for child to play with at home*
(total no. families helped = 32)

(d) *Transport help: car purchase/ hire, tax exemption, parking facilities*
(total no. families helped = 63)

Type of intervention

discussion/information/advice

liaison with services/professionals

getting practical help: equipment/grants/transport

Figure 4.3 Intervention connected with recreation and leisure opportunities.

However, twenty-nine families needed more active intervention than just the provision of information. This usually meant making an application on the family's behalf to the social services department or the Family Fund for financial help towards the cost of holiday accommodation or transport.

One-half of the families in the project were given some kind of help with joining specialist voluntary organizations for disabled children and their families, or with obtaining a place in a playscheme or other leisure club for their child (Figure 4.3(*b*)). Again this help most often consisted of the provision of information and advice:

> Gave information about playgroup at toy library – Mrs F. will take Geoff . . . Discussed hobbies – Geoff very interested in horses. Mrs F. hadn't heard of Riding for the Disabled. She will check with [consultant] if this would be appropriate, while I'll locate nearest branch.

> Suggested MENCAP summer playscheme for 'special care' children and gave brief details.

Just under one-third of the 107 families received help from the resource workers with obtaining toys and other recreational equipment to use at home (Figure 4.3(*c*)). Most were given information and advice:

> Parents intend to plan a bit of garden for Heather. I said I would send book called *The Garden and the Handicapped Child* . . . Gave Mrs G. details of gardening aids . . . gave information on gardening from Disabled Living Foundation.

With a small number of families the resource workers also liaised with other professionals about the suitability of a particular recreational item for a specific child, or helped obtain financial assistance to buy it:

> Talked about James's hyperactivity . . . he's very fond of slides. Suggested we ask Family Fund for a slide. There's room in the backyard.

Sixty-three families were helped with transport problems (Figure 4.3(*d*)). Here the resource workers were almost as likely to take an active part in obtaining practical help as they were just to give information. This active help included arranging volunteer transport to holiday playschemes and evening clubs or for hospital visits; applying to the Family Fund for financial help towards additional transport expenses; and obtaining specially adapted car seats or harnesses for older disabled children.

49

(*a*) *Lifting/carrying child in the home*
(total no. families helped = 24)

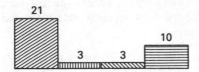

(*b*) *Incontinence and laundry*
(total no. families helped = 69)

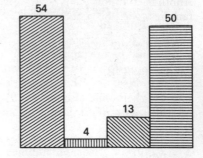

(*c*) *Washing/feeding/bathing/
dressing* (total no. families
helped = 61)

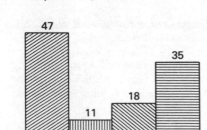

(*d*) *Supervision/behaviour problems
during day or night/independence*
(total no. families helped = 56)

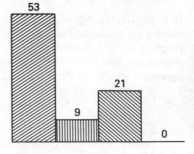

(*e*) *Obtaining special/extra clothing/
footwear/bedding*
(total no. families helped = 50)

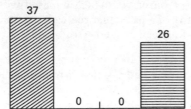

Type of intervention

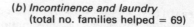 giving information/advice

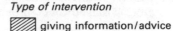 referral for treatment,
training

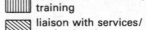 liaison with services/
professionals

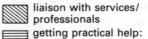 getting practical help:
equipment/aids/services

Figure 4.4 Intervention connected with practical problems of daily care.

PRACTICAL PROBLEMS OF EVERYDAY CARE

Another common focus of intervention, among 93 per cent of the 107 families, was the practical problems of everyday care which arose as a result of the child's disability (Figure 4.4). Only twenty-four families needed help to improve their child's mobility inside the home (Figure 4.4(a)). Most frequently this help was comprised of information and advice about, for example, services or appropriate aids:

Suggested Mrs P. contact local St John Ambulance for advice on lifting Beryl properly.

Talked with parents about stairlifts – showed them various illustrations – and about lifts that can go round corners. They are prepared to pay for lift themselves if social services are not supplying that particular model. Will arrange for [stairlift company] rep. to come and give free advice and estimate.

In contrast, sixty-nine families were given help in connection with their child's incontinence or with the additional laundry this generated (Figure 4.4(b)). Here the resource workers were as likely to take action themselves to obtain practical or material help as they were just to advise parents:

Gave Mrs J. details of Kylie sheets and stainproof carpet.

Contacted health visitor, discussed provision of Kanga pants. Health visitor said Mrs V. had received nine pairs in 12 months whereas entitlement was six ... Discussed case fully with community nursing officer, who said she'd arrange that Mrs V. should have as many as she required.

Mrs J. wondered if Family Fund would help with washer and tumble drier. I suggested she applied, and said I'd write as well if she wished.

The resource workers helped over one-half of the 107 families with problems arising from their child's lack of independence in self-care activities such as washing, feeding, dressing and bathing (Figure 4.4(c)). Again advice and information were the most common forms of help given, but liaison with other professionals was sometimes also necessary (for example, with speech therapists and teachers about a child's poor eating ability). The resource workers were also directly involved in obtaining practical services or aids for thirty-five families:

Steve is growing out of improvised high chair – mother and I looked in catalogue at possible ones. Will write off [to firm] for more details and will approach social services about possibility of them meeting the cost.

Obtained specially designed shower seat and toilet rails from REMAP ... Leon is able to support himself now on the toilet which, apart from being a tremendous help to Mrs B., is also a great boost to his self-esteem.

The resource workers gave help with the disabled child's behaviour, either with its more problematic aspects or with maximizing her or his independence, to fifty-six out of the 107 families (Figure 4.4(*d*)). Not surprisingly, information and advice-giving were the most common forms of help:

Gave Mrs S. leaflet produced by Family Fund on hyperactive children – said she'd like to keep it for ideas.

Discussed Gill's demand for independence – has asked to be allowed to go to shop by herself and to park with friends. Mrs P. has refused so far. Discussed how realistic her anxieties are and agreed as starting-point that Mrs P. should allow Gill to go to local shop alone, as she can watch her from the gate.

Fifty families were helped to find specialized sources of clothing or footwear for children who had unusual requirements, or to obtain financial help to buy the extra items of clothing, bedding and footwear which disabled children often need (Figure 4.4(*e*)). The resource workers gave twenty-six of these families direct help – for example, by assisting with applications to the DHSS or Family Fund for financial grants; by obtaining specialist equipment such as an angled bed for a child with chronic chest problems; or by pressing for the prompt repair of special orthopaedic boots.

HOUSING PROBLEMS AND AIDS TO DAILY LIVING

Altogether the resource workers helped 77 per cent of the 107 families they visited with some kind of housing or environmental problem – for example, by trying to obtain minor or major housing adaptations; by trying to improve the safety or accessibility of gardens; by helping with plans to move to more suitable accommodation; or by obtaining aids to daily living (Figure 4.5). It is clear from Figure 4.5(*a*) and (*b*) that few families were given information and advice alone about their housing problems; the majority also needed help in dealing with other agencies and professionals to obtain the items or services they needed. Hence the resource workers were often additionally involved in making formal referrals to other agencies for assistance; in liaising – sometimes between

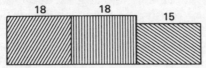

(a) *Minor adaptations to house and/or garden*
(total no. families helped = 26)

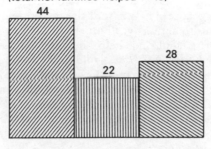

(b) *Major house adaptations/moving house*
(total no. families helped = 48)

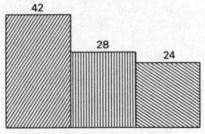

(c) *Personal equipment/aids to daily living*
(total no. families helped = 52)

Type of intervention

giving information/advice

referring/applying to other agency

liaison/advocacy with other agency

Figure 4.5   Intervention to resolve housing problems and to obtain adaptations and equipment for the home.

a number of different agencies where major adaptations were concerned; and in acting as advocates on a family's behalf when delays occurred. With a small number of families, a very great deal of work was done in connection with their housing problems; this is further described in Chapter 7.

Similarly, many of the families who were given help with obtaining daily living aids (Figure 4.5(c)) needed more than just information or advice:

> Social services are arranging for special chair to be made for Martin ... Phoned social services occupational therapist [OT] to ask whether chair was ready. Was told the matter had been passed to Mr Z., area health authority. Phoned Mr Z. ... was told he knew nothing about it, could not help and referred me back to social services. Telephoned OT ... was told that Mrs W. [social worker], who had visited Martin five months ago and made original request for chair, was on holiday but would be given my message ... Left message for OT about Martin's chair twice ... Phoned OT and stressed the urgent need for the chair.

FAMILY FINANCES AND BENEFITS

In contrast, a very high proportion of the help given by the resource workers in connection with families' financial and benefit problems consisted simply of information and advice-giving (Figure 4.6). Information and advice was given on a wide range of financial topics: benefits for the disabled child such as child benefit, education welfare benefits, and non-contributory invalidity pension and supplementary benefit on reaching the age of 16 (Figure 4.6(b)); benefits for the whole family like supplementary benefit, family income supplement, invalid care allowance and housing benefits (Figure 4.6(c)); and counselling about debts and other financial worries (Figure 4.6(d)):

> Talked to Mrs G. about allowances, etc. when Peter reaches 16.

> Went through welfare rights handbook with parents, trying to sort out their entitlements. Left book with them and asked them to write down their needs and we would then write to DHSS.

> Mrs R. hadn't heard about rating reductions when there's a disabled person in the house – gave her a leaflet.

Only in connection with the disabled children's mobility and attendance allowances (Figure 4.6(a)) did the resource workers have to provide a noticeable amount of help with appeals and reviews – that is, to sixteen of the thirty-nine families given help with these benefits:

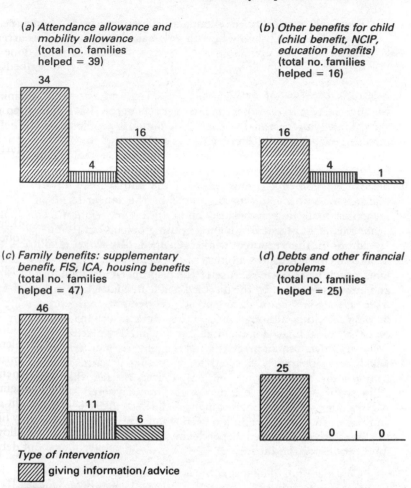

(a) *Attendance allowance and mobility allowance* (total no. families helped = 39)

(b) *Other benefits for child (child benefit, NCIP, education benefits)* (total no. families helped = 16)

(c) *Family benefits: supplementary benefit, FIS, ICA, housing benefits* (total no. families helped = 47)

(d) *Debts and other financial problems* (total no. families helped = 25)

Type of intervention

giving information/advice

help with application

help with appeal

Figure 4.6 Intervention in connection with family finances.

Mrs Y. phoned; attendance allowance has been reduced to day rate. She does not agree that the care Lucy needs has lessened and says she wants to appeal – will I help? We drew up a routine of when Lucy is well and otherwise ... to send in a letter to Attendance Allowance Board. Asked GP to write a letter in support. Sent with my covering letter to Attendance Allowance Board ... Mother genuinely grateful to get attendance allowance raised to higher rate again. Says she'll know how to go about things if situation arises again.

FAMILY AND PERSONAL PROBLEMS

Finally, the resource workers gave 88 per cent of the 107 families help of some kind with personal, social, or emotional problems. This help included enabling nineteen parents to go out on their own without their child or children by, for example, arranging suitable baby-sitting facilities; counselling twenty-seven parents with marital problems; discussing problems connected with the employment of thirty-two mothers or fathers; discussing some of the longer-term emotional responses to having a disabled child with thirty-eight parents; and dealing with the physical or mental health problems of fifty-one parents. In addition, the resource workers helped fifty-three families with problems concerning the siblings of the disabled child – usually problems which had arisen because of the disproportionate amount of care and attention needed by the disabled child. In connection with all these issues discussion, counselling and advice-giving were the predominant helping activities, although the resource workers also made six referrals on behalf of siblings (for example, for day nursery places).

The relatively small proportion of the resource workers' intervention which was apparently devoted to discussing parents' feelings about having a disabled child undoubtedly reflects the fact that none of the children in the study were newly born or diagnosed – a time when parents may well experience a much greater need to discuss their feelings and reactions. A more common need among this sample of parents was to discuss the continued dependency of their disabled child and its implications for the future:

> Consideration of adapting the house has made Mrs C. consider the full implications of Charles's handicap long term – she says it's easier emotionally to live on a day to day level ... Mrs C. feels overwhelmed by the enormity of the whole issue and very ambivalent about the residential/stay at home issue ... Encouraged her to be more positive about the future and learn from the past.

This analysis of the content of the resource workers' intervention – the types of problems they dealt with and the ways in which they dealt with them – reflects clearly the specialized focus of their activities. Only in relation to financial matters and general family problems did the resource workers deal to any extent with issues which were not directly concerned with the disabled child, but even here their intervention tended to be limited to the provision of information and advice. (It is of course possible that the incidence of acute financial and family problems among the families in this study was lower than it would be among the clients of a generic social work agency.) However, despite their specialist role, there is evidence from the resource workers' records that their professional social work background enabled them to deal with such problems when they did arise.

The Resource Workers' Contacts with Other Agencies

The analysis thus far has shown that the most frequent types of intervention by the resource workers with the families themselves were general discussion and counselling about problems, and the provision of information and advice about possible solutions to those problems. However, the previous sections have also suggested that work directly with parents and children formed only part of the intervention. In addition, the resource workers were also involved in referring families to other services, liaising and co-ordinating services and acting as advo- cates. All this work was carried out on the families' behalf, sometimes entailing contacts with a number of different organizations or officials in resolving one particular problem. Other summary measures of the resource workers' intervention, therefore, are their contacts with a range of other agencies and professionals, and the relative frequency with which each was contacted on behalf of the families in the project. Details of these contacts – whether in person, or by telephone or letter – were obtained from the resource workers' records. They provide an impressive picture of the wide variety of formal and informal, statutory, voluntary, local and national resources upon which the resource workers drew during the project.

CONTACTS WITH HEALTH SERVICES PERSONNEL

To begin with, Table 4.2 shows the range and frequencies of the resource workers' contacts during the project with professional practitioners and service administrators in the health services. The resource workers were in contact with health visitors or the community nursing services on behalf of more than one-third of the 107 families; most of these contacts were in connection with the supply of incontinence equipment or other nursing aids. Hospital consultants, physiotherapists, community medical officers (including school doctors) and hospital appliance centres were each contacted on behalf of about one-quarter of the families. For those families on whose behalf such contacts were made, the average number of contacts was not large, apart from the average of five contacts with psychologists about the developmental or behaviour problems of six children.

Table 4.2 *Resource Workers' Contacts with Health Services Personnel*

Contact with:	Number of families on whose behalf contact made	Average number of contacts per family
Health visitor or community nurse	41	3
Hospital consultant	34	3
Physiotherapist	27	3
Community medical officer	27	2
Hospital appliance centre	27	3
GP	19	2
Speech or occupational therapist	15	3
Psychologist	6	5
Ambulance service	1	3

(Total number of families = 107)

CONTACTS WITH WELFARE AGENCIES

The resource workers' contacts with welfare and personal social services agencies show a very different picture (Table 4.3). The resource workers were in contact with local authority generic social work staff – social workers, social work assistants and team leaders or managers – on behalf of almost three-quarters of the 107 project families. The number of contacts per family was also high; on average seven per family, and up to thirty-three contacts on behalf of two families. Contacts were made

Table 4.3 *Resource Workers' Contacts with Welfare and Personal Social Services*

Contact with:	Number of families on whose behalf contact made	Average number of contacts per family
Local authority		
generic social work staff	77	7
aids officer/OT	52	5
hospital social worker	36	2
other specialist social worker (e.g. for deaf, blind, mental handicap)	10	3
Other welfare agency (e.g. probation)	8	5
Hostel/home	7	3

(Total number of families = 107)

with social services aids officers or occupational therapists on behalf of one-half of the families visited by the resource workers. Again the average number of such contacts – usually about the supply of aids, or adaptations to the house or garden – was relatively high, and included six families where ten or more contacts were made. The relatively small number of contacts with hostels and homes does not reflect the full scale of the work done in finding short- or long-term residential placements, but only those instances in which the resource workers themselves were in direct contact with an establishment.

Table 4.4 *Resource Workers' Contacts with Education, Training and Employment Services*

Contact with:	Number of families on whose behalf contact made	Average number of contacts per family
School		
by resource worker alone	94	4
by resource worker and parents	13	2
School psychologist/welfare officer	21	3
Education department official	12	3
Careers/employment adviser	10	2
(Total number of families = 107)		

CONTACTS WITH EDUCATION, TRAINING AND EMPLOYMENT SERVICES

Table 4.4 documents the resource workers' contacts with the range of professionals who were involved with the education, training, or employment of the 107 disabled children. Although their contacts with the children's schools were not especially frequent (in no instance was a resource worker in contact with any school more than eight times during the project), they were extensive and were made on behalf of all but nine of the school-age children in the project.

CONTACTS WITH HOUSING AND PLANNING SERVICES

While the majority of childen were receiving (or began during the project to receive) some kind of education, fewer of them had housing problems with which they and their families needed help from the resource workers. Table 4.5 shows the range of the resource workers' contacts with housing organizations during the project (some housing problems, particularly those concerning the adaptation of private sector housing, were of course the responsibility of social services departments

Table 4.5 *Resource Workers' Contacts with Housing and Planning Services*

Contact with:	Number of families on whose behalf contact made	Average number of contacts per family
Housing department		
about moving house	15	5
about adaptation/repair	12	2
Planning/architect's/environmental		
health/chief executive's departments	10	3
Other housing agency	2	3

(Total number of families = 107)

and so were among the contacts documented in Table 4.3). Problems about moving house and adaptations to local authority dwellings involved contacts with housing agencies on behalf of altogether about one-quarter of the 107 families. As well as district council housing departments, contact with environmental health, architect's, planning and chief executive's departments could be necessary. Exceptionally contacts with non-statutory agencies, such as housing associations and a building society, were also made. Usually few contacts per family were necessary, apart from rehousing problems where up to fourteen contacts were made.

Table 4.6 *Resource Workers' Contacts with Sources of Financial Help*

Contact with:	Number of families on whose behalf contact made	Average number of contacts per family
Department of Health and Social Security about		
supplementary benefit		
basic entitlement	4	3
additional needs and payments	6	6
other welfare benefits	7	1
attendance or mobility allowance	11	2
Local authority about housing or education benefits	9	1

(Total number of families = 107)

CONTACTS WITH SOURCES OF FINANCIAL ASSISTANCE

The help given by the resource workers in connection with social security benefits and other financial problems is documented in Figure 4.6 opposite. Table 4.6 shows the range of organizations which the resource workers contacted in order to deal with these problems.

In total, the resource workers were in contact with DHSS or local authorities about welfare benefits on behalf of one-quarter of the 107 project families. Discretionary additions to supplementary benefit stand out as occasioning a particularly high average number of contacts per family. (The project took place before the implementation of the 1980 Social Security (No. 1) Act which replaced exceptional circumstances additions and exceptional needs payments by additional requirements and single payments.)

CONTACTS WITH VOLUNTARY ORGANIZATIONS

As well as the various statutory sources of help, the resource workers also drew heavily on the resources and facilities of voluntary organizations at both local and national levels. Table 4.7 documents the wide array of problems about which the resource workers consulted national voluntary organizations for disabled children and their families. These organizations included, most commonly, the Spastics Society, the Association for Spina Bifida and Hydrocephalus (ASBAH), and MENCAP (the National Society for Mentally Handicapped Children and Adults). Specialist sources of information such as the Disabled

Table 4.7 *Resource Workers' Contacts with Specialist Voluntary Organizations*

Contact about:	Number of families on whose behalf contact made	Average number of contacts per family
General information on national facilities and local groups	28	2
Holidays for disabled children	23	3
Mobility aids and aids for daily living	24	2
Incontinence equipment	10	2
Medical information about a disability	10	1
Assessment and education facilities	10	4
Housing adaptations	6	6
Short-term or permanent residential care	5	3

(Total number of families = 107)

Living Foundation, NAIDEX, REMAP (Rehabilitation Engineering Movement Advisory Panels), the Disability Alliance and the Royal Association for Disability and Rehabilitation (RADAR) were also frequently consulted.

In all, the resource workers were in contact with national voluntary organizations on behalf of almost two-thirds of the 107 families, most often for general information about the voluntary organization and the special services it offered, or for information about holiday facilities for disabled children. In addition, the resource workers were in contact with locally based voluntary groups on behalf of twenty-eight families, most frequently to find out about recreation facilities, or to obtain volunteer transport, baby-sitting, or financial help from local charitable sources.

These data clearly show that the regular visits to the 107 project families, and the counselling, information and advice given to parents during those visits, formed only part of the resource workers' activities during the intervention. In addition, their liaison, referral and advocacy work brought them into contact with a very wide range of national, local, statutory and voluntary agencies and officials. The agency with which the workers were in contact on behalf of most (88 per cent) of the 107 families was the disabled child's school. Local authority generic social work staff were contacted on behalf of three-quarters of the families; national specialist voluntary organizations on behalf of two-thirds; and local authority social services aids officers on behalf of almost one-half the 107 project families.

The Total Amount of Time Spent on Different Kinds of Problem

At the end of the intervention the resource workers completed a pre-coded questionnaire for each family they had visited. This questionnaire asked them to assess the amount of time they had spent, in whichever way and for whatever reason, on a range of topics and problems. The results of this assessment, presented in Figure 4.7, represent a summary of the data in the preceding sections of the chapter. Figure 4.7 incorporates the prevalence of different types of problems among the 107 families; the intensity of the work which was done to alleviate the problems; and the contacts through visits, letters or telephone calls which the problems necessitated between the resource workers, the families and various statutory and voluntary agencies.

With around three-quarters of the families they visited, the resource workers considered that they had spent a fair amount or a great deal of time working on problems concerning the disabled child's educational placement, progress and the quality of home–school relationships; the day to day care and development of the child; the parents' present, past and anticipated future feelings about the child; and the child's health,

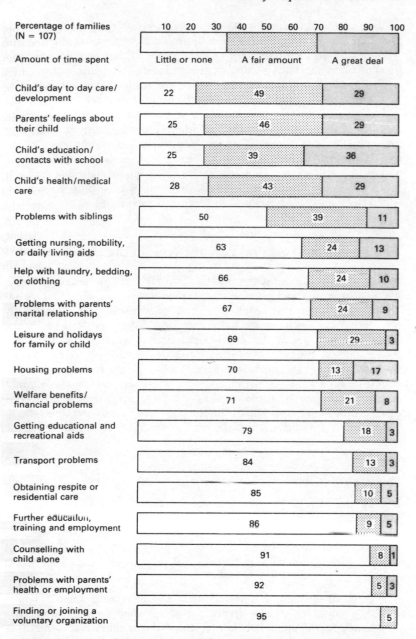

Figure 4.7 Total amount of time spent by resource workers on different types of problem.

medical care and treatment. At the other extreme, time was spent with less than one-tenth of the families on problems concerning the parents' own health and employment, or on enabling families to join and participate in specialist voluntary groups for disabled children.

The varying amounts of time which the resource workers spent in work on each of the different kinds of problem reflect, first, the prevalence of particular types of need and difficulty among a sample of families with severely disabled childen; secondly, the recurrent or protracted nature of certain issues; and thirdly, the complexity of the work involved in their resolution. This in turn indicates the range of knowledge and expertise – and the relative importance of particular kinds of knowledge and expertise – involved in providing a specialist social work service to disabled children and their families.

The Resource Workers' Perspectives on the Intervention

Intervention concerning the practical, social and emotional problems which arise from the day to day care of a severely disabled child does not necessarily mean that such problems will always be successfully resolved. Achievements and outcomes may have been limited by the intractability of problems, whether practical or emotional; by resource factors outside the control of the project workers; or by restrictions on the intensiveness and duration of their involvement. In this section the effects of any such constraints, and conversely any factors which might have enhanced the resource workers' achievements, are discussed. The discussion will draw principally on the semi-structured interviews which were carried out with each of the resource workers after the end of the project.

Positive Influences

During the interviews, the resource workers were asked to describe their own overall goals during the two-year intervention. Two common goals were clear; the development of a supportive relationship with the parents and children visited, and ensuring that each family received all the practical, financial and professional help from which they could benefit:

> With all of them, I achieved some sort of relationship ... where they could talk quite freely ... about their feelings about the handicapped child ... And most of the families had something material out of me going ... I wanted to make sure that, if they needed anything, they jolly well got it in the two years.

Improving relationships within the family ... [and] to enable a group of people who generally get less than they're entitled to from the services – not just the cash services, but social services, hospital treatment, good medical care, general community-based services, good education, etc. – who are generally at the end of the queue for the lot, to get a better deal out of it – which is fair, it's just what they're entitled to.

One conventional goal and criterion of success of the intervention might have been the prevention of a disabled child's admission to residential care. However, the resource workers considered this to be an inappropriate objective; for some children, the regular use of residential care facilities had been the only way of relieving intolerable family stress:

There were families where I used residential care to prevent the possible total breakdown of the family.

In only one instance did a resource worker consider that, had she not been available during a family crisis, the disabled child would have been admitted to permanent residential care.

Four particular features of the intervention stood out, in the resource workers' minds, as having been particularly important in contributing to its success and also to their own job satisfaction. The first was the opportunity to maintain regular contact with the families:

We provided a regular service. Families knew they could rely on us appearing every six to eight weeks without them having to contact us.

We've highlighted that need of regular visiting, even if it was only every three months – as long as they knew that in three months' time somebody would be coming.

I found parents saying to me, 'Well, I was worried about so-and-so two weeks ago' or 'I felt a bit low two weeks ago, but I knew you'd be ringing me up and coming within the next few weeks, so it was all right'. Because they knew I'd be coming within the foreseeable future, they could contain whatever it was that was bothering them.

The second positive feature of the intervention was the regular supply of relevant information about developments in policies and services for disabled children, which was provided for the resource workers by the backup team at Dr Barnardo's:

We were supplied with vast quantities of information 'hot from the press', which meant we didn't have to go searching for leaflets, etc., which is very time-consuming. Also we had our own – so one didn't have to run round an office for them or go to the local ministry with all the delays.

We were superbly equipped with information, weren't we?

The third positive feature of the intervention was the opportunity it gave the resource workers to improve the quality of parent–school contacts, which they thought had been of benefit to children, parents and teachers (and also the latters' attitudes towards social work):

> Either establishing or maintaining a contact with the schools – that is one of the things I think was very, very important . . . Some of the families had a tenuous sort of contact with the school; some had none; some had had rows with the school and in two particular cases one would hope that was mended . . . and both the school and the mother were very, very grateful.

I think it has opened the eyes of school staff about what a social worker is and what they have to offer. That has been a particularly positive side.

The fourth positive factor affecting the intervention and its outcomes was one which paradoxically also had some negative consequences. Working on an entirely independent intervention and research project meant that the resource workers had neither the access to material resources and services nor the authority and established credibility of an employing welfare agency. All material resources for the families therefore had to be negotiated and obtained from other agencies, as did official legitimation of the resource workers' intervention from other professionals and administrators. However, the resource workers thought that these negative consequences of their independence had easily been counterbalanced; first, by the regular stream of specialized information they had received from Dr Barnardo's:

> I think all we could offer was our expertise and knowledge. This was a great help with the masses of information which came from Dr Barnardo's.

> I should think there are few social services departments who have got as much information as I've got in my little office upstairs

and secondly, by the greater freedom of action which their independence had given them:

> I found it an advantage not to be part of the set-up in a lot of ways. You could go into the interdepartmental things, be taken notice of

by both sides because you didn't belong to any authority. You could go to councillors which you couldn't do with social services ... We didn't have to wait for approval of senior staff, committees, etc.

I'm sure we were more imaginative and persistent that we would have been if we'd been part of [the social services] scene.

Constraints and Limitations

Certain organizational features of the project undoubtedly did place restrictions on the activities of the resource workers and may well have limited their overall achievements. The isolation of working alone from home (apart from the regular bi-monthly meetings with staff at Dr Barnardo's) created a certain amount of strain, as did the considerable distances which two of the resource workers in particular had to travel to maintain contact with scattered caseloads. The amount of travel also limited to some extent the length of time out of their fifteen hours a week which the resource workers were able to spend in more direct intervention, as did the fact that, working from home, the resource workers had very little of the clerical and administrative support usually available to office-based social workers. These restrictions do seem to have limited their overall achievements to some extent. At the end of the project the resource workers thought that, had they had more time during the two years such that their intervention had been more intensive, they could have achieved a little more with 57 per cent of the 107 families and a great deal more with 23 per cent.

The other major constraint on the outcomes of the intervention was of course its two-year duration. Certainly, as Chapter 7 will show, some very intensive efforts by the resource workers to help families carry out housing adaptations or move house had still not come to fruition by the end of the intervention:

> The first thing that comes to mind is the sense of urgency in trying to get some of the things off the ground or completed in the two years, which really perhaps was not very sensible because there were things which should have been done little by little and slowly.

Secondly, two of the resource workers thought that much of their input during the first year of the project had concentrated on the development of relationships with the parents and children they were visiting rather than on more practical problems. This again had limited the range and number of tangible outcomes:

> It took some of them a very long time to decide that I was worth trusting. Had I just had 12 months with the Jones family I could have done nothing at all.

Thirdly, some of the resource workers admitted to a reluctance to tackle some problems which arose towards the end of the period of intervention because they did not expect to be able to resolve them in the remaining time. They were also aware that additional time had been taken up with preparations for their withdrawal at the end of the two years:

> The difference came towards the end, if new needs came up that you didn't have any length of time [to deal with] . . . I didn't want anyone to feel devastated. If you know it's two years, you can work towards that and never let anyone become dependent.

Of course a period of intervention lasting only two years for a project which had aimed, among other things, to provide support for the families of severely disabled children was somewhat unnatural and inappropriate. While families' current needs might be met, their needs for moral support, information, advice and practical assistance would clearly continue:

> When it came to the end of the two years, it seemed to be a very artificial ending. When you terminate a social work contract, usually it's because the family's better or they move; but to stop the project on a certain date . . . is very difficult.

The effect of the limited duration of the project was, in the resource workers' opinion, to have restricted their potential achievements. Had the period of intervention been longer than the two years, they thought that they could have achieved a little more with one-half of the 107 families and a great deal more with another 35 per cent.

Immediate Outcomes

In the final pages of this chapter the resource workers' overall evaluation of the results of their intervention is discussed, the immediate outcomes for the 107 project families are described and the overall costs of the intervention calculated.

Certain unique organizational features of the project clearly had both advantageous and constraining effects on the outcomes of the resource workers' intervention, as described in the preceding sections. Taking all these into account, how did the resource workers view the net overall success of their intervention with the families they visited? With only two of the 107 families did the resource workers consider that they had achieved nothing at all: one where the already well-informed parents were in touch with the local ASBAH social worker, and one where the child's Perthes disease and asthma had improved greatly since the parents' application to the Family Fund. (Interestingly, although the former family concurred at the end of the project that the intervention had made no impact at all, the latter parents felt that the resource worker's intervention had made a very great deal of difference to their lives.) With one-third of the families, the resource workers thought that they had made small achievements, and with one-half, they considered they had achieved a fair amount. Further, with 15 per cent, they thought they had achieved a great deal. Not surprisingly, there was a statistically significant association between the number of visits made to a family and the resource workers' assessment of their level of achievement with that family; the greater the number of visits, the higher the resource workers' self-assessed levels of achievement. (Here again it is likely that the number of problems and needs experienced by the families during the intervention was a common underlying variable.) There was also a tendency for the resource workers to feel they had achieved more with those families whose children were older. With only 18 per cent of the under-5s did the resource workers consider that they had achieved a very great deal, compared with exactly one-half of the over-10s, again possibly reflecting the greater needs of this older age-group. There was, however, no relationship between the resource workers' assessments of their levels of achievement and the children's impairment; they were as likely to have achieved a little, a fair amount, or a great deal with families whose children had mental handicaps as with those whose children had physical or multiple impairments.

For the 107 families, the end of the project certainly did not automatically mean the withdrawal of all social work support. The resource workers discussed with them their needs for continuing support and as a result formal referrals, sometimes accompanied by a joint visit or case conference, were made on behalf of eighty-five families. Forty-two of these referrals were made to social services departments; twenty-five to Dr Barnardo's team which had provided professional support to the resource workers during the project; and the remaining eighteen to education welfare officers, voluntary welfare agencies, or hospital social workers. Interestingly, the twenty-two families for whom no arrangements were made had apparently had less help from the resource workers during the previous two years; they had received significantly fewer visits than those families who were referred for ongoing help. They were also significantly more likely than the referred group to be among those families with whom the resource workers considered they had achieved only a little or nothing at all during the course of the project. Again there were no differences in the impairments of the children in those families who were and were not referred for continuing help. However, those with children aged between 5 and 10 were much less likely to be referred: only 31 per cent were referred for continuing support compared with 88 per cent of both the oldest and youngest age-groups.

Finally, there remains the crucial question of the cost of the intervention. Was it an extravagant luxury, providing an expensive service to a group of privileged families? In spite of the high travelling costs incurred by two of the resource workers, the total cost of the intervention – the resource workers' salaries, travel expenses, telephone, and postage and clerical costs – averaged no more than £109·50 a year per family at 1978 prices. To take account of inflation that sum would have to be increased to about £220 a year or £4 a week in 1985.

This chapter has documented in detail the range and focus of the resource workers' intervention. It provides a unique picture of the activities involved in providing specialist social work support to families of severely disabled children. In Chapter 5 we begin to examine the impact of that intervention, first of all as described by the parents themselves.

CHAPTER 5

Outcomes: The Parents' Views

'Consumer' Opinion in Social Work Research

A noticeable trend in social work research since the mid-1960s has been the increasing focus on the recipients' perceptions of the processes and achievements of social work intervention. This trend is important for two reasons. First, examining the opinions of those who receive a service is an important complement to – and indeed may directly challenge – professional perceptions of 'client' needs and behaviours, and the professional practices which derive from those assumptions (Robinson, 1978; Oliver, 1983). Secondly, any rigorous and comprehensive evaluation of the effectiveness of social work intervention must clearly take account of the views of the beneficiaries of that intervention:

> Most studies of the outcome of social policy rely on objective or indirect criteria of success . . . However, where a service is intended to produce direct benefits for the recipient and where the results can be expected to materialise in the short run, there is every reason for using the client's own evaluation of the help received as a central measure of success. (Hadley, Webb and Farrell, 1975, p. 133)

Some evaluative studies of social work intervention (for example, Mayer and Timms, 1970; McKay, Goldberg and Fruin, 1973; Sainsbury, 1975) have focused exclusively on clients' expectations of, and satisfaction with, social work help. Other studies (Rees, 1978; Sainsbury, Nixon and Phillips, 1982) have examined the processes of social work intervention from the sometimes varying viewpoints of the major participants, social workers and their clients. Yet a third group of studies (for example, Goldberg, 1970; Bayley, 1973; Hadley, Webb and Farrell, 1975) have examined the views of clients as part of a broader strategy of outcome evaluation, to complement data which have been obtained from other sources using different research methods. It is in this latter context, as an integral part of an overall research strategy to assess the impact of the resource workers' intervention, that 'consumer' opinion will be used in this study.

The opinions of social work 'consumers' may, however, be influenced by a number of factors, apart simply from the quality or usefulness of the help they actually receive. Their previous experience of asking for, or being given, help; their expectations of the service being given; and their own definitions of the help they think they need will all affect their evaluation of a particular social work service. Furthermore, the importance of the 'casework' relationship between social worker and client and the fact that practical and material help may also be delivered through that relationship both mean that the quality of the personal relationship with the social worker may also colour the recipients' opinions of social work intervention.

The questions asked during the second series of interviews with the 107 project families tried to take account of these various influences by, first, asking a series of pre-coded questions in which parents assessed the amount and type of help they had received from the resource workers in relation to a number of specific problems. These questions were complemented by some further open-ended questions in which parents were invited to describe the subjective impact of the intervention. The analysis of the answers to these questions constitutes the main part of this chapter. It is followed by an assessment of the longer-term impact of the intervention, based on the follow-up postal questionnaire which was sent to the project families nearly two years after the intervention had ended.

The Help Received from the Resource Workers

During the second interviews after the end of the intervention parents were asked to assess how much help the resource workers had given them in connection with eight different types of problem. Respondents were encouraged to be as frank as possible in these assessments and were repeatedly assured of the confidentiality of their replies. There is therefore no reason to suspect them of having been constrained in expressing negative or critical comments. Some of the negative responses which were received did, however, also include instances in which help with a particular type of problem had not actually been needed by an individual family during the project. As it was not always possible to distinguish and exclude these respondents from the analysis, the data in the following pages do underestimate the perceived *helpfulness* of the resource workers. The data are, on the other hand, reliable indicators of the extent, amount and types of help which parents recalled having received during the project, and their estimations of the value of that help.

Help Received in Connection with Specific Problems

DISABILITY AND MEDICAL CARE

For example, it appears from Figure 5.1 that the help received from the resource workers in dealing with issues connected with their child's

Percentage of parents who found resource worker
(N = 107):

Figure 5.1 Help received from resource workers in connection with child's
disability and medical care.

disability and medical care may have been less significant to parents than
the help received from other professional sources. The disabled child's
handicapping condition and health care were issues likely to have arisen
with virtually all the 107 families, but only one-half of the parents said
that the resource workers had actually given them help with either or
both of these matters. The most common form of help reported by those
families who had received it was simply information and advice (recalled
by thirty-five of the fifty-four parents receiving help); twenty-seven
parents said that they had been given books or pamphlets by the resource
worker about their child's disability; and twenty-two said the resource
worker had helped by liaising with other professionals about their child's
disablement or medical care.

DAY TO DAY CARE AND DEVELOPMENT
Similarly, issues about their child's day to day care and general
development were likely to have been common among the 107 families,
but only sixty-four parents said that they had received help from the
resource workers in connection with them (Figure 5.2). Again this help
was most likely to have consisted of direct information and advice-giving
by the resource workers (recalled by forty-six of the sixty-four parents
who had received help). In addition, twenty-six parents recalled the

Percentage of parents who found resource worker
(N = 107):

Figure 5.2 Help received from resource workers in connection with child's
day to day care and development.

help given by the resource worker in the form of referrals to other
sources of advice, and six specifically cited the resource workers' liaison
with their child's school over these problems.

The number of parents who said that the resource workers had helped
them in connection with their child's health or general development is
surprisingly low in view of the considerable and widespread inputs
recorded by the resource workers. It is, however, possible that parents'
assessments of the relative helpfulness of the resource workers included
implicit comparisons with the help they had received during the same
period from other professionals such as doctors, paramedical therapists
and teachers, who were directly responsible for the child's medical and
developmental care.

AIDS, EQUIPMENT AND HOUSING

Clearly, only a proportion of the 107 families in the project group were
likely to have experienced housing difficulties severe enough to necessi-
tate major adaptations or removals; consequently only 40 per cent
reported that the resource workers had helped them with these problems
(Figure 5.3 (*a*)). On the other hand, three-quarters reported that the
resource workers had given help with obtaining aids and equipment for
their disabled child (Figure 5.3 (*b*)). In both instances the majority of

(a) *Adaptations or moving house*
Percentage of parents who found resource worker
(N = 107):

Very great deal of help
23

Fair amount of help
9

Little help
8

No help
59

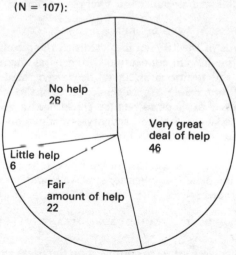

(b) *Aids and equipment*
Percentage of parents who found resource worker
(N = 107):

No help
26

Very great deal of help
46

Little help
6

Fair amount of help
22

Figure 5.3 Help received from resource workers in obtaining aids, equipment, or suitable housing.

Percentage of parents who found resource worker
(N = 107):

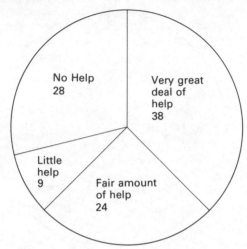

Figure 5.4 Help received from resource workers in dealing with financial problems and benefits.

those who reported that the resource workers had helped in some way thought that this had amounted to a very great deal of help.

FINANCIAL PROBLEMS AND BENEFITS

Over two-thirds of the 107 families said that the resource workers had given them some help in connection with general financial problems or with meeting the additional financial needs generated by their child's disablement (Figure 5.4). Again the majority of these parents thought that the resource workers' assistance constituted a very great deal of help. Most (sixty-eight of the seventy-seven parents receiving help) recalled having received information and advice from the resource workers about financial and benefit problems; forty-seven said the resource workers had helped them complete forms or write letters in connection with benefit applications as well; and six cited help with benefit appeals or reviews.

LIAISON AND ADVOCACY, FAMILY PROBLEMS AND PERSONAL
COUNSELLING

Finally, parents were asked to comment on three less tangible aspects of the resource workers' intervention: the help that they had received from the resource workers in liaising and negotiating with officials and

(a) *Liaison and advocacy*
Percentage of parents who found
resource worker
(N = 107):

(b) *Family problems*
Percentage of parents who found
resource worker
(N = 107):

(c) *Personal counselling*
Percentage of parents who found resource
worker
(N = 107):

Figure 5.5 Help received from resource workers with liaison and advocacy, family problems and personal counselling.

professional people generally on matters concerning their disabled child; the discussion of problematic relationships within the family and devising ways of reducing some of the impact which the disabled child could have on these relationships; and the clarification of some of the parents' own feelings and anxieties about their disabled child. As Figure 5.5 (a) shows, 80 per cent of the 107 parents had had help from the resource workers with liaison and advocacy; 87 per cent had received help with family problems and relationships (Figure 5.5 (*b*)); and 95 per cent had been helped by discussing their own feelings and worries with the resource worker (Figure 5.5 (*c*)). Not surprisingly, in this latter instance there was a clear relationship between the frequency with which parents recalled having talked with the resource worker during the project about their own feelings and anxieties and the extent to which they had found this helpful; those who said they had talked often were significantly more likely to have found it a very great help.

SUMMARY OF AMOUNTS OF HELP RECEIVED

Figure 5.6 summarizes the data on the amount of help received. From it, it is possible to compare the proportion of the 107 parents who thought that the resource workers had given them at least some degree of help, and the proportion who said that they had given a very great deal of help, in each of the eight subject areas. Clearly, the vast majority of parents felt that they had received most help from the resource workers in their role as counsellors: discussing relationships within the family and the

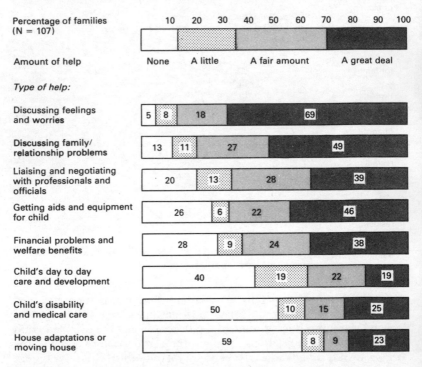

Figure 5.6 Proportions of families who received a little, a fair amount and a great deal of help of different kinds.

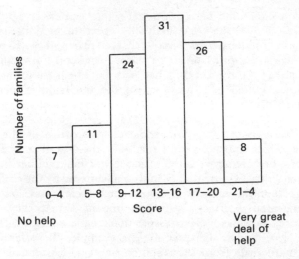

Figure 5.7 Overall score of total amounts of help received from the resource workers.

attitudes and feelings of other family members about the disabled child, and talking through their own feelings and worries. Liaison and advocacy, obtaining aids and equipment, and help with financial or benefit problems followed in importance. Parents were less likely to have found the resource workers helpful in connection with their child's health and medical care, with her or his day to day care and development, or with housing problems.

Variations in the Amount of Help Received from the Resource Workers

From parents' answers to the eight questions asked about the amount of help that they had received from the resource workers in connection with particular kinds of problem an overall score was computed for each family, by assigning a value of 1 to each response of the resource worker having given a 'little help', 2 to a 'fair amount of help' and 3 to a 'very great deal of help'. This score produced an indication of the overall amount of help received from the resource workers as perceived by each family. The distribution of these total scores, out of a possible maximum of 24, is shown in Figure 5.7. Only one of the 107 parents said that the resource worker had not been helpful in relation to any of the eight types of problem. The distribution of the remaining 106 parents' scores was slightly skewed, with slightly more than one-half (56 per cent) having scores higher than the mean of 14.

This score of parents' perceptions of the total amount of help received from the resource workers was analysed further, to see if there were any associations with particular family characteristics or with particular levels or types of input from the resource workers. For example, did certain kinds of family feel they had had more help from the resource workers than others? To what extent did the families' perceptions correspond with the resource workers' own assessments of their intervention?

There were in fact no discernible characteristics of the families themselves which appeared to be related to the overall amount of help they reported receiving from the resource workers. Neither the type of impairment (physical, mental, or multiple) suffered by the child nor the child's age, nor the manual or non-manual social class status of the family, appeared to affect the overall amount of help they received. There were, however, clear associations with some of the input measures described in Chapter 4. For example, those families who received more visits from the resource workers also tended to report having received a greater amount of help. There was a significant relationship between the resource workers' own assessment of their achievements with each family and the total amount of help which the family reported receiving: those families with whom the resource workers thought they had achieved a fair amount or a great deal also reported having received significantly more help (as measured by their 'overall help' scores) than those families where the resource workers felt they had achieved only a little. While this close match between resource worker-assessed input and parent-assessed outcome is reassuring, it is in fact likely to reflect the common underlying factor of the extensive and severe problems experienced by some of the families in the project. Indeed those families who reported having received a great deal of help (as indicated by their high 'overall help' scores) were also those with whom the resource workers felt their achievements had been limited by the two-year duration of the intervention – had they had a longer period, they could have achieved even more.

The Amount of Contact with the Resource Workers

Finally, in this section, we examine parents' opinions on the amount of contact they had with the resource workers during the project. Most parents (81 per cent) said that they thought that it had been 'about right'; 16 per cent said they would have liked to have had more frequent contact with the resource workers; and only 3 per cent thought that they had had more contact than they had actually needed. There was, however, no significant difference in the average number of visits actually made by the resource workers to these three groups of families.

Parents' Voices

At the end of the second interview parents were invited in an open-ended question to identify the one most important feature of the resource workers' intervention. This was not always easy; fourteen parents were unable to identify any single feature which was more important than the rest, and twelve parents mentioned two important features. These 'most important' features fell into four broad groups, as shown in Table 5.1.

Table 5.1 *The Most Important Feature of the Resource Workers' Intervention*

	Percentage of parents
'Having somebody to talk to'	42
'The information, advice and practical help we received'	41
'Knowing there was someone there if I needed help'	23
'The reliability of the regular visits'	8

Total number of parents = 93
Percentages do not sum to 100 because 12 parents cited two features

In all, thirty-nine parents said that the most important feature of the resource workers' intervention had been the feeling of personal support they had derived from having someone to whom they could talk about their disabled child and the problems arising from her or his care:

Being able to talk to her. It used to make me feel better once she'd been and we'd sat down and talked.

Being able to talk to her and unburden myself. It relieved the tension. Nice, just knowing she's there on the phone.

Being made to feel human and not on your own. She helped keep me sane, feeling that I could talk to her. I did feel very much on my own until [the resource worker] started to call.

The value of 'having someone to talk to' seemed to have been enhanced by two particular factors. First, there was the fact that the resource workers clearly knew and appreciated the practical and emotional consequences of childhood disablement:

Her understanding. I think she fully appreciated what I was trying to say to her, and I enjoyed her coming.

You feel someone has an interest in Gerald, her interest was very genuine. She understood what his condition involved.

Secondly, the talking was done within a relationship which had been allowed to develop during two years of regular contact:

> Having one person who gets to know you very well, and you develop a trusting bond between you.

> I think that as she came each time, you got to know her very well and so you could relax and talk to her, whereas when a stranger comes along you feel you have to watch your p's and q's.

> It was like having a friend I could lean on, who could put me in touch with anyone who could help me. She seemed to be able to advise me on any problem. She had a lot of experience.

> She was more like a friend than a social worker.

The second most frequently cited 'important feature' of the intervention was the information, advice and practical help which parents said the resource workers had given them. Implicit in many of their comments was an appreciation of the fact that this help had been offered routinely and spontaneously or in response to very general queries rather than, as in parents' previous experience, only in answer to precisely formulated requests:

> We've got to know more in the last two years than we ever knew.

> She knew where help could be got and was prepared to guide me.

> She found out about everything, whereas the social services don't – if you ask them about one problem, they will find out about that; but that's all, they never give you any other information. I didn't even know about the mobility allowance, and I still wouldn't have done if it hadn't been for [the resource worker] telling me. Social services never bother to let you know anything if you don't go and ask.

> Mainly all these lists of things she's given me. I've got a stack of addresses to look through where I can contact different organizations when I have a problem. She seemed to know a lot about Pamela's handicap and even if I asked her a question and she couldn't answer, she would always go away and find out about it and let me know.

> She has been the only one who helped us. No one else has bothered but she knew what we could get.

Other parents cited more specific instances of practical help as the most important feature of the intervention:

> The fact that she sorted out Larry's supplementary benefit. She wrote me a letter telling me that she thought Larry would be eligible for it, and I had to use her letter when I saw the supplementary benefit people to prove my point.

> The holiday for Desmond stands out.

> She put a lot of pressure on the housing department.

> She started the ball rolling about our claim to the Vaccine Damage Claims Unit.

The spontaneity and precision of the information-giving which parents so clearly appreciated seems likely to have been a consequence of the resource workers' specialized caseloads and the specialist information with which they were briefed before and during the intervention. This enabled them to make unprompted suggestions or respond effectively to very generalized queries.

Almost one-third of the parents said that they found the reliability of the resource worker's regular visits, or her accessibility should the need for help arise, to be the most important features of the intervention:

> I found it a great comfort knowing [the resource worker] was coming to visit.

> I knew there was someone there to help if I ever needed it.

> She would say, 'If you ever need me, just ring up', and it's a great relief to know that there is someone there.

Parents were also asked whether there were any kinds of help which they would like to have had during the previous two years, but which the resource workers had been unable to give them. Only seven of the 107 parents were able to cite any outstanding needs. Four of these would have liked more help with practical problems – adaptations, finance and a holiday for the disabled child; one mother would have liked more help to enable her to develop a social life of her own; and two mothers said that they would have appreciated more opportunity to talk to the resource worker.

We were also interested in parents' views on the appropriateness of a specialist social work service as a means of providing help and support to families with disabled children in general. Only eight parents said they thought that other types of help would be more useful – though most of these were cited in addition to, rather than instead of, the help given by the resource workers. Four parents called for more financial help, a specialist baby-sitting service, more provision for disabled teenagers and more advice for people with mental handicaps. Two parents thought that more help should be forthcoming from the statutory services:

> I only wish that people like [the resource worker] could have enough authority to be able to tell people like social services and social security that they have an obligation to do certain things – she could only go and ask.

One parent said that she derived a great deal of help from talking with other parents, while the eighth simply 'did not know'.

The question about appropriate forms of help for disabled children and their families prompted many parents to amplify their earlier comments on the value of the service given by the resource workers. These comments fell into three main groups. First and foremost, parents had clearly appreciated the personal contact with an informed but independent person, with whom they could discuss any problems:

> You need someone like [the resource worker] to talk to and ask advice. An outsider can sort out a problem, they can see it from a different angle.

> Her help was good – it was an independent sort of help, you can't always talk to your doctor or friends.

> The fact that she isn't part of the family, and sees things differently from what I do.

Other parents valued the kind of service provided by the resource workers because it had involved routine and regular contact without a formal request for help having to be made:

> I think you need someone like [the resource worker] to visit you on a regular basis – someone you can talk to on a regular basis. It makes you feel you are not being forgotten. The social worker only comes if you ask them to come.

> Yes, [you need someone like the resource worker] from time to time – but one person. You need to be able to build up a relationship with one person, instead of all different people coming in.

However, for the majority of parents, it was the resource workers' ability systematically to offer appropriate information and advice which lay behind their endorsement of the service:

Definitely we need someone like [the resource worker]; I don't think people are told enough about the handicaps, and the benefits they can get.

It was good to have her calling from time to time. It's so useful to have someone to tell you what things there are available to help.

Two specific aspects of this information and advice-giving service were singled out for particular comment. One was the way in which the resource worker had acted as a 'single door', a person who could be approached about a wide range of problems, and who would direct parents to the most appropriate source of help:

It helps to be in touch with someone like her because we don't always know who to go to.

You need to be in touch with someone like [the resource worker] because you are cut off from the world and you don't know how you can get help.

Secondly, a number of parents felt that the quality of the resource workers' information and advice-giving was the result of their specialist expertise, and that specialization was therefore an essential feature of a good support service for disabled children and their families:

[The resource worker's] type of help is good. Other people like the health visitor, who see other people, their knowledge is so broad that they have not got specialist knowledge of handicapped people. Their knowledge is connected with normal people.

Everyone ought to have someone like [the resource worker] who is just dealing with handicapped people and not with old people as well.

I think we need someone to give help and advice. [Families with disabled children] need someone – particularly someone with specialist advice for the *mentally* handicapped.

Although parents were not specifically asked about it, it was clear from their comments at the end of the project that for many of them the help provided by the resource worker had been their first experience of receiving any regular professional support:

I think families do need someone like that to come. I didn't have anybody before she came, and I think it's been a good thing altogether. I shall miss her.

85

> I think you need someone just to call in, you need someone to be there occasionally who will bother. I'd never been in contact with anyone before.

> Apart from [the resource worker], there is no one else who calls.

In the light of these answers it is perhaps not surprising that the vast majority (94 per cent) of the 107 parents felt that overall the intervention had made some difference to their lives. Sixteen per cent thought it had made a little difference; 28 per cent thought it had made a fair amount; and exactly one-half – 50 per cent – thought it had made a very great difference.

The positive impact made on these 107 families by the resource workers' intervention is undeniable. First, the intervention enabled them to share anxieties and resolve problems in the context of regular contact with an informed counsellor; secondly, it led to them obtaining an apparently unprecedented amount of useful information and advice. These two features are reflected in the opinions expressed by recipients of other forms of social work intervention. Younghusband's (1978) review of research on 'consumer' reactions to social work concluded that clients' positive opinions are affected, first, by the practical concern and sympathetic understanding shown by social workers, and secondly, by the social workers' ability to give practical advice and obtain material assistance.

It is of course possible that parents' subjective evaluation of this particular intervention was distorted by the affective content of their relationship with the resource worker; it may have been her personal attributes or the quality of the relationship she had developed with them which contributed to so much of their positive feelings. While this was undoubtedly true to some extent (all but one of the 107 parents said that they liked the resource worker as a person), these feelings would have constituted a serious source of bias if only one project worker had been involved. Instead the same opinions were expressed about five workers with different ages, social backgrounds and professional histories. This suggests that parents were responding much more to the common elements in the service which the resource workers were providing than to their personalities or characters.

Retrospective Reflections

Any doubts about the validity of parents' subjective opinions of the intervention were also mitigated by the results of the follow-up postal survey, which was carried out twenty-two months after the end of the intervention. By this time the impact of the resource workers' personal characteristics might be expected to have faded. The results of the follow-up survey, which was intended to assess the longer-term impact of the intervention, were consistent with the views expressed by parents immediately after the project ended. This again suggests that the service itself, rather than the personalities of the people who provided it, was the source of parents' positive opinions.

Eighty-two completed questionnaires were returned out of the 107 posted to project group families (a further six were returned uncompleted because families had moved or their disabled child had died, giving an effective response rate of 77 per cent). Parents were, first of all, asked to identify their main sources of advice and help since the end of the project, and to compare this help with the amount received from the resource workers. Only 15 per cent of the eighty-two parents thought that they were now getting more help (either because their needs had increased or because of the resource workers' long-term mobilization of local services). Thirty per cent said they were receiving the same amount of help as before, but 48 per cent of parents thought they were now receiving less help than during the project although their needs had not diminished. The main sources of the help which was currently being received were various – voluntary organizations, the Family Fund, social services, schools and Dr Barnardo's – and multiple – 20 per cent of parents named more than one such source. However, 26 per cent could not identify any current main source of help, even though there was no evidence that they no longer needed it.

Exactly two-thirds of the eighty-two parents said that the information and advice they had received during the project was still proving useful almost two years later. One-half also said that they were still finding other kinds of help like practical services or equipment which they had obtained during the intervention to be of use.

Finally, the follow-up postal questionnaire asked parents to choose whether they would prefer to have a service like that provided by the resource workers, or its equivalent value in the form of a weekly or annual cash grant. The vast majority (89 per cent) of parents chose the service. Most of the 11 per cent who opted for the cash grant said they would prefer it in an annual lump sum rather than as a weekly allowance. When asked to assess the preferences of families with disabled children *in general*, again a majority (69 per cent) of parents thought that others would also prefer the supportive service to a cash allowance. A typical comment was the following:

Money just does not replace the support needed from day to day.

These findings clearly confirm one of the main hypotheses which underlay the establishment of the resource worker project, that severely disabled children and their families lacked – and would benefit from –

regular contact with a specialist social worker who could provide information, advice and support. The practical help which families obtained as a result of the intervention was important, and unprecedented, for very many of them. Even those parents who felt that they had needed little practical assistance had appreciated the regular contact and counselling help available from the resource workers. Clearly, then, the support provided by this kind of service helped parents to feel less isolated and more able to cope, and seemed to improve their morale in caring from day to day for a severely disabled child.

However, parents' opinions – crucially important though these were – are not the only dimension on which the project was evaluated. The interviews with the project and comparison groups before and after the intervention were designed to assess the impact of the intervention according to a large number of other criteria. By comparing the circumstances of the two groups at the beginning of the project and again at the end, any differences which emerged could be attributed to the intervention of the resource workers. In Chapters 6–10 these comparative outcome measures are described and discussed.

CHAPTER 6

Outcome Measures 1: Disability and Day to Day Practical Care

In this chapter we begin to examine the impact of the resource workers' intervention by comparing the needs and circumstances before and after the project of the families they visited with the needs and circumstances of the comparison group of families. Both the project group families and those in the comparison group were asked identical questions in the interviews which were carried out before the intervention began and again after it had ended. The data obtained from the first set of interviews in effect served as a baseline: first of all, it was possible to check whether there were any differences between the two groups of families before the intervention began; and secondly, it was possible from the baseline to measure the changes which took place in each group of families in the subsequent two years.

With a carefully controlled scientific experiment, any changes which are detected in the experimental group but not in the control group can, with a reasonable degree of confidence, be attributed to the experimental treatment or intervention. Within the context of social work research and other types of experimental social intervention strictly controlled conditions are clearly not possible; families will be affected by a wide range of influences and circumstances in addition to the specific intervention whose impact is being studied. In this instance families in both the experimental and comparison groups continued to receive a wide range of help from doctors, teachers, local authority social workers, occupational therapists, health visitors, voluntary organizations and others, *in addition* to the special intervention of the resource workers with one group of families. Any changes in the experimental group can therefore be attributed with less reliability to the intervention of the resource workers, so these comparative data have been complemented by additional information about those aspects of the intervention which may have caused the changes. In the following five chapters the outcome measures which compare the two groups of families before and after the intervention are prefaced by quantitative and qualitative data from the resource workers' records of the actions they took.

Disability, Handicap and Health Care

Disability and Handicap

Clearly, the role played by the resource workers in relation to the children's disabilities and their treatment was marginal, and supplementary to the activities of doctors, nursing staff and remedial therapists. Yet as Chapter 4 showed, 81 per cent of the 107 project group families were given some kind of help with this topic, most often (with 77 per cent of the 107 families) in the form of information and advice:

> Mrs A. asked if I knew of any short articles on Down's syndrome ... I said I had a list in a MENCAP booklet and will let her have it – all on different aspects of care, what to expect, etc. Assured her they were for parents, not experts.

> Suggested Mrs B. ask the school physiotherapist if she could suggest anything Mrs B. could do to help clear Alan's chest while he is off school.

> Mrs C. worried about Alvin's left foot seeming to turn inwards again ... wanted an earlier referral to [orthopaedic surgeon] – Alvin not due to see him for ten months. Mrs C. asked me about correct procedure. I suggested physiotherapist at school refer him through school medical officer, or directly.

Less frequently (with 36 per cent of the 107 project families) the resource workers liaised directly with medical professionals about individual children, or initiated referrals for assessments or treatment:

> Discussed difficulties of getting medical information with the paediatrician's social worker. She felt that the paediatrician would be more than willing to see the parents again and go through the results of the tests with them ... Both parents were pleased to have opportunity to discuss the results with the consultant, providing 'it will be no trouble'.

The outcomes of intervention of this kind are very difficult to assess. Any such assessment would need to involve measurement of the extent to which parents in the intervention group had become perhaps better informed about their child's disability, or more satisfied with the treatment she was receiving, than parents in the comparison group. Such measurements would probably not be very reliable, and might also be at odds with the opinions of doctors or other medical professionals who were involved with the children and their families. It is, however, reasonable to assume that this particular area of intervention by the resource workers contributed to the general appreciation of the information and advice parents were offered during the project, which was documented in Chapter 5.

Apart from the disabling condition itself, the resource workers were also concerned to help parents alleviate some of the handicaps commonly associated with severe disability, by giving information and advice themselves or by increasing parents' and children's contacts with remedial professionals. For example, many severely disabled children (including almost two-thirds of both the project and comparison groups at the start of the project) may be unable to speak as well or as clearly as others of the same age. The resource workers helped sixteen families with this problem, by giving information and advice, by liaising with speech therapists and other professionals, or by liaising between professionals and parents:

> Discussion with speech therapist in relation to recommended exercises in the book *Let Me Speak*, as I feel regulated interaction between Mrs P. and Ray could improve their relationship. Therapist . . . will give Mrs P. some general speech development exercises to do.

> I am very grateful to have had the opportunity of meeting the speech therapist and seeing her work with the child . . . I tried to impress upon parents and [sibling], who is 9 and involved in playing and speaking with Chris, the importance of Chris being encouraged to use expressive language. It is so easy for the parents and [sibling] to anticipate what Chris wants, but this way she is not going to 'speak for herself'.

However, at the end of the project the number of parents who reported that their child's speech had improved over the last two years was exactly the same – 42 per cent – in each group. The resource workers also appeared to have affected only slightly the frequency of children's contacts with speech therapists; 29 per cent of the resource worker group parents said that their children had had speech therapy during the two years of the project compared with 27 per cent of comparison group parents.

Another handicap experienced by many severely disabled children is in the acquisition of basic literacy skills. Of the 100 children in each group over 5 years old at the end of the project, only 29 per cent of the resource worker group and 28 per cent of the comparison group were said by their parents to have a reading ability which was normal for their age. The resource workers recorded giving help to seventeen of the remaining parents about their child's reading problems, either through the provision of information and advice or through liaison with other professionals:

> Mr M. has disciplined Mick into doing reading homework again and they feel part of the problem is the infantile level of the story content of books which are for Mick's reading ability. Contacted National Children's Book Club about the possibility of a suitable book list ... Mentioned the reading problem to [educational psychologist. He] has a book list available compiled by the school remedial service, so he will discuss this with parents.

This input was reflected in the subsequent outcome measures. Of the sixty-eight resource worker group children whose reading ability was below normal for their age, 27 per cent were reported to have improved during the project as against only 19 per cent of the seventy-two comparison group children.

Visits to Hospitals

For a substantial proportion of severely disabled children, primary responsibility for their health care, treatment and therapy lies with specialist hospital-based medical services. Many disabled children do experience prolonged or repeated in-patient admissions for assessment, operations, or treatment, and most can also expect regular out-patient appointments with a paediatrician or other specialist.

IN-PATIENT ADMISSIONS

A child's admission to hospital as an in-patient, in addition to causing parents some degree of anxiety and emotional stress, is likely to give rise to a number of practical problems as well. Transport for visiting has to be arranged. Whether or not a private family car is available, such transport will invariably incur additional financial costs. Both parents may lose time and earnings from work, and special arrangements will have to be made for the care of other children in the family. Help with many of these problems may normally fall within the relatively specialized remit of a hospital-based medical social worker. However, as described in Chapter 4, the resource workers found at the start of the project that only 6 per cent of the families they were to visit reported being in even occasional contact with a hospital social worker.

Fifty-four per cent of the 107 resource worker group children and 56 per cent of the 103 comparison group children were in fact admitted to hospital (for one or more nights) during the two-year project, about one-half of each group on two or more occasions. The resource workers helped relatively few families, however, with any problems which arose at these times: four families were helped to find out or speed up the date of their child's admission; two were given advice about how to keep the child amused during a long spell in bed; and eight families were helped with transport to and from the hospital:

> Coral waiting to go into hospital, on urgent list, for operation. (Orthopaedic surgeon] retires in eight weeks, no successor appointed yet ... I spoke to community health council secretary. He phoned later to say that they are expecting to do the operation before [the surgeon] retires.

> Vera will be operated on in Children's Hospital and go for convalescence to Weston. This creates problems for visiting – 6-hour journey to spend 1 hour with child. Contacted medical social worker – she will definitely see about help with cost of visits.

> Aron to be admitted to hospital [50 miles away] tomorrow. Ambulance will take mother and Aron but not father. Mrs D. can't manage Aron on own in ambulance [he is hyperactive]. GP has phoned ambulance station and they will not agree to take both parents. Mrs D. says she dare not go on her own. Can I help?

The resource worker dealt with this immediate crisis by meeting the parents and child at the bus station halfway between their home and the hospital and driving them the rest of the way there. She then set about devising a more satisfactory solution:

> Phoned ambulance station, spoke to supervisor. Whoever had answered the parents' call had been quite correct in refusing request as per regulations; but exceptions can be made and he eventually said one should have been made in this case ... I explained there might be a similar situation on return journey. Rang social worker at hospital, who said she'd try and see if something can be done about transport on return ... [as] Dr N. wants to see both parents before Aron discharged.

The resource workers' intervention did appear to make some impact on the proportion of families who reported experiencing difficulties in connection with their children's hospital admissions. In the two years before the project began difficulties were experienced by 38 per cent of the fifty-six resource worker group families and by 21 per cent of the sixty-one comparison group families whose children had been in hospital. The proportions who later reported having experienced difficulties during the project decreased in both groups, but to a slightly greater extent among the resource worker group families.

OUT-PATIENT APPOINTMENTS

Between 82 and 85 per cent of the children in each group had to attend hospitals or clinics on an out-patient basis for check-ups or treatment during the project. Transport could again be costly, particularly if a child had to attend a specialist clinic some distance from home, while ambulance journeys might be circuitous or poorly timed in relation to hospital appointments. According to the resource workers' records, seven families were helped during the project with problems of transport to out-patient appointments, either by being given information and advice or by direct liaison:

> Mr C. wants to go [to out-patient appointment] but cannot go in ambulance with Mrs C. Suggested that if necessary Mrs C. could ask social services, who may provide help or ask the WRVS.

> Rang [paediatrician's] secretary. Explained problems of getting Mel to and from hospital appointments and asked for [ambulance] transport. Secretary rang back to say Dr X. had agreed to transport 'for time being'.

Of those families who normally used the ambulance service to get to hospital appointments, the proportions experiencing difficulties declined in both groups during the project, but again the decrease was slightly greater among the resource worker group families.

Disabled children and their families sometimes experience other problems with the organization or timing of out-patient appointments, or in communicating satisfactorily with medical staff. A total of fifteen families were helped with these difficulties by the resource workers, who gave information and advice or liaised directly with the hospital:

> Mandy's behaviour – linked with epilepsy? – is worsening. Not due to see paediatrician again for six weeks. Mrs J. doesn't think she can wait that long. Has phoned hospital but paediatrician away. I spoke to paediatrician's secretary and explained situation. Dr S. back on Monday and appointments full. After discussion, she said that Mandy could be fitted in.

> Seems great confusion over hospital visits. Mrs P. has had appointments in Easton for electroencephalogram, at Weston Royal Infirmary and also several appointments at Northton for kidneys and epilepsy. Offered to try and sort out why so many hospitals involved. Phoned Weston Royal Infirmary doctor's secretary, Easton and Northton ... Received phone call from Northton. Unless emergency, Marlene will only have appointments there, apart from orthopaedics and teeth. Other hospitals have agreed.

In order to assess the impact of the resource workers' intervention those parents in each group whose children had had recent out-patient appointments were asked the following series of questions, both before and after the intervention, to assess their overall satisfaction with the arrangements for appointments:

(1) Do you usually see the same doctors when you go?
(2) Do you think the doctors there are interested in the problems you have with ——?
(3) Do you think they give you enough information at the hospital about ——'s handicap?
(4) Do you think you are given enough information at the hospital about ——'s treatment?
(5) Do you think that —— is receiving the right treatment for his/her disability?
(6) Do you usually have problems caring for your other children when you go to the hospital with ——?
(7) Do you or your husband usually have to take time off work when —— has a hospital appointment?
(8) Do you have to wait for a long time at the hospital?
(9) Do you find that the journey to hospital is expensive?

Each answer indicating a lack of difficulty or dissatisfaction was assigned a value of 1, and these were added together to produce an overall 'satisfaction' score. There was, however, no difference between the two groups of families, each group having an average score of between 5 and 6 both before and after the intervention.

The Personal Care of the Disabled Child

This section looks at three major aspects of the disabled child's personal care: washing and bathing; dressing and feeding; and toileting and incontinence. It assesses the impact of the resource workers' intervention on the management of the child's lack of independence in personal care, to ease the burden which this dependency placed on others.

Washing and Bathing

Both before and after the intervention, over 80 per cent of the children in each group needed more help with getting washed and bathed than would be expected for a non-disabled child of the same age; around 60 per cent were still entirely dependent on help from others. Washing and bathing a disabled child can be eased by a variety of special aids, such as taps, rails, bath insets, hoists and showers, or by structural alterations to a bathroom to create more space for a wheelchair and helper. Of the eighty-nine families in each group whose children needed more help than normal with washing and bathing, 33 per cent in the resource worker group and 27 per cent in the comparison group already had one or more such aid before the project began.

Altogether thirty-nine families were given help by the resource workers with obtaining bathroom aids and alterations. With twenty-six of these families, the resource workers did more than just give information and advice, they referred families for help or liaised on their behalf:

> Mrs K. interested in Sunflower [bath] aid and also hoists. She'll phone social services, and I said I'd write as well for Sunflower aid and general advice. Mrs K. has friend with handicapped boy who has Sunflower aid but she did not realize where it came from or that it was more generally available.

> Question of bathing – parents wonder if bath aid would be sufficient. Mr W. would like to see housing department and social services about this, and see what can be done to give Mary some degree of independence and help Mrs W. Agreed I'd write to housing and social services departments and send him copy of letter, and then he'll go himself and try and get an appointment with housing manager.

Sometimes a considerable amount of perseverance was necessary:

> March 1978. Local authority social worker had suggested to Mr and Mrs J. that Family Fund might install a shower (in their council house). I explained this was social services' responsibility. Asked if I should phone social worker and tell him Mrs J. would like a shower. It was agreed I should.
> November 1978. Social services still not visited about shower. Promised to contact them again in stronger terms.
> December 1978. Wrote to housing department about shower, with copy to social services. Social services telephoned, and agreed that shower was necessary and will support application. Social services are writing to housing department.
> May 1979. Shower not installed. Rang social services to let social worker know there's been no progress. She will phone housing department.
> Rang housing department. Officer who had visited family has retired and no one seems to be doing his work. Spoke to Ms X., who said that shower had been delivered at end of February and was

waiting to be installed. She promised to speak to building inspector.

Direct works department rang – waiting for plumber to install shower. Explained urgency; building inspector suggested writing and explaining case again. Wrote again to housing manager.

July 1979. Shower still not installed. Suggested local councillor approached. Mr J. will go and see him. Mr J. finds it increasingly difficult to get Lyndon in and out of bath – effort is too much and Mrs J. cannot manage at all.

Wrote to local councillor.

August 1979. Shower now installed, shortly after father's visit and my letter to councillor.

As a result of this intervention, 29 per cent of the resource worker group families whose children needed help with washing or bathing obtained aids during the project, as against 26 per cent of the comparison group. These twenty-seven resource worker group families between them obtained thirty-one items; the twenty comparison group families obtained a total of twenty-four items. In both groups shower installations and alterations to the layout of the bathroom were the most frequently obtained forms of assistance.

However, this help did not appear to make any substantial impression on parents' subjective feelings about their child's lack of independence in washing and dressing. Parents were asked during each set of interviews to indicate on a 7-point scale how much of a burden they felt this dependency to be. There was a slightly greater increase in the proportion of resource worker group parents who felt it did not constitute any burden at all, and a greater decrease in the proportion who felt it to be a very great burden, than among the comparison group families. However, there were no differences between the two groups in the extent to which the scores of individual parents increased or decreased during the project.

Dressing and Feeding

Before the project began, about 85 per cent of the children in each group needed more help to get dressed than would be usual for a non-disabled child of the same age; almost 60 per cent of each group were completely unable to dress themselves. In addition, 60 per cent of the comparison group children needed either specially prepared food or help with feeding, as did 53 per cent of the resource worker group children.

The resource workers recorded giving twenty-five families help with feeding or dressing problems, mainly in the form of information or advice about sources of practical help:

Talked about what Laura can do – dresses herself well under supervision, but cannot manage hooks and eyes and buttons at back, especially on bra. Gave details of bras Laura might be able to manage ... Mrs P. very pleased with suggestions I made ... has tried Velcro which Laura can manage to fasten and unfasten, and is looking for a front-fastening bra. I suggested Mothercare might stock them.

Alison also has problems of holding eating utensils, so I gave information about the new attractive ranges of wide-handled utensils which are available.

Will find out about large-size Pelican bibs and large plastic bibs covering shoulders ... Wrote to Disabled Living Foundation for address of suppliers.

Mother would like to know where she can obtain a suction-bottomed egg cup ... I ordered one through the occupational therapist at the child development centre.

Parents in both groups whose children needed any extra help with feeding or dressing were asked whether they had obtained any aids or special equipment for this during the project, but despite the resource workers' intervention, as many comparison group families reported having obtained between them almost exactly the same number of items as the resource worker group families.

The provision of aids and equipment is of course only one method of easing the burden of dependency; a first priority will be to enable children themselves to develop their own independence and personal care skills. Before the project began, around one-fifth of the parents in each group reported that their children were taking part in structured learning programmes, usually at school, to improve their independent living skills. Despite the intervention of the resource workers (who recorded liaising with other professionals about the management or training of eleven children with self-care handicaps) the proportion of children who were reported by their parents at the end of the project to have recently received such training was identical in each group.

Therefore it is perhaps surprising that slightly more resource worker group than comparison group children seemed to have become relatively independent in getting dressed during the project – a 10 per cent (as against a 5 per cent) increase in the proportion who were reported to be able to dress themselves with no more than a little help. However, there were virtually no changes before and after the project in the proportions of children in each group said to need special help with feeding. Similarly, when asked to indicate on a 7-point scale their subjective feelings about the burden of dressing their disabled child, the mean scores of the parents in each group were the same both before and after the intervention.

Toileting and Incontinence

TRAINING PROGRAMMES AND TOILET AIDS

Coping with incontinence and toileting a disabled child are among the most trying problems which parents have to face. Of the 188 children aged 5 and over at the start of the project, 61 per cent were doubly incontinent and a further 12 per cent were partially incontinent (the proportions in each group were the same).

As with other self-care skills, the problems of incontinence can be improved for some children by structured training programmes or by advice to parents and children on management techniques. The resource workers recorded giving information and advice on incontinence and toileting problems to fifty families. Some of this information concerned personal incontinence aids and equipment, which will be dealt with later; but some was concerned with toilet training and the general management of incontinence:

> Problem of odour caused by leakage from catheter. Mrs H. is unaware of special deodorants. Sent her the ASBAH leaflet on the subject.

> Suggested to Mrs T. that she ask headteacher about methods they use to train Sam.

With fifteen families, the resource workers actively liaised with other professionals about, or referred children for, structured training programmes:

> Phoned clinical psychologist. She has started a parents' group, teaching behaviour modification programmes to parents of handicapped children. Could she help Carrie with toilet training? Psychologist willing to help.

> No progress being made with toilet training, so we discussed the possibility of using a programme devised by clinical psychologist over summer holidays. We agreed I'd arrange a preliminary discussion between Mrs G. and psychologist . . . [Later.] Psychologist would prefer to have a medical referral as she is going ahead with treatment. Would like some indication of Rhona's developmental progress over the past eighteen months. Agreed with Mrs G. I could write to paediatrician.

However, this intervention did not seem to lead to a greater use of toilet training programmes: at the end of the project twenty-six comparison group children were reported to have had some treatment or training to help with their incontinence during the previous two years compared with only eighteen resource worker group children. There was also no difference in the proportions of parents (20 per cent in each group) who thought their child's incontinence had improved during the project.

Children with disabilities may also have difficulty in getting to the toilet, getting on and off it, or sitting on it without support. Seventy-eight children in each group were able to use the toilet to some extent before the project, but of these 72 per cent and 65 per cent in the resource worker and comparison group respectively needed more help than usual for a child of the same age. However, rails, bidets, special toilet seats, commodes and other aids may all help to ease a child's problems of physical manoeuvre and increase her or his independence. Of those children who used the toilet but needed more help than normal, 15 per cent in the resource worker group and 42 per cent in the comparison group already had aids of this kind before the project began. Information and advice about toileting aids was included in that received by the fifty families who were given information and advice about incontinence and toileting problems:

> Because Betty's arms are so weak, she needs to be lifted on to toilet or bedpan. Mrs B. is unable to do this without someone's help ... it is vital that some way is devised by which some greater degree of independence can be achieved. I suggested a device whereby a bedpan could be slotted in and out of back of a commode.

Sixteen families needed more active help from the resource workers to obtain suitable toilet aids:

> Discussed toilet seat problem with social services occupational therapist. She knows of no inset other than Mothercare trainer seat. She will contact Multiple Sclerosis Society to see if they can help. I contacted Spastics Society occupational therapist – she knows of no suitable inset seat. I suggested use of Amesbury commode which can be fitted over existing toilet.

> Wrote to social services about potty chair. Social worker for the handicapped phoned – had never heard of Watford potty chair. Explained that [social services] central division office issued them and promised to let her have literature.

As a result, thirteen resource worker group families but only five comparison group families said they obtained toilet aids during the project, either for the first time or in addition to those they already had.

In each group the same proportion of these aids was provided either wholly or partly by the health or social services. However, these aids did not seem to make any impact on the children's overall degree of independence in using the toilet, as perceived by their parents. By the end of the project 27 per cent of both the fifty-six resource worker group children and the seventy-seven comparison group children who had needed extra help to use the toilet were thought to have become more independent.

PERSONAL INCONTINENCE AIDS

The day to day management of incontinence can of course be made much easier with the help of disposable nappies or pads, plastic pants and protective bedding such as mattress covers and drawsheets. Although local health authority community nursing services are empowered to provide these items, parents are frequently unaware of the range of items available, and sometimes have difficulty obtaining enough suitable items for their child's needs. The remainder of this section will examine the impact of the help given by the resource workers with obtaining these personal aids to ease the day to day management of incontinence.

As well as giving information and advice, the resource workers had to take active steps to help thirty-five families obtain incontinence equipment which was suitable or sufficient for their child's needs. Obtaining suitable nappies was a frequent problem; some parents simply did not know that disposable nappies were available from their local clinic:

> Told Mrs F. she'd be able to get disposable nappies for Len and she should inquire at health centre ... I asked health visitor to let family have a supply as they were not aware they could get them.

Other parents preferred to use towelling nappies, not normally available through the community nursing services, but found it difficult to obtain large enough sizes for their children:

> Gave details of large towelling nappies ... Mrs J. has now bought large-size towelling nappies and is delighted with them.

The most frequent (and often the most protracted) problems arose in maintaining a regular supply of disposable nappies from the health authority:

> Mother hasn't received any disposable interliners this month and is now reduced to nine towelling nappies – has made various attempts to investigate this by phoning health centre without success. I phoned health centre – not surprised mother made no progress as I was passed round four extensions. Eventually it was discovered

she'd been 'missed' from this month's delivery. Arranged for a box to be left at desk for mother to collect and a full delivery made as soon as possible.

Problems about disposable nappies – they were delivered to the home from the clinic, but now clinic has run out and Mrs P. is buying disposables at 86p a packet every other day. Contacted handicap liaison health visitor – she will make an early visit.

Similar help was needed with the supply of plastic pants, particularly with obtaining those suitable for a growing child:

Mrs M. is finding plastic pants are getting too small. Took incontinence pants samples. Mrs M. very interested in these, took name down, will ask at health centre . . . [Later.] My talk with Mrs M. on incontinence pants has done some good. Mrs M. has asked again at clinic and has rather grudgingly been given a few when she goes. She is satisfied.

A third type of item often needed by an incontinent child is protective bedding such as mattress covers, drawsheets, or disposable pads. The resource workers gave a number of parents information about these types of protective bedding:

Took new incontinence bed pads sent by [private firm]. Mrs N. will try them out and let me know what she thinks – had never seen bed pads before.

Discussed various incontinence aids and I was able to give name of manufacturers of one-way absorbent sheets which may well be of great help to Mrs O. as she is trying to get Melvin to sleep without nappies.

The resource workers also recorded sixteen instances where they referred families to, or liaised with, health authorities over the provision of such items:

Rubber mattress cover is rotting – existing cover was bought with a bedding grant from supplementary benefit. Phoned handicap liaison health visitor. She visited family and provided plastic mattress cover and Incopads for the bed to replace mother's home-made drawsheets.

Mrs S. has a rubber sheet almost the whole length of the bed but the mattress still gets wet as Alex moves about – a completely enclosed waterproof mattress or zipped cover would solve the problem. Rang clinic, who can supply Sandra mattress cover . . . Mrs S. has been in touch with clinic about Sandra mattress cover and been badly bitten. The man to whom she spoke said she could only get a cover on production of a doctor's note. This wasn't the impression I got when I rang and had not been told about any medical note. It has put Mrs S. off doing anything more about it. Getting to the surgery is a bus ride and her GP charges for doctor's notes ... Phoned clinic. In view of Mrs S.'s circumstances she can have a Sandra mattress cover without GP's note, and one is ready for collection.

In order to measure the impact of the intervention those parents whose children were over 4 years old but had some kind of incontinence problem were asked at each interview whether they used disposable nappies or pads, waterproof pants, or protective bedding; and if so, whether they usually obtained all or some of these from the health authorities. As Figure 6.1 shows, the overall proportions of incontinent children using each item increased in both groups during the project, apart from the use of waterproof pants by the comparison group. There was a very marked (22 per cent) increase in the proportion of resource worker group children using mattress covers, drawsheets and other protective bedding. Changes in the percentages of those who obtained some or all of their aids from the health authorities varied with different items. There was little change in the proportions of either group who usually obtained their disposable nappies from the health authorities. There was a small drop in the proportion of comparison group families with incontinent children who obtained waterproof pants from the authorities. However, the proportion of resource worker group families who obtained their protective bedding from the health authorities doubled during the project, while the proportion of comparison group families stayed virtually the same.

What impact did the resource workers' intervention have on parents' subjective experience of looking after an incontinent child? Those parents whose children were over 4 but who had some kind of incontinence problem were asked at each interview whether there were any incontinence aids – disposable nappies, waterproof pants, or protective bedding – which they thought they needed but did not have. Comparatively few parents in either group reported an outstanding need for disposable nappies, either before or after the project; but the proportion of resource worker group parents who reported a need for waterproof pants halved, while the proportion of comparison group parents reporting a need for protective bedding nearly doubled.

Finally, as with other aspects of self-care, parents were asked to indicate on a 7-point scale the extent to which they found it a burden coping with their child's incontinence. The mean score of the comparison group increased slightly during the project, but there was a

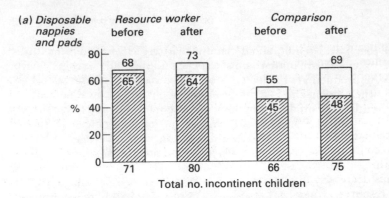

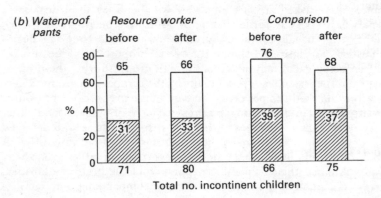

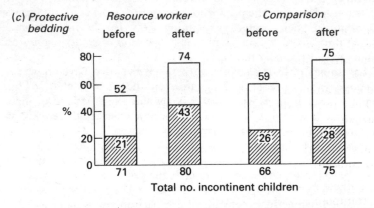

Figure 6.1 Use of incontinence equipment and its supply from the authorities.

significant decrease in the average score of the resource worker group of families. When the scores of individual families before and after the intervention were compared, 38 per cent of comparison group families felt their child's incontinence had become more of a burden as against only 22 per cent of the resource worker group.

In summary, those families who were visited by the resource workers obtained more toileting aids than the comparison group families. They also continued to use, and receive from the health authorities, protective clothing for their incontinent child, while the use and receipt of these items decreased among the comparison group. Thirdly, the proportion of resource worker group families receiving help from the health authorities with protective bedding doubled during the project. The impact of the resource workers' intervention was also apparent at a subjective level; the severity of the burden of coping with incontinence which was experienced by the resource worker group families had decreased significantly by the end of the project.

Giving Extra Attention and Supervision

Supervision during the Day

Many disabled children need more attention or supervision during the day than would normally be required by a non-disabled child of the same age. Children with mental handicaps may have very short concentration spans or little awareness of danger, or may damage themselves or their surroundings, or may have a tendency to run away. Children with severe physical limitations, on the other hand, often need extra amusement to alleviate frustration and boredom. Before the project began, around 56 per cent of the children in each group were thought by their parents to need extra attention or supervision for these reasons.

Thirty-three of the families visited by the resource workers were given information or advice about their child's behaviour problems or need for extra attention, and twenty-two were helped by the resource worker liaising with other agencies or professionals about ways of keeping the child amused:

> Talked about toys to occupy Rupert. He's very fond of the trampoline at school. I suggested Family Fund might buy one. Mrs B. will think about this and probably write herself.

> Visited child's school. I was shown suitable toys for Tom and said I'd pass this information on to parents and try to get him to play with these.

105

Mentioned writing to various sources of help with special indestructible toys – offered to write for information. Mrs S. would like me to do this.

Alistair [blind child] does not get cassette tapes, nor is he a member of tape library. Mrs H. confirmed it would be very beneficial if Alistair could belong to tape library. Contacted mobility officer for the blind.

Not surprisingly, in view of the continuing dependence of their severely disabled children, the proportion of parents who thought their children needed more attention or supervision than normal had risen in both groups by the end of the project, although the increase was slightly greater among the comparison group (a 22 per cent as against a 17 per cent increase in the resource worker group). Parents' subjective feelings about the severity of the problems created by their child's need for extra attention mirrored this pattern. When parents' scores on a 7-point scale of severity were compared, there was a slight increase in the mean score (and therefore the severity of the problems) reported by the comparison group parents and, in particular, in the proportion with the highest scores. Meanwhile the mean score of the resource worker group families fell, as did the proportion with the highest scores. In addition, the individual scores of more comparison group than resource worker group parents increased during the project. This indicates that the resource workers' intervention had made some impact on the growing burdens of providing extra daytime attention and supervision to a group of severely dependent children.

Attention at Night

Broken nights caused by the medical or behavioural problems of disabled children are frequent occurrences: 79 per cent of resource worker group parents and 80 per cent of comparison group parents said before the start of the project that their child needed more attention at night than other children of the same age. The resource workers recorded only twelve instances in which they gave help with this problem, mainly to the parents of mentally handicapped or deaf children who woke very early and would not stay in bed:

Mrs G. asked about bed with cot sides. Explained that she should ask GP or health visitor about this. She will do so when she goes to clinic next – Andy climbs out of bed.

Mrs B. talked about the difficulty of keeping Jane warm as she kept getting in and out of bed. This meant she was up and down covering her up. Mrs B. asked advice about duvets as she'd never used one. I said I'd lend her one belonging to my child and see how Jane managed with it . . . Mrs B. found duvet very good and Jane kept covered up at night.

At the end of the project the proportion of children reported to need extra attention at night had decreased in both groups, but by a greater amount (10 per cent) in the resource worker group than in the comparison group (3 per cent). Similarly, the impact on parents' subjective experience of their child's need for extra night attention appeared to be small but noticeable. The mean score of the comparison group parents' assessment, on a 7-point scale, of the severity of the problem increased but remained the same in the resource worker group. On an individual level 47 per cent of comparison group parents thought the problem was more severe at the end of the project than before compared with only 29 per cent of resource worker group parents.

The Overall Burdens of Care

A measurement was devised of the overall severity of the burdens experienced by parents in caring for their disabled child. This was calculated by combining parents' answers to the five separate questions in which they had been asked to indicate how much of a burden they found their child's need for extra help with dressing, bathing, coping with incontinence, providing extra supervision during the day and giving attention at night. Their answers, on a 7-point scale ranging from 1 ('no burden at all') to 7 ('a very great burden'), reflected the perceived severity of each problem. When combined, these scores indicated the overall severity of the burdens felt by parents in caring for their disabled and dependent child (the higher the score, the greater the felt burdens).

The mean scores of each group of families, out of a possible total of 35, showed small (but non-significant) differences before and after the intervention: that of the resource worker group dropped from 18·3 to 17·0, while that of the comparison group increased from 18·0 to 18·5. The individual scores of more comparison group parents than resource worker group parents increased during the project. Comparison group parents were also more likely to have large increases in their scores, suggesting a greater increase in the overall felt burdens.

We then looked to see whether, underlying these small differences in the severity of the burdens of care experienced by the two groups of parents, there were some larger differences in the scores of specific groups of families before and after the intervention. For example, had families with young children experienced a greater decrease in the overall burdens of care as a result of the intervention than families with older children, or were particular types or levels of intervention by the resource workers apparently more effective in reducing the severity of the burdens of personal care?

First of all, the two groups of families were divided into a number of subsamples according to the predominant impairment of the child (physical, mental, or multiple); the child's age (under 5, 5–10, or 11 and over); and the social class of the head of the household (manual or non-manual). There were no significant changes in the average 'overall severity of burdens' scores of families of different social classes or whose children had different types of impairment. However, there was a significant decrease in the scores of those parents with children aged 11 and over who had been visited by the resource workers. This suggests that the intervention had substantially eased the problems experienced by the carers of this eldest group of children. This result is consistent with the earlier finding (in Chapter 4), that families with older children had also received more help from the resource workers, as measured by the number of visits made to their homes during the project. It is also consistent with a second significant result, that those families with whom the resource workers themselves thought they had achieved 'a very great deal' also had significantly lower 'overall severity of burdens' scores by the end of the project. In other words, there was a clear association between the level of input from the resource workers and the impact which this made on parents' experience of caring for an older, more heavily dependent child.

Practical Problems at Home

Some of the practical problems created by the care of a severely disabled child have already been indicated; here we consider some of those less directly related to the child's continuing dependence in self-care activities. Many of these are essentially problems of physical management: providing mobility inside and outside the house for a child who is unable to walk; doing the extra laundry caused by incontinence, sickness, or general clumsiness; replacing rapidly worn-out bedding, clothing and footwear; heating the house of a child who is in poor health; and so on. Alleviating some of these practical problems formed, according to the resource workers' records, a substantial part of their intervention. To what extent was the impact of this intervention discernible when contrasted with the comparison group?

Help with Extra Laundry

The majority of severely disabled children generate more laundry and cleaning than is usual for a non-disabled child of the same age; 74 per cent of resource worker group parents and 83 per cent of comparison group parents reported at the start of the project that they had extra washing or drying to do because of their child's disability. Incontinence is the most common cause of this extra laundry, but sickness, clumsiness and spending a lot of time sitting or crawling on the floor may all be contributory factors.

The resource workers helped thirty-one families to obtain or replace laundry equipment, mainly washing machines or tumble dryers. In the vast majority of instances this help consisted of encouraging parents to apply to the Family Fund for a grant for laundry equipment and, where necessary, writing as well in support of that application:

> Parents asked if Family Fund would provide tumble dryer. I warned about the cost – drying cabinets are cheaper to run. Parents will look at both in the shops and then write to Family Fund.

> Mrs D. wondered if Family Fund would help with washer and tumble dryer. I suggested she applied and said I'd write as well.

In the minority of instances in which the help given by the resource workers to obtain laundry equipment did not involve an application to the Family Fund, the resource workers gave advice or referred families to the Department of Health and Social Security or their local social services department for help with wiring and plumbing in new washers and dryers.

However, there was virtually no difference in the proportion of each group of families who received help with laundry equipment during the project. Of those families whose children caused extra laundry, 60 per cent of resource worker group families and 63 per cent of comparison group families had already received a grant from the Family Fund for a washing-machine or tumble dryer before the start of the project; 37 and 38 per cent respectively obtained one during the project. Only in the *number* of items of laundry equipment obtained from the fund during the project did the resource worker group families appear to have fared better, of the 30 families who obtained help with laundry equipment from the fund during the intervention, 43 per cent received two items, whereas only 22 per cent of the thirty-two comparison group families did.

Parents' subjective experience of the burdens caused by their child's extra laundry also showed some changes which could reflect the resource workers' intervention. All those with extra laundry problems rated their feelings on a 7-point scale, ranging from 'I don't feel it's any burden at all' to 'I feel it's a very great burden'. The mean score of the resource worker group families fell from 4·9 to 4·4 after the proejct, while that of the comparison group families increased from 4·8 to 5·0. These changes were mainly accounted for by a fall in the number of resource worker group families with the highest scores and an increase in the number of high-scoring comparison group families.

Replacing Worn Clothing, Bedding and Footwear

Frequent laundering results in extra wear and tear on clothes and bedding. This can also occur if children are overactive or destructive, wear aids such as callipers or braces which rub on their clothes, or spend much of their time crawling or shuffling on the floor. As well as extra bedding, special beds or cots may be needed, or special bedding to prevent pressure sores. Children who are an unusual shape or size may need expensive specially made clothes, while those with walking difficulties may need specially fitted boots or shoes. At least one extra need of this kind was reported by 70 per cent of resource worker group families and by 79 per cent of comparison group families before the project; subsequently 70 and 79 per cent respectively said that such a need had also occurred during the intervention.

Parents may experience difficulty in meeting regular extra needs of this kind from their own financial resources, and may need advice about applications to the Family Fund, health authorities, social services departments, or the Department of Health and Social Security. Information about, and liaison with, suppliers of specialized bedding or footwear may also be needed. Fifty families were given help with these problems by the resource workers. Twenty-four of these families needed only information and advice:

> Promised to send Mrs N. the Disabled Living Foundation leaflet on clothing because of wear and tear on James's clothes from Milwaukee brace.

> Heavy wear on Helen's shoes – gave information on plastic-coating shoe guard.

Ten families were helped to make successful applications to the Family Fund to help meet their child's needs for extra bedding or clothing:

> There is not enough money to allow Max several changes of bedding – his bedding needs changing every day which puts pressure on his mother to wash straight away, to make sure there is enough clean at next bedtime. Applied to Family Fund – family given £50 grant for bedding.

The National Health Service was another source of help with which the resource workers liaised on behalf of sixteen families, particularly where special beds, bedding, or footwear were required:

Phoned clinic and discovered that sheepskins [to avoid pressure sores in bed] can be obtained on receipt of recommendation from GP ... I telephoned area health visitor for the handicapped who I know has some in stock.

School physiotherapist wondered if I could make inquiries about 'drainage bed' [to prop up child and keep chest clear]. Visited local aids centre with Mrs Y., Georgina and physiotherapist. Manager of aids centre was very helpful, and said once we had the bed, he'd work out what rails were needed. Rang community nursing officer. She said it would be sufficient if I gave details on phone ... [Later.] Letter from area health authority saying bed had been ordered.

Orthopaedic boots very shoddy, joints keep breaking, therefore not giving ankle support. I suggested I write to firm with copies to physiotherapist and orthopaedic consultant. Parents thought this would help ... [Later.] Fitter from firm was at hospital, saw Alice and took a great deal of care in fitting. New boots arrived within a week – much better.

Social services departments, voluntary organizations and private firms were also contacted by the resource workers on behalf of five families:

Contacted child assessment centre at hospital to obtain address of plastic toe-capping manufacturers. Wrote to manufacturers ... Carole's toe-caps worn through already. Suggested mother tries to go to firm herself and take Carole to see [shoe] fitter, to see what he can suggest.

Figure 6.2 shows the impact of this intervention on families' receipt of additional help with their children's special or extra clothing, bedding, or footwear needs. The proportion of resource worker group families who reported having received help from the Family Fund or the statutory authorities increased during the project in relation to all three types of item. There were particularly marked, and statistically significant, increases in the proportions receiving help with their child's needs for extra clothing and bedding. In contrast, the proportion of comparison group parents receiving help towards their child's extra clothing needs increased by only 5 per cent during the project, while the proportion who reported having had help with extra bedding and footwear actually declined.

Telephones and Heating

Anxiety about a disabled child's health, particularly if she or he is prone to sudden illness or convulsions, means that for some parents a

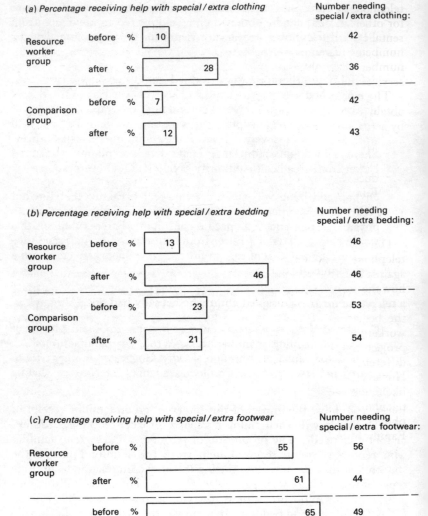

Figure 6.2 Help received from authorities with clothing, bedding and footwear.

telephone in the home is a necessity. Many will have a telephone already for other reasons but for some parents the cost of the installation and rental can be prohibitive. It was therefore important to look at both the numbers of families who obtained a telephone during the project and the numbers who obtained financial help (from the Family Fund, social services department, or charitable sources) with the cost of this.

The resource workers recorded helping a total of sixteen families to obtain a telephone, most frequently by giving information and advice or by actually assisting with an application for financial help:

> Mr W. to start spell of night duty soon and parents asked if there could be any help with a telephone as there is no way of contacting doctor at night [for an epileptic child] – wanted to know if Family Fund could help. Explained that fund could not consider it until social services have been approached. Rang local authority social worker.

During the project thirty-two resource worker group families had a telephone installed or connected because of their disabled child as against only twenty-one comparison group families. Figure 6.3 shows how these acquisitions affected the proportions of those families needing a telephone for their disabled child who actually had one. Although at the beginning of the project only just over one-half of the resource worker group families who needed a telephone had one, by the end of the project this had jumped to over three-quarters and the initial, significant difference in the unmet needs of the two groups had almost disappeared. However, the resource workers did not appear to have increased the likelihood of families obtaining financial help towards the cost of their telephones. Only one-third of the families in each group who obtained phones during the project had any financial help, mainly from the Family Fund.

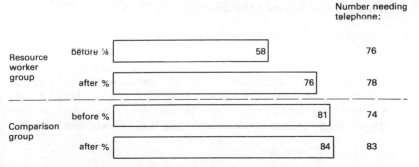

Figure 6.3 Ownership of telephones among families needing a telephone because of their child's disability.

Similarly, it was difficult to demonstrate that the resource workers' intervention made a noticeable impact on the extra heating which many families needed because of their child's poor health or restricted mobility. The help which the resource workers gave with this was often in the context of a much bigger set of problems concerning housing adaptations or modernization and, as we shall see in Chapter 7, solutions to these problems were sometimes delayed beyond the end of the project. Nevertheless the resource workers did record some instances where obtaining additional heating was a discrete, simple task:

> Mrs S. very worried because Peter has such poor circulation and 'is always cold' – no heater in bedroom. Gas heater costs £65·20. Mrs S. to see her GP [to obtain a letter about the child's need for extra warmth] ... Received GP's note from Mrs S. about heater, and approached social services.

> Sent letter to Family Fund supporting request [for portable gas fire] ... Reply from Family Fund received. Told Mrs T. to give fund exact details and she will get a cheque.

Altogether thirty-one resource worker group families obtained some form of extra heating during the project, of whom eleven had help with some or all of the cost. Thirty-two comparison group families also obtained extra heating, but only seven had help towards the cost. (In both groups the most common source of help was the Family Fund.) However, there was still virtually no difference between the two groups, either before or after the project, in the proportions who felt they had enough extra heating, had some extra heating but needed more or who had no extra heating appliances at all to meet their disabled child's need for additional warmth.

Getting About outside the Home

Over 80 per cent of the children over 2 in each of the two groups were unable to walk as far or as well as non-disabled children of the same age; over 40 per cent were unable to walk at all at the start of the project. In this final section we examine the help which these children received from the resource workers with obtaining wheelchairs and other personal mobility aids, and the help which their families were given with transport to relieve the potential restrictions caused by the child's lack of mobility.

Personal Mobility Aids

With such a large proportion of children experiencing difficulty in walking, the use of personal mobility aids – wheelchairs, crutches, callipers, buggies, tricycles, walking frames, and so on – was common. Eighty-five per cent of the children with walking difficulties regularly used at least one such aid before the project began; indeed those in the resource worker group between them used an average of 2·2 aids, and those in the comparison group each used 1·7 aids on average. Many of these aids are provided by the National Health Service through hospitals and specialized appliance centres (ALACs). Some may also sometimes be obtained from social services departments, schools, or community health services, while some voluntary organizations provide very specialized aids for children with particular disabilities. Alternatively, parents may choose to by-pass all these sources and buy mobility aids and accessories on the private market.

Although other professionals (such as occupational therapists and physiotherapists) and agencies (such as hospitals) were directly responsible for assessing, ordering and supplying personal mobility aids, the resource workers were nevertheless able to inform parents about the range of items available, direct them to the appropriate sources of supply and, on occasions, help them to deal with errors and delays in delivery. Altogether fifty-two families were given help of this kind, most commonly (in forty-six instances) with information about different types of aids or advice about how to obtain them:

> Mrs J. mentioned exercise bike. Explained that hospital could supply this – Mrs J. to ask.

> Adam is too large for his major buggy – cannot be placed and secured firmly. I suggested Mrs K. sees her GP about a wheelchair.

> Mr L. wanted information about a tricycle – showed him the type for spina bifida children and left information; also about good quality collapsible wheelchair as their NHS one doesn't collapse. Spoke of Zimmer children's growing chair – Mr L. will write for catalogue.

However, thirty families needed more active intervention to obtain mobility aids for their children. Some of these were new items, the need for which arose for the first time during the project:

> Wrote to headteacher for advice about trolley ... [Received] letter from headteacher recommending 4–8 trolley – will show trolley to Mrs D. at school ... Discussed with Mrs D. She has seen 4–8 trolley at school and Ashley has used it – thinks he would like it very much, though are unable to afford £57. I said I could approach Family Fund – agreed.

Peter still very attached to baby walker but has outgrown it – no larger one is made. Offered to make inquiries . . . Phoned ALAC – aid on wheels can be supplied on doctor's recommendation . . . Wrote to paediatrician.

In three families new mobility problems arose after the birth of a second, non-disabled child, when an ordinary wheelchair or buggy was no longer appropriate for transporting two non-ambulant children:

Mrs J. would like a double buggy but doesn't know where to obtain one. Advised her to contact ALAC, and if a new prescription is required, I'll contact the physiotherapist . . . Mrs J. has contacted ALAC – they'll issue a double buggy when baby is 6 months old.

However, a good deal of time was also spent helping parents to replace existing mobility aids with ones which were more suitable for their child's current size or condition, or to obtain repairs or adjustments to existing chairs and buggies:

Mrs X. finds Gavin heavy to push in his heavy wheelchair. Explained that lightweight Zimmer wheelchairs are now available from ministry – family unaware of this . . . Discussed wheelchair problem with physiotherapist and school medical officer. It was agreed I should approach ALAC to ask for a home visit by a technical officer.

Mrs Y. is dissatisfied with new pushchair – it is large, clumsy, difficult to handle and an eyesore . . . Phoned physiotherapist. He agreed with Mrs Y.'s feelings when I described the chair and feels technical officers should sort it out. If an appointment is made at the ALAC, he will try to attend. Wrote to technical officer.

New wheelchair is too heavy to be lifted into boot of the car and a folding, smaller chair has been refused by ALAC. Agreed I should write and try to see if we can change this decision. Wrote to ALAC asking for lighter chair for travelling . . . [Later.] Family very pleased with new lighter chair which had arrived as a result of my request to ALAC.

Sometimes a considerable amount of perseverance was necessary to obtain a mobility aid which was suitable for the child, or to prevent a whole family being immobilized by a long delay in delivering equipment:

Major buggy has foot strap broken and back wheels are beginning to bend and wobble. Mr Z. had phoned ALAC at Eastwich, asking for help and was told to expect a visit from them to assess repairs. That was three weeks ago and nothing has happened. I phoned Eastwich ALAC and was told they knew nothing about it and to try Southwich ALAC because they cover the area in which Kali's school is. Rang Southwich and explained situation, stressing that family is due to go on holiday in three weeks. No promises made but a referral for a visit would be passed on ... Major buggy was delivered a week later.

Phoned Mrs J. to confirm the meeting at clinic with her today. She said she had no chair for Amanda – her present one having broken, she has been loaned a totally useless one – i.e. it is too big and doesn't collapse. How can Mrs J. take Amanda in car? Phoned ALAC – there's been a hold-up from manufacturers of chairs, so no delivery to Blackpool. Can give no definite date for delivery of new chair. I pointed out total uselessness of loaned chair and asked for replacement today, so that child could go with Mrs J. to hospital: ALAC said impossible. I simply said I'd expect a new chair to be delivered by 1.30 p.m. Met Mrs J. at clinic – wheelchair had been delivered ... Amanda simply thrilled with chair and the mobility and independence it gives her.

To assess the impact of this intervention three outcome measures were used: the number of aids obtained during the project by each group of families; the (public or private) sources of these aids; and the numbers of children in each group who still needed (further) mobility aids.

Of those children with some degree of walking difficulty, 51 per cent in the resource worker group and 48 per cent in the comparison group obtained at least one new mobility aid during the project. Between them these forty-five resource worker group families obtained sixty-seven different aids, while the forty comparison group children obtained a total of fifty-seven new mobility aids – an average of 1·5 and 1·4 new aids per child respectively. The vast majority of these aids were obtained free of charge from the health and social services or through the child's school, although slightly more parents in the resource worker group reported having contributed themselves towards the cost of an item which had been obtained during the project. When parents were asked to identify any mobility aids which their child needed but currently did not have, 42 per cent of the resource worker group families whose children had walking difficulties between them reported a need for thirty-eight (further) mobility aids as against the twenty-three (further) aids needed by only 27 per cent of similar comparison group families. These more extensive unmet needs among the resource worker group families after the end of the project may simply reflect an increased awareness of, and desire for, aids about which they had been informed by the resource workers. Alternatively, they may reflect applications for mobility aids which had been initiated by the resource workers, but which had not actually been delivered by the end of the project; there is some evidence from the resource workers' records to support this latter explanation. However, it was not possible to assess the extent to which, had these items been delivered earlier, they would have affected this particular outcome measure.

Vehicles, Accessories and Concessions

Children with limited walking ability often experience serious problems in using public transport, particularly if large buggies or wheelchairs are involved. Public transport can also be difficult to use with children who are hyperactive, or who have severe behaviour or health problems. Consequently without access to private transport the mobility of children, parents and siblings can be restricted to within walking distance of the home. Over three-quarters of each group of families reported some difficulty of this sort. The remainder of this chapter looks at the help given by the resource workers with transport problems and at the impact which this help made. (Families' take up of the mobility allowance will be discussed along with other cash benefits in Chapter 9.)

According to their records, the resource workers helped thirty-three families during the project to acquire or replace a car, usually by informing them about sources of financial help, price concessions, leasing or hire-purchase schemes and, occasionally, by helping to complete application forms:

> Explained to family a little about Motability and also about cheaper rates on new tyres for those getting mobility allowance.

> Last week the family heard from Motability that Maurice's age-group is now eligible – delighted as they've been saving the mobility allowance for many months now, anticipating a substantial advance rental. Mrs B. asked me to help her complete the application form.

However, there was no evidence that this intervention made any significant impact on families' ownership of, or access to, a vehicle for taking out their disabled child. Before the project began, 65 per cent of the seventy-nine resource worker group families and 71 per cent of the eighty-three comparison group families who experienced difficulties in using public transport with their disabled child owned or had regular use of a vehicle. By the end of the project the proportions of these families had increased by only 3 and 5 per cent respectively, with the resource worker group families remaining relatively disadvantaged. There was also no evidence that the thirty-five resource worker group parents who had acquired or replaced a car during the project had had more financial help to do so; only 6 per cent reported having taken advantage of special hire-purchase facilities compared with 15 per cent of the forty-seven comparison group families who had bought a car. There was, however, some evidence that the resource worker group families whose children had difficulty using public transport were better equipped with information at the end of the project to help them plan future vehicle purchases. Although there were no marked differences in the proportions of each group of families who had heard of the Motability scheme or were thinking of applying to it, seventeen resource worker group parents recalled having been given advice about the scheme – in every case from the resource worker – as against only one comparison group family.

Making provision for a child's safety in a car can be a problem for children who cannot sit up unsupported, especially once the normal range of child car seats and harnesses has been outgrown. However, this was a relatively infrequent problem: only seven families were given information by the resource workers about suitable items or advice about sources of help with the cost; and only one resource worker group family and two in the comparison group reported at the end of the project that they had acquired a special car seat or harness during the previous two years.

There were three other specific ways in which the resource workers tried to help those families whose children's disabilities created transport problems. First, some families did not know about, or had experienced difficulty in obtaining, an orange parking badge which would allow a car being used for the disabled child's benefit to have access to specially designated parking facilities. The help given by the resource workers varied, from straightforward information and referral:

> Mrs M.'s father is buying a smaller car, so he can transport Noreen and Mrs M. Mrs M. wondered if I knew if the orange badge scheme would apply to a grandfather's car as well as a parent's. Rang social services about it.

> As there is no disabled sticker on car, I asked if Mrs B. had asked for one. No, as Lucy can walk, she didn't think she could get one. Lucy lurches and cannot go far, needs help or overbalances. I contacted social services

to more complex negotiations:

> Mrs A. asked if I'd take up a problem she has over the car-park on the sea front. Attendant said that [special] facilities are only for

disabled driver, not if passengers are disabled . . . I wrote to Mr X. who's in charge of car parks, asking him to establish position on disabled badges . . . Mr Y. phoned – all attendants have been told to be more strict and, unless driver was disabled, not to allow free parking or disabled places to be used. This was not an inflexible rule, though – there could be exceptions and Craig should have one. Mr Y. would see the attendant concerned.

A second concession available to children with severe mobility problems is an exemption from road tax on a vehicle which is used primarily for their benefit. Again a number of parents needed information and advice about this:

Headteacher has advised parents not to claim exemption and tied this up with car insurance; but I would view these matters entirely separately and advised parents to look again at the matter of exemption as it would be reasonable to assume that the car also enables Mrs C. to cope more easily with care of her handicapped child, and that with regard to the insurance, this should be taken up separately with the company.

Altogether a total of eighteen families were given some kind of help by the resource workers in connection with one or both of these concessions. However, according to the evidence from the interviews with parents at the end of the project, the impact of this help appeared to have been variable. For example, of those families who had a car available for taking their disabled child out, 78 per cent in the resource worker group and 72 per cent in the comparison group had an orange parking badge at the end of the project; and similar proportions of each group reported having received some information or help with this during the previous two years. On the other hand, a significantly higher proportion of resource worker group families (84 per cent as against only 64 per cent of the comparison group) who appeared to be eligible for road tax exemption were in fact getting this at the time of the second interview.

Thirdly, the resource workers recorded giving seventeen families with transport problems information about, or help with, an application to the Family Fund. As a result, eleven resource worker group families received grants from the fund for items which included driving lessons, car hire and taxi fares as against eight comparison group families. However, the average amount received by each resource worker group family towards these extra transport expenses was some £60 lower than that received by the comparison group families. (This and other help received from the Family Fund during the project will be more fully analysed in Chapter 9.)

The Alleviation of Transport Restrictions

This chapter has by no means examined all the sources of help with mobility and transport problems which the children and their families received during the project. We know from the resource workers' records, for example, that help with obtaining adequate garaging facilities, concessionary fares and transport from voluntary sources was given to twenty-six families. Similarly, some families experienced transport problems in connection with their children's education, holidays and use of leisure or respite care facilities; the impact of the resource workers' intervention on these latter problems will be examined in Chapter 8.

However, the help given by the resource workers to obtain and pay for a car and other additional transport expenses, or to take advantage of other concessions available to people with mobility problems, might be expected to have had some impact on the restrictions which families experienced in going out with their children, doing shopping and participating in other social activities outside the home. In both interviews therefore those mothers (or other main carers) who had reported difficulties in taking their disabled child on public transport were asked how much they felt restricted by the child in going out during the day to do things like shopping. Before the intervention, 33 per cent of the main carers in each group said that they felt only occasionally restricted or not at all; by the end of the project the proportion without restrictions had risen to 42 per cent of the resource worker group, but dropped to only 26 per cent of the comparison group. Similarly, the proportion of resource worker group carers who said they felt restricted all the time fell during the project (from 29 to 23 per cent), but rose in the comparison group (from 29 to 35 per cent).

Secondly, all those parents whose children were difficult to take on public transport were asked during both sets of interviews about the extent to which they felt that outings by the family as a whole were restricted. Here, however, there were virtually no differences between the two groups; between 43 and 48 per cent of each group said they felt fairly, or very, restricted both before and after the intervention.

It seems therefore that the impact of the resource workers on families' felt restrictions was rather patchy. While more of the children's main carers felt less restricted (and more comparison group carers felt more restricted), the impact on restricted family outings was minimal. However, some of the help given by the resource workers (for example, with claiming exemption from road tax, or with taking advantage of hire-purchase concessions) would not in any case necessarily have contributed to reducing these felt restrictions. Help of this kind, by offsetting some of the extra costs arising from severe childhood disability, may on the other hand have made an impact on families' financial well-being, or on the incidence of anxieties about coping financially. (These outcome measures will be analysed in Chapter 9.) In Chapter 7 the impact of the intervention on families' housing and environmental problems is described.

CHAPTER 7

Outcome Measures 2: Homes and Gardens

A surprising range and number of housing and other environmental problems can arise for disabled children and their families. Some of these problems will be caused by physical disablement: a non-ambulant child may be unable to manoeuvre her or his wheelchair in and out of the house, for example, because of front steps or an uneven garden path; many bathrooms are too small to admit a wheelchair plus, possibly, an adult helper. Other – perhaps less obvious – difficulties may arise for families with mentally handicapped children who can find that they need secure fencing around their garden to prevent the child wandering off, or an extra bedroom for a child whose behaviour is too disruptive to share with a sibling. Problems such as these will obviously affect only a proportion of families with even the most severely disabled children at any one time. However, when they do they can be serious, necessitating radical alterations to the home environment or even moving house altogether, both of which may involve the assistance of a large number of local authority and other statutory and voluntary organizations, and considerable expense and worry by parents themselves.

This chapter examines parents' satisfaction with their homes at the start of the project and their assessment of the dwelling's suitability for the disabled child. The intervention of the resource workers to help resolve parents' housing problems will then be described. This intervention included helping parents to move house, adapting and extending existing dwellings and altering gardens or yards to make them safer or more accessible for the disabled child. The outcome measures, comparing the numbers and adequacy of the various solutions achieved by the two groups of families, will then be analysed. This analysis will, however, fail to reflect the full extent of the resource workers' intervention because of the length of time which could often be involved in designing and carrying out major adaptations or moving house. The resource workers' records show that a great deal of time was spent on some particularly difficult or complex housing problems but that these had not been resolved by the end of the intervention, nor were they expected to be resolved until after the second set of interviews had been carried out.

Before the intervention began, parents in both groups were asked whether they thought their house was currently suitable in view of the

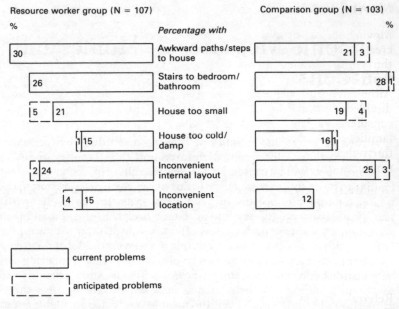

Figure 7.1 Current and anticipated housing problems at the start of the project.

special needs of their disabled child, and whether they expected any problems (or additional problems) to arise during the next couple of years. Just over one-half of each group considered their house was currently suitable but about one-third of each group expected that housing problems (or additional problems) would arise in the near future. Figure 7.1 shows the range of problems identified by those families who considered their house currently was, or would become, unsuitable. There was little difference in the type or number of problems identified by the families in each group; in both groups difficulties of access into the house from outside, stairs up to the bathroom and/or bedroom and an internal layout which prevented easy movement of a wheelchair were the most common problems cited. Among those families who cited current or anticipated housing problems, the seventy-six resource worker group families identified an average of 2·7 problems each and the sixty-seven comparison group families an average of 2·6 problems per family.

The following section documents the various efforts made by parents to resolve their housing problems, describing the contributions made by the resource workers and examining the impact which this intervention had made by the end of the project.

Moving House

Moving house altogether is one means of resolving the difficulties created by an unsuitable physical home environment. A total of thirty-nine families moved house during the project, and a further thirty-six were planning to do so by the time of the second interviews. Although not all of these moves were prompted primarily because of the disabled child, her or his particular needs clearly had to be taken into consideration when finding alternative accommodation. Among the families they visited, the resource workers recorded helping a total of thirty-three families with actual or anticipated moves, most commonly (in thirty-two instances) by giving information or advice:

> Mr T. asked me about schooling for Pearl and housing in [the town to which the family was going to move]. I was able to assure him that there was a school for Pearl and promised to send details of rented housing, and estate agents' names if they wanted to buy.

> Sent letter to parents giving addresses of [local] housing associations.

Referral to, and liaison and advocacy with, local authority housing departments was undertaken on behalf of sixteen of the families who needed to move house:

> Mrs B. rang – they have been offered three transfers, none suitable – too small, cramped accommodation. Very anxious, could I help? ... [I arranged] interview with transfer section manager. I clarified the fact that this family needs a 4-bedroomed house mainly because of Connie's incontinence.

> [Family wants to move nearer to child's special school for the blind but cannot get their name on housing transfer list.] Found out the area where family would prefer to live. Said I'd contact Royal National Institute for the Blind and get a recommendation from them. Mrs C. to let me have medical note from GP. Asked [local authority social worker] for a letter to include in my report to the housing department, asking them to accept the family on their transfer list.

Seven families were helped by the resource workers to apply to the Family Fund, or to the Department of Health and Social Security for an additional supplementary benefit payment, to help meet the costs of moving house because of their disabled child:

> Family worried about removal charges and transfer of phone to new house. Explained that DHSS could pay removal charges – three

estimates would be needed. Suggested DHSS also approached about transfer of phone, also social services . . . [Later.] Family are so pleased about removal expenses grant from DHSS that they'll pay the cost of phone transfer themselves.

Offered to approach Family Fund for help with removal costs . . . [Later.] Mrs S. received letter from fund promising a grant on receipt of solicitor's bill and removal firm's bill.

The resource workers also helped seven families who had moved to a different area by putting them in touch with some of the new services for disabled children:

Wrote to [new local education authority], asking about special schools in area . . . Told Mrs T. of a special school near to their new home which present headteacher had said Pearl would attend, and gave Mrs T. the name and phone number of the new headteacher so she could contact her once they've moved.

Gave information on mental handicap schools in [new city]. Mr A. will look at them while he's there visiting.

Interestingly some of the help given in connection with moving house was commented on spontaneously by parents during the second set of interviews:

She's written and been down loads of times to the Housing – she even went to see the head man specially.

She advised us on what to do about moving, what help we could get – she gave us addresses of whom to let know when we leave. She advised us about a resettlement grant which we could get if we were leaving town.

The impact of this intervention was assessed in two ways. First, we looked at all those families who moved during the project, to see whether those in the resource worker group were more likely to be satisfied that the new house was suitable for their child's needs. Altogether twenty-six resource worker group parents had moved, nineteen of whom thought their new house was suitable. In contrast, only thirteen comparison group families had moved, and only seven of them to a suitable house. Even when those families who had moved for reasons unconnected with their disabled child were excluded, there was still a noticeable difference between the two groups in the proportions who were satisfied with their new homes.

Secondly, we looked at the extent to which moving house had solved the housing problems which parents had been experiencing at the time

Table 7.1 *Moving House as a Solution to Earlier Housing Problems or Anticipated Problems*

Had, or anticipated problems and subsequently:	Resource worker group	Comparison group
	(%)	(%)
Moved to suitable house	21	9
Moved to unsatisfactory house	9	9
Planned to move but not yet done so	20	16
Done nothing	50	66
Base (= 100%)	76	67

of the first interview or which they had expected to arise in the near future. Table 7.1 shows what had happened to those families by the time they were interviewed again two years later. More than twice as many resource worker group than comparison group families who had had, or anticipated having, housing problems had moved to a suitable house by the time of the second interviews. Again this indicates the impact which the resource workers' intervention made on families' chances of satisfactorily resolving their housing problems by moving.

Adaptations to the Home

Moving house is a fairly radical step to take in order to obtain a physical environment which is more suitable for a disabled child. For many families, the first step in resolving any housing problems will be to see whether their present home can be modified or adapted in some way. This might involve simply building a ramp up to the front door, the installation of extra heating appliances, or the fitting of handrails. Sometimes, however, extensive structural alterations may be needed such as the rearrangement of internal walls and doors, the installation of a stairlift, or even adding a new extension to accommodate a downstairs bathroom and bedroom for the disabled child.

In addition to the actual building work, such adaptations can entail lengthy prior negotiations with local authority social services, housing, planning, architect's and environmental health departments; and with building societies, finance companies, the Family Fund and private building contractors. A joint Department of Health and Social Security/ Department of the Environment circular (DoE/DHSS/Welsh Office, 1978) which was issued during the fieldwork of the resource worker project clarified the respective responsibilities of social services and housing departments for the adaptation of privately and publicly owned housing. However, considerable problems of interagency co-ordination may still be experienced (Keeble, 1979; Borsay, 1982). Several examples of these were recorded in the records kept by the resource workers during their intervention, and for a few of the families they visited, carrying out major adaptations to their homes proved to be a time-consuming and nerve-racking experience.

Altogether forty families were helped by the resource workers in connection with carrying out adaptations to their homes. Only eighteen parents needed no help other than information and advice:

> Mrs T. wanted advice on an application being made to the council for help to extend the dining room, and resurface the drive to their house which is badly cracked and a danger to Mark when he is walking ... Rang social services headquarters. They advised getting rid of savings if family want help from social services ... Parents afraid they'll be asked for details of income and savings; would rather struggle and pay themselves ... I suggested they apply for a grant and see what happens.

> I asked Mrs J. if she had thought of having a downstairs toilet built ... I told her about the service whereby the county architect's department gives free advice and plans – this could be useful whether or not they also received a grant for the work.

In addition, twelve families were helped by the resource workers with applications or referrals to social services, housing, architect's or environmental health departments (for financial help, for specialist expertise in designing appropriate adaptations, or improvement grants); or to the Family Fund or specialist voluntary organizations (again for financial help or specialist design advice):

> Mrs H. mentioned the need to make bathroom door into a sliding one – bathroom combines with toilet and is very small. Door opens in from hall, almost touching bath and sink ... Referred to social services department occupational therapist. She will refer direct to architect's department.

> Alan's wheelchair will only just go through the doors in the house – there's no room even for his fingers, so he can't manage to get through himself and move from room to room. A narrower chair isn't practicable ... Mrs I. is agreeable for me to write to REMAP and ask if she can be visited.

> Need for a ramp at the front door as Mrs K. is unable to negotiate the wheelchair at the back door. Wrote to social services department about a ramp.

However, a referral on its own was often not enough; on behalf of thirteen families the resource workers carried out protracted negotiations and liaised with a large number of statutory and voluntary agencies to co-ordinate their respective activities and cut down delays. The case of Sue W., who had spina bifida, illustrates this work. At the start of the project Sue, then aged 7, and her family had just moved into a new bungalow, to which they wished to add a bathroom, toilet and bedroom extension:

[February 1978]. Mrs W. visited rating office to inquire about reducing their rates in order to be able to apply for an improvement grant. Resource worker discussed case with social services occupational therapist (OT); not much money available from social services to help family with adaptation. Discussed facilities and difficulties of having to toilet Sue in the dining-room and share a bedroom with her brother.

[May 1978.] Discussed case with OT; architect's department drawing up plans for an extra room to include shower; OT had put case forward for joint funding from area health authority and this had been accepted in principle. Gave Mrs W. a copy of an article in *Link* magazine explaining housing grants.

[June 1978.] Rang OT; no news from architect. Rang architect . . . Mrs W. said she'd received plans from architect but they'd put shower in bathroom, not in bedroom as she wanted. Extension would cost £4,000 and it did not look as if they'd receive any help. Felt they'd given up having their holiday for nothing.

[July 1978.] Drafted letter of support to social services area director for grant for adaptation.

[September 1978.] Grant from social services approved, depending on amount of intermediate grant.

[November 1978.] Talked to Mrs W. about possibility of asking for help and advice from Spina Bifida Society and Family Fund if there was a gap between the intermediate and social services grants and the family's contribution.

[January 1979.] Builders started work on extension. I said we could ask Family Fund for help with carpet and furniture.

[September 1979.] Life was so much easier now Sue had her own room with bathroom and shower installed. Toileting was now so easy and Sue had more independence. It had been worth all the upheaval. Mrs W. was delighted to show me Sue's room finished. She'd carpeted and decorated it, and bought new furniture with Family Fund grant. She was so relieved the work was done and so appreciative, and said that it had made the world of difference to their lives – Sue now got up by herself and went to the toilet.

The particularly complex housing adaptation problem of the Jackson family which necessitated extensive and protracted liaison and advocacy by the resource worker involved is summarized in the Appendix to this chapter.

The evaluation of this intervention involved comparing the numbers of adaptations actually carried out by each group of families during the project; the extent to which financial assistance had been obtained towards them; and the numbers of adaptations planned but not yet completed by each group of families.

Before the start of the project, one-quarter of each group of families had already carried out some adaptations to their homes. During the following two years about one-sixth of each group adapted their homes in some way for the first time, made further adaptations to their homes, or had special alterations carried out on a new house to which they had moved during the project. The proportions of each group who carried out adaptations for the first and a subsequent time were very similar. So too were the proportions of each group who had said at the start of the project that their house was unsuitable or who expected it soon to become unsuitable, and who subsequently carried out alterations: about one-fifth of each group with initial or anticipated problems had completed adaptations by the end of the project. There was, however, some difference between the two groups in the number or extensiveness of the adaptations they carried out. Between them the eighteen resource worker group families carried out twenty-four different adaptations, while the sixteen comparison group families carried out a total of nineteen different alterations (Figure 7.2(*a*)).

Because of the length of time involved in planning, obtaining financial help for and carrying out major adaptations, the evaluation of the resource workers' intervention also had to take into consideration the number of adaptations which had been planned or begun during the project but which had yet to be completed by the time of the second interview. Almost equal numbers of families, around two-fifths of each group, were planning (further) adaptations. However, with the exception of building extra rooms, the families in the resource worker group were planning to carry out more of each type of adaptation despite the fact that this group of families had already completed slightly more adaptations during the previous two years (Figure 7.2(*b*)).

Those parents who had had adaptations to their homes carried out and completed during the project were asked, for each adaptation, whether it had been provided or paid for completely by the statutory authorities or some other organization; or whether they had paid for some or all of it themselves. Of the twenty-four adaptations carried out to the homes of families in the resource worker group during the project, at least some financial help had been obtained for fifteen of

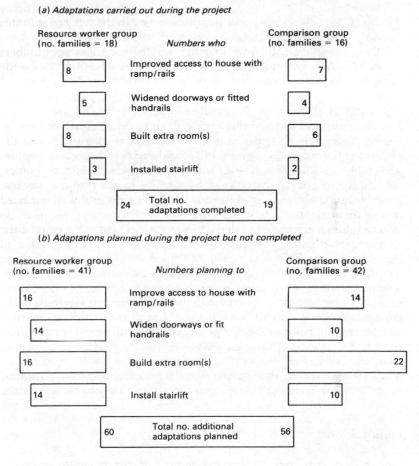

Figure 7.2 Adaptations carried out or planned during the project.

them. Only nine of the eighteen adaptations completed by the comparison group families had been carried out with the help of funds from statutory or voluntary sources. The most common source of help from both groups were social services departments but housing departments, improvement grants and the Family Fund were also mentioned. Some families cited more than one source of financial help but there was no difference between the two groups in the numbers of sources cited.

Outside the House

The need for adaptations and improvements can extend beyond the interior of the house. Gardens may need to be paved or driveways levelled to enable a child with mobility problems to move about more easily. Children with mental handicaps may need secure fencing and gates, so that they can play outside the house without needing continual supervision.

Around 21 per cent of the families in each of the two groups had already made alterations of this kind to their gardens before the project began. Nevertheless, 34 per cent of the resource worker group and 23 per cent of the comparison group still considered that their gardens were unsuitable, or would become so within the foreseeable future. Therefore, not surprisingly, twice as many families in the resource worker group as in the comparison group had alterations made to their gardens during the project.

Like internal adaptations, alterations to gardens and yards could take a considerable time to complete satisfactorily (as, for example, in the case of Caroline Barton which is described in the Appendix to this chapter). It was therefore appropriate to include in the evaluation those alterations which were planned but not completed by the end of the project. Again many more resource worker than comparison group families had garden alterations planned. Altogether significantly more – 42 per cent – of resource worker group families had either completed or were planning to alter their gardens as against only 25 per cent of the comparison group. However, there was no difference in the proportions of each group who recalled having received financial help from statutory or voluntary sources with the garden alterations they had carried out.

Conclusions

One way of assessing the overall impact of the resource workers' intervention is to compare changes in the numbers of families who expressed satisfaction with the suitability of their homes before and after the project. Before the project began, just over one-half of each group considered their house was suitable for the disabled child. By the end this had decreased from fifty-five to forty-five of the comparison group, while remaining the same in the resource worker group. When the answers of each family before and after the project were compared, it was found that the houses of 19 per cent of each group had apparently become unsuitable for their disabled child during the intervening two years. On the other hand, when those families who had initially considered their homes to be *unsuitable* were compared, only 9 per cent of comparison group families had become satisfied with the suitability of their houses by the end of the project. In contrast, 20 per cent, a significantly higher proportion, of resource worker group families appeared to have resolved their earlier housing problems by adapting or moving, and now had a home which was suitable for their disabled child.

The impact of the help given by the resource workers to families who moved during the project is apparent in their greater likelihood of moving to a suitable and satisfactory home. The effect of the help given to those families who planned or carried out alterations to their gardens is also clear. However, the impact of the intervention on the alterations to the inside of the families' houses is less easy to detect. Certainly, this is at least partly due to the complex and protracted negotiations which such alterations could involve, necessitating a considerable amount of liaison and advocacy by the resource workers but without immediate results. The two case studies appended to this chapter illustrate these problems.

Appendix

George Jackson

When the resource worker first visited the Jacksons (January 1978), George, who had cerebral palsy, scoliosis and very limited independent mobility, was nearly 14. He lived with his parents and two younger siblings in an owner-occupied house. The Jacksons had first applied to their social services department for help with adapting the house in 1975; they were having difficulty getting George up and down stairs, and there was an additional problem of limited wheelchair access to the washbasin in the upstairs bathroom. A detailed assessment had been made and plans for an extension devised by a social work student who, when his placement ended, had handed the case back to the social services department occupational therapist (OT). No action was subsequently taken. Before the start of the project, the Jacksons had also applied to the social services department (SSD) for help with paving their driveway to make it level for George's wheelchair.

February 1978. Resource worker (RW) made referral to SSD about the Jacksons' housing problems.
March 1978. Social services OT visited family and prepared an application to SSD for bath hoist, tarmac drive, stair lift and toilet aids. The OT then discovered that before SSD fieldwork panel would consider the grant application:

(1) local authority architect's department must approve plans;
(2) environmental health department must be approached about an intermediate grant;
(3) medical report must be obtained from medical officer;
(4) child must be registered with SSD.

None of these things had been done. Problems about siting the stair lift – RW suggested that OT should ask advice of council architect's department.

April 1978. Housing department officer visited family about intermediate grant. The RW approached Job Creation Programme (JCP) about possibility of using JCP workers to lay paving flags on drive; RW asked George's headteacher to support application to SSD by confirming that he would continue to live at home after leaving school.

June 1978. Parents still awaiting visit from council architect about moving internal walls for stair lift installation; they are anxious about the delays as they cannot do other repairs, nor decorate until plans are finalized. Time is also running short for organizing labour under JCP to help lay flagstones in garden, if SSD are not going to do it.

July 1978. The RW rang SSD; case had been handed back to OT a month ago, still waiting for architect's report; RW wrote to SSD divisional officer explaining that there was a time-limit for organizing labour from JCP if SSD will not lay garden flags, and advising him of the distress caused to family by the delays. Area officer SSD phoned RW; he was concerned to help the family and would like to deal with the garden paving immediately as a gesture of goodwill on part of SSD and as a morale booster to family – will try to organize grant to buy materials for paving if RW can organize volunteer labour.

The RW phoned council of voluntary service; no JCP group could tackle the paving, but community service order (CSO) volunteers might help. The RW rang CSO organizer, and informed SSD area officer that volunteer labour had been arranged; RW pointed out that unless the council architect approved the necessary movement of walls to install a stair lift, paving the garden would be academic as the plans would have to be altered to build a downstairs extension – and this would cover the area of garden to be paved. The SSD area officer later rang RW – architect had visited family with OT and had decided it would cost £3,500 to install a stair lift and move internal walls, so a downstairs extension would be preferable. However, SSD divisional officer decided it would be justified to go ahead with paving the garden in the meantime, anyway.

The OT rang RW and complained about having to start again preparing an application for help to build an extension; RW obtained estimates of number of paving flags available from the council, the amount of ash and sand and the cost of extra paving flags needed. She collected information from Mrs Jackson about cost of ash, second-hand paving flags from the corporation and delivery charges. Delivered the estimate to SSD divisional officer, who signed it and agreed to pay out the money to Mrs Jackson the following day.

August 1978. Everything going well with the paving, using CSO volunteers; parents doing some themselves during the evening. The RW rang SSD area officer and informed him of this progress. Area officer assured RW that as soon as the plans for the extension arrive at SSD he will ensure that the OT proceeds with all haste.

September 1978. The RW rang area officer; SSD has still not received plans from the architect's department and phone calls to ascertain their whereabouts are not returned. Area officer has issued one strong memo and will send another, and also notify the SSD divisional officer of the delay and lack of co-operation. Later, RW saw area officer at SSD; plans have now been received and, after argument between architect's department and SSD, architect's department is now collecting tenders for the work.

October 1978. The RW phoned SSD area officer about garden paving; agreed that RW should approach divisional officer for the balance of the grant, on the grounds that it would be therapeutic for the Jacksons to organize and finish the job, and it would also prove cheaper than if it went through the architect's department and social services committee.

The RW spoke to divisional officer; after some persuasion, he agreed to pay the Jacksons £30 for the balance of the flagstones – however, it has to be done officially through SSD panel. Asked RW to pass on his instructions to OT to present it to panel.

The RW visited Jacksons who have heard nothing from SSD about £30 grant: the CSO volunteers are arranging to come and lay flags this weekend in anticipation of the money being through. Architect has called and told family officially that plans have been passed, but he thought SSD was organizing estimates. The RW encouraged Mrs Jackson to phone OT.

November 1978. The RW discussed the case with SSD area officer and OT. Area officer has had various meetings with the architect's department to improve policy (based on problems with this family); architects have now accepted responsibility for obtaining estimates for the Jacksons' extension and are doing so.

The RW visited Jacksons, who had had a visit from environmental health officer about an intermediate grant; RW promised to make inquiries about a maturity loan and try to pin down SSD to a rough estimate of what the family's contribution to the cost of the extension is likely to be.

December 1978. The RW spoke to environmental health officer about maturity loans; environmental health officer is investigating other forms of local authority help, should it be required by family.

The RW spoke to the SSD OT and area officer; no indication of amount of family's contribution can possibly be given at this stage. The OT promised faithfully to put application before SSD panel this month. January 1979. The OT asked parents to obtain two estimates – in region of £8,000 – before application could be submitted to SSD panel.

March 1979. The RW rang OT; the application for the Jacksons' extension has been passed by the divisional fieldwork panel, and will be put before the metropolitan district fieldwork committee after the environmental health officer has visited to ascertain amount the family can afford to contribute; RW rang environmental health officer, who feels it will take some time to negotiate à loan (towards the extension and to pay off an existing second mortgage) from the local authority. Environmental health will give maximum grant of £2,500, so this will leave SSD some £5,000 to find – a sizeable proportion of their annual budget.

The RW rang social worker at the Spastics Society; the society would probably be able to make a contribution of £1,000–£3,000. If the Jacksons agreed to yet another person being involved, the Spastics Society social worker suggested SSD contact her direct if they wish to apply for a grant.

The RW visited Mrs Jackson; she was prepared for the Spastics Society to visit but did not want to make the actual application – SSD must do this. She said they 'just cannot face taking out their begging-bowls again'.

The OT phoned RW; she wished to apply for Spastics Society grant and assured RW that even if she had not had a definite answer from the Spastics Society, she would present the application to SSD metropolitan district fieldwork panel as soon as completed.

. Spastics Society social worker phoned RW; she had had a very confused phone call from OT asking for grant – could RW clarify situation? The RW suggested she write asking OT to send details, in writing; RW informed environmental health officer of likelihood of Spastics Society grant.

The RW rang Mrs Jackson; SSD have not notified the Jacksons of their approach to Spastics Society.

May 1979. Spastics Society social worker rang RW; had received message from OT asking for details of Spastics Society grant as the SSD fieldwork panel meets on Monday. Spastics Society still has nothing in writing and wants to know how much SSD will be granting.

June 1979. The RW rang Mrs Jackson; SSD fieldwork panel had been most sympathetic but needed to have more detailed information on the estimates before deciding. Parents puzzled as the estimates already contained information which had been requested by SSD in the first place.

The RW rang the local council and Citizens' Advice Bureau about the procedure for complaining to the Ombudsman and to the chair of the social services committee.

The RW visited Mrs Jackson, who had spent the last two days trying to sort out detailed estimates for the extension. Mrs Jackson asked RW to contact SSD deputy director (who had presented the application to SSD fieldwork panel); RW rang environmental health officer who read out the panel minutes. Agreed with environmental health officer that without external intervention the application will continue to go round in circles. The RW rang Mrs Jackson, who agreed to RW's writing to chair of social services committee, asking for a decision at the next panel meeting. Failing that, the Jacksons would take the matter to their MP or the Ombudsman.

July 1979. The RW visited family. Estimates had not arrived at SSD, and OT had not chased them up in any way. After much encouragement from RW, Mrs Jackson phoned deputy director; he said the fieldwork panel met last week, so the estimates had not been available. Mrs Jackson pushed very strongly for a decision at the next meeting in two weeks' time. The RW wrote to the chair of social services committee, explaining delays in obtaining estimates and asking for full consideration at the next meeting.

It transpired that social services committee had not wanted to contribute towards work which had to be undertaken as a condition of the intermediate grant but the Jacksons had not been told this. The RW rang Spastics Society; the society and Family Fund will each contribute £500 towards family's contribution. (The SSD OT had made Family Fund application two months before.)

The RW visited family; SSD deputy director had phoned to say social services committee had passed the application. The Jacksons had also received notification of the grant from the Family Fund and were very annoyed because OT had asked permission to apply and they had refused. The Jacksons now felt very embarrassed as they had already had so much help from the fund.

September 1979. The RW visited Mrs Jackson, who was negotiating with builders. The builders wanted paying in three instalments, but metropolitan district will only pay when work completed; RW discussed problem with environmental health officer.

October 1979. The RW visited the Jacksons. The building had still not started as verbal assurance of an interim payment from SSD was not sufficient. Deputy director was supposed to write at the beginning of the week to the builders with a copy to Mrs Jackson, but it had not yet arrived.

POSTSCRIPT

The building work on the Jacksons' extension eventually began after the end of the project in November 1979, and George was finally able to move into his new downstairs bedroom in the autumn of 1980. The resource worker, who visited the family again to see the work, commented that 'the extra space is marvellous – well worth fighting for', and there is ample room for full wheelchair navigation should George's condition deteriorate. The entire job took five years from initial application to completion.

Caroline Barton

Caroline, aged 8 at the start of the project, had cerebral palsy. She could walk with the help of a frame on level ground only. She and her family lived in a semi-detached owner-occupied house. The family's first contact with the resource worker (RW) was in December 1977. At that time they were awaiting the outcome of an application made seven months previously, to their local social services department (SSD) for help towards the cost of resurfacing their driveway which was cracked, uneven and dangerous for Caroline to walk on.

March 1978. The RW rang local authority social worker (SW); path should be done soon. The current delay was because the county council legal department was preparing an undertaking for the Bartons to sign, agreeing to repay grant if they moved house in the next five years. The SW said that the social services department occupational therapist (OT) was also trying to improve family's downstairs toilet facilities as Caroline has to use a commode.
May 1978. The RW visited family; legal undertaking had been signed and returned. The RW discussed the possible involvement of a specialist architect from the Spastics Society to give advice on the design of a downstairs bathroom and toilet.
June 1978. The RW wrote and later phoned county council legal department about the lack of action on the path; officer said he had been told that repairs to the path had been started.
July 1978. The RW received a letter from the Town Clerk saying that the estimate supplied by Mrs Barton was too low for a satisfactory job, so work on the path had been put out to tender. The RW rang Mrs Barton; six firms had visited to give estimates for resurfacing the drive.

The RW rang Town Clerk's department and was told that the matter was now in the hands of SSD, so she could not find out which firm's tender had been accepted; RW rang SSD divisional administrative officer – a tender had been accepted and the firm asked to repair drive urgently.

August 1978. Repairs to driveway still not started; RW rang SSD administrative officer and was told that the contract had been given to H. & H. Co., but SSD would not give their address and the firm could not be found in the telephone directory. The RW asked for work to begin urgently; RW also rang SW, who promised to phone architect's department.

September 1978. The SW rang RW; the architect had phoned H. & H. Co., but could not obtain a firm starting date. After further pressure from SW, the architect had promised to get a starting date from the building firm. The SW had then contacted building firm herself and spoken to the owner's wife, who could give no idea of starting date. Mrs Barton then contacted her local councillor (now sixteen months after her first approach to SSD); RW also phoned local councillor; he promised to contact legal department and architect's department.

October 1978. Councillor rang RW; work on driveway to start this week. Contractors arrived and began work on driveway. The RW visited the Bartons with the Spastics Society architect to discuss their downstairs toilet and bathing facilities. The architect will send drawings and then draw up proper plans if Mr and Mrs Barton approve.

The RW rang SW; SW said SSD would put forward a recommendation for a 50 per cent grant from district council towards the toilet and bathroom adaptations.

December 1978. The RW visited family; cracks were appearing in the newly surfaced drive, which Caroline's walking-frame got stuck in. Also loose cement and dust were coming off the surface. Mrs Barton had complained to architect's department and SW – SSD were consequently refusing to pay the contractor's bill; RW rang SW and architect's department, who were annoyed that SSD had not paid the bill.

January 1979. The RW visited Bartons; path was now much worse, broken by frost. Mrs Barton had contacted councillor again.

The RW rang SW; SSD was putting pressure on architect's department to inspect the path, and was still refusing to pay the bill.

February 1979. The RW rang chief executive's department and SSD administrative officer. As architect's department had accepted the tender for the work, they were responsible for getting the contractor back to redo the job.

March 1979. The SSD agreed to inspect the path again. Plans received from Spastics Society architect.

The RW discussed bathroom and toilet extension plans with SW – may take two years to build, but SW will strongly recommend that the cost be split between SSD and district council; RW also saw senior SW, who promised strong support for application for extension. The RW rang planning department and asked for copies of an application for planning permission to be sent to Mr and Mrs Barton; RW offered to help fill in the application form.

The RW rang Spastics Society architect as plans for extension need alteration; Mrs Barton had found out from the planning department exactly what alterations were needed to the plans. The RW rang, and Mrs Barton wrote to, architect with this information.

March–May 1979. The RW rang administrative officer at SSD head-quarters three times to try and get driveway resurfaced.

May 1979. The RW phoned councillor, who had been given the impression by County Hall that the path had been resurfaced; councillor will make further inquiries in architect's department about the lack of action. As a result of these inquiries, the council architect and the contractor visited to see the path, but did not speak to Mrs Barton.

June 1979. Still no action on path, so with Mrs Barton's agreement RW wrote to local MP; SW informed of this.

July 1979. Mrs Barton received further plans for the extension from the Spastics Society architect and discussed them with the environmental health officer.

As a result of the RW's letter to MP, SW informed RW that an investigation into the affair of the driveway was taking place. While RW happened to be at the Bartons' house the senior architect visited to apologize about the path; their records had been lost, and the contractor had refused to do the work until paid. Contractor finally repaired the driveway, but instead of taking it up and re-laying it, a skim of more cement was laid, thus raising the level of the path by 1½ inches. This left a 2-inch drop to the three manhole covers in the drive and a 4-inch drop to the lawn, for which the contractor had made two ramps. Mrs Barton was worried that the raised level of the drive would now cover the damp-proof course of the house next door, which was currently for sale. The RW rang the legal department at the Town Hall to find out whether the Bartons would be held responsible for this.

Mrs Barton rang RW; resurfacing was now finished but white dust was coming up again and covering the house. The RW rang senior SW, who spoke to area officer. Senior SW visited to see the path; said he was horrified and was not prepared to pay the contractor. Mrs Barton rang RW; architect from council had visited after receiving a complaint from the senior SW. Architect was very angry about the fuss over the drive, though he admitted that it had not been done correctly. He said that another skim would be put on the surface.

August 1979. The RW rang SW about financial application for extension; RW and Mrs Barton drafted a letter to MP about the driveway, although Mrs Barton was now terrified that the trouble over the path would jeopardize their plan for the bathroom and toilet extension.

September 1979. The RW made an appointment for Mrs Barton to see a solicitor at the local Citizens' Advice Bureau about their possible responsibility for any damage to the damp-proof course of the next-door house.

Architect visited Mrs Barton; promised to re-lay or reskim path and said that any damage to next-door's damp-proof course was the council's responsibility. The SSD OT has recommended extension plans as urgent.

October 1979. Case conference with SSD. Extension plans will go to social services committee in December 1979 and should be approved.

The RW visited Citizens' Advice Bureau solicitor with Mrs Barton; with his help, RW drafted a letter to SSD chief administrative officer at County Hall about liability for any damage to next-door's damp-proof course.

November 1979. The question of liability for damage to the damp-proof course was raised again with chief administrative officer in a letter from RW.

December 1979. Letter received by RW from chief administrative officer accepting responsibility for any damage caused to neighbour's property.

POSTSCRIPT

A year after the end of the project (December 1980), the extension had still not been started, nor had any date been given for work to begin. Meanwhile Caroline was still having to use a commode downstairs because she could not get to the upstairs toilet.

CHAPTER 8

Outcome Measures 3: Education, Leisure and Respite Care

The resource workers gave almost all the families they visited help of some kind in connection with their child's current school placement; with finding future placements for those children who were due to change school or who were approaching school-leaving age; with obtaining educational equipment and toys for children to use at home; or with arranging recreational activities and respite care for the children and holidays for the whole family. This chapter describes this intervention and examines its impact, by comparing various aspects of the families' circumstances before and after the project with those of the comparison group of families who received no such specialist intervention.

Educational Issues

Before the intervention began, 85 per cent of resource worker and 80 per cent of comparison group children were attending school full time. (Of the remainder, most were either attending on a part-time basis or were too young to have started school yet.) By the end of the project the proportions in full-time education had increased to 92 and 89 per cent respectively, the largest group of non-attenders by now being those who had left school because they were over 16.

Working relationships between special school staff, families and social workers appear to vary widely. In some local authorities a close relationship is facilitated by the attachment of a specialist social worker to each special school. However, without such special appointments, it appears that liaison with special schools, and between schools and families, is not a common feature of generic, community-based social work. For example, one evaluative study of special school social work attachments found that they were welcomed by school staff precisely because the schools 'had experienced difficulties in obtaining social work input' (Kiernan, 1982, p. 2.6).

Within the five resource worker local authority areas there were no such special school appointments. Moreover, the resource workers themselves indicated that their work with schools was regarded as unusual and innovatory. School staff appeared to have had few previous opportunities to discover what kind of social work support families were receiving, and home–school liaison did not seem to have featured high on local authority social workers' priorities:

> Headmaster and staff are fully aware now of the home situation but really only because they've been able to be closely in touch with me – there hasn't been a social worker involved in this family before.

> Discussed the situation with the local authority social worker – he felt it was a good idea for him to take Mrs J. to school, but it is something he can only do if there's a special reason.

The resource workers also indicated (see Chapter 4) that they felt their work of liaising with schools and improving home–school contacts had been particularly worthwhile and rewarding. To what extent was this apparent in the outcome measures used to detect changes in the resource worker group of families? These outcome measures focused on parents' satisfaction with their children's schools, the arrangements for getting there and the education they received there, and on the frequency and quality of parents' contacts with the child's school – all issues which may have been influenced by the intervention of the resource workers.

Satisfaction with the Child's School and Education

As with any child, parents may have strong views on the suitability of a particular school for their child – the more so, perhaps, in view of the special needs and varying abilities of many severely disabled children. There may be difficulties therefore in finding a school which parents feel satisfied with, or arranging a transfer to another school should the child's (or the family's) needs change. A second set of problems can arise because of the large catchment areas of many special day schools (and the even larger catchment areas of residential schools). These can result in long journeys and complex transport arrangements to and from school.

Altogether sixty six families – two-thirds of all those whose children were currently in education – were given help by the resource workers in the form of counselling, information and advice about general issues concerning their child's education and school progress:

> Darren was at home today because of half-term. This visit was really worthwhile because we all talked at some length about the difficulties Darren is having at school, and how to face and conquer them. Darren is the only handicapped child in this rather large secondary school and feels that no one quite knows how to respond

to him and treat him as a normal boy. We were able to talk about the necessity of accepting disability, how difficulties can bring out strengths in a person that otherwise might remain hidden.

Sonia has poor school attendance record – again tried to impress on Mrs A. the importance of her attending school.

However, a more active liaison role was usually needed when a child was due either to start school for the first time or transfer to another school. Five families were helped by the resource workers to make contact with, and introduce their child to, a new school:

Visited local special school, spoke with headteacher about possibility of Shirley commencing, say, one day a week after Christmas. Headteacher very keen and we agreed that I'd try and bring Mrs H. and Shirley down to school.

Nineteen families were helped in their efforts to find a different, more suitable, school placement, or with assisting their child in adjusting to a school transfer which had been recommended by the education authority:

I reminded headteacher that family is prepared to consider weekly boarding-school and would definitely prefer this to Anton being transferred to local ESN(S) school ... parents would like to learn more about Spastics Society assessment and provisions, so that they can ask education department to explore this as an alternative should they decide on ESN(S) placement. Agreed I'd ask Spastics Society social worker to visit and give more information. I'll write to headteacher confirming their opinion about ESN(S) school and putting forward their suggestion that Anton should be given an extra year at present school and that they should be present at the case conference ... [Later.] It only remains for education department to finalize details – Anton will attend as weekly boarder from September.

District education officer, at a meeting with parents, had said would they consider Paula being residential – said it would probably be South Hall School or Brown Farm School. I promised to find out exact differences between the two schools – phoned district education office for details.

Mother worried about child's transfer to Townend School in the autumn – would like to see the school. I suggested that she spoke to present school head about this but she doesn't want to be a nuisance, so I said I'd speak to headteacher at Townend School.

Fifteen families were also helped when problems arose over the transport arrangements between home and school:

> Ashley is listed as a full-time boarder at his new school which means
> the family will have to meet the costs and make the arrangements
> for him to come home at weekends. I strongly advocated parents'
> writing to special services officer [in education department] and I
> will write in support. Mrs L. will also discuss the problem with
> special schools adviser . . . [Later.] Ashley had now been granted an
> LEA taxi every weekend.

> Bill is at residential school, and his parents are planning to move to
> a new area. If he is the only child in the new area at his school, I
> suggested Mrs B. looks into the question of using her car to take
> him to and from school and claiming an allowance.

The impact of such intervention was, however, hard to detect. In both
sets of interviews those parents whose children were attending school
either full or part time were asked whether they were satisfied with the
type of school their child attended; the teaching she or he received at
school; the number of hours she or he attended school; and the transport
arrangements for getting to and from school. Over three-quarters of the
families in each group expressed satisfaction with each of these items
both before and after the project, and about two-thirds of each group
said they were satisfied with all four items both before and after the
intervention. There was no discernible evidence therefore that more
resource worker group families had in fact become satisfied with their
child's school, teaching, or transport arrangements as a result of the
intervention, or that they were more likely to have resolved any
problems which arose during the project.

Relationships between Home and School

One area in which the resource workers felt their work had been
particularly important was in fostering the development of closer and
mutually trusting relationships between parents and the staff at their
children's schools. On the one hand, the resource workers were able to
discuss with school staff any problems being experienced by a child or
family which might benefit from the school's help; on the other hand,
they could interpret and explain the school's goals and methods of
working to parents who were poorly informed or out of touch. According to the detailed analysis of their records, the resource workers visited
the schools of virtually all the children who were currently receiving
education at least once during the project. More than one visit was made
to over three-quarters of the children's schools, and additional contacts

by telephone or letter were also made on behalf of fifty-five families. The most common reason for these contacts was to discuss the disabled child's general development and progress, with the resource workers liaising on behalf of eighty of the ninety-two families. Less frequent reasons for contact were health or behaviour problems which the disabled child had developed, other family problems, or the provision of suitable aids and equipment for the disabled child.

The resource workers also took a more active part in trying to improve the home–school relationships of thirty-three families, by encouraging and enabling parents themselves to develop closer contacts with their children's schools:

> Suggested to headteacher that I should try and persuade Mark's parents to visit more often – she thought this a good idea ... Suggested to parents they should visit – they didn't realize they were welcome at school apart from official days or just to collect Mark.

> Headteacher said they'd never seen Mr and Mrs T – I wondered if they really understand they can visit the school. I said I was going to see them later that day and would talk to them ... Parents were very interested – Mr T. said he'd take his wife up more frequently. He knew he could go to school but hadn't realized the importance of actually seeing what Alice is doing there.

> After much discussion with local authority social worker about Mrs G.'s strong feelings that she receives no help or support from school and that possibly she thinks they consider her a rather poor mother, we decided to visit headteacher together and try to work towards a closer relationship between school and Dennis's home, as well as definite practical ways in which Dennis can be encouraged and taught at home to follow on from school teaching. Social worker to make appointment with headteacher; I'll tell Mrs G. what we plan and hope she'll feel encouraged to come to school with us in near future.

For thirteen of these families, closer contact with their disabled child's school was fostered by the parents' actually visiting the school with the resource worker. The resource workers' reports of these joint visits suggest that they benefited the parents, school staff and disabled child alike:

> Collected Mrs A. and baby, took them to school and took them and Charlene home. Most productive visit. Teacher showed mother Charlene's audiograms and for the first time Mrs A. understood

that Charlene has quite good low-frequency residual hearing. She was instructed how best to help her at home, especially with getting more sounds. Mrs A. was quite emotionally overcome – I feel this will be worth repeating next term.

Headteacher said since I'd contacted her and taken Mrs C. to school, she has a different attitude to the family – previously thought Mrs C. was not a very caring mother. Now knows differently – thanked me for this.

Took Mrs B. to see Billy at school – it was very moving to see Billy's reaction on seeing <u>his</u> mother come into the classroom for the first time. He immediately came to her, put his arms round her, spent whole morning being cuddled. Staff were very kind and welcoming and overjoyed Billy had his mother. It made me feel very sorry I had not brought her sooner, and determined to make the effort again – Mrs B., a person of little confidence, was made to feel very important.

Apart from the possible educational benefits for the disabled child of closer home–school relationships, the resource workers were also concerned in some instances to establish the child's school as an easily accessible source of help and support to parents after the end of the project:

Agreed with headteacher that because mother has very little contact with social services department, we must continue to encourage her to come to school.

Mother feels that the school is now her most important link and is grateful for my liaison, enabling her to go freely to school.

However, the effects of this intervention were surprisingly not apparent in any of the various outcome measures. When those parents whose children were currently attending school were asked before the start of the project whether they were satisfied with the amount of contact they had with their child's school, 90 per cent of resource worker group parents and 87 per cent of comparison parents said that they were. By the end of the project the proportions in each group had declined by a slight – but almost identical – amount. There was also no difference between the two groups in the actual frequencies with which parents said they met staff and other parents at their child's school. Indeed, when asked at the end of the project to assess whether these contacts had become more or less frequent during the previous two years, slightly more comparison group than resource worker group parents reported that their contacts with both staff and with other parents at their child's school had become more frequent. Furthermore, there were apparently no differences between the two groups of families in the quality of these contacts: almost identical proportions of each group said that they felt able to discuss their child's school progress with staff; that they could share with school staff any other anxieties they had about their child; and that they found it helpful to talk with other parents at their child's school. The failure of these outcome measures to pick up any effects of the resource workers' intervention suggests that their substantial intervention might not have resulted in any actual changes at all. A second possible explanation could be that the comparison group families were already receiving the kind of intervention (for example, from social workers attached to their children's special schools) which was initiated by the resource workers with the families they visited. Information to support this hypothesis was unfortunately not available, for reasons which will be discussed in Chapter 11, but it seems unlikely in view of the apparent absence of differences in the support received by the two groups before the start of the project. A third explanation is that the outcome measures which were used were simply inappropriate or insufficiently sensitive to detect any changes which did occur.

Leaving School and After

Placements after School

The process of leaving school and finding a suitable daytime placement or occupation can be stressful for both parents and child and requires support, counselling and practical help. When the project began, the oldest children in each group had just reached 16; by the end of the project four in the resource worker group and three in the comparison group had left school. All of the four resource worker group families were given help during the project with finding out about alternative opportunities and facilities, and with making contact with appropriate professionals and agencies:

> I explained the role of the disablement resettlement officers, and what they should be able to help with, as well as the various residential and non-residential assessment courses, training courses and independence centres. With parents' permission, I'll contact a local disablement resettlement officer for preliminary advice on what Ella should be thinking about first . . . [Later.] Suggested to careers adviser that possibly an assessment by an educational

psychologist might be helpful with a view to a suitable placement on leaving school. Adviser will contact psychologist.

Agreed with headteacher that ... I should contact social services and see what alternatives they had to offer ... Social services special placement officer said it was not worth me coming to see him as he had nothing to offer Ken when he left school – the adult training centre was not equipped to deal with such a severely handicapped boy and he thought Ken was the area health authority's responsibility ... Discussed with school medical officer ... Phoned GP, who said he'd give any help he could ... Phoned adviser for the handicapped at social services – she had no suggestions to make about day care, but said we could ask social services to pay if we had to have a place in the voluntary sector ... Visited the sister in charge of community nursing for the consultants at the local subnormality hospital ... Talked to the headmistress at the subnormality hospital school ... Visited medical social worker at City Hospital ... Fully discussed 'rotating care' with mother; told her of my idea to sound out Cheshire Home. Mrs K. said she'd talk to matron about possibility of 'rotating care'. I said I too would write ... Took Mrs K. to see matron of Cheshire Home – she was very willing to accept Ken for 'rotating care' ... Joint visit with local authority social worker to Mrs K. Social worker said she'd ask her authority if they'd be willing to pay for 'rotating care'. [This was approved. Later.] Mrs K. feeling unsettled about Ken and 'rotating care', finding it difficult to get used to completely different routine and unable to get used to the idea she was free to go out if she wanted. We fully discussed these feelings and how she'll need time to adjust.

By the end of the intervention two of the four school-leavers in the resource worker group had obtained employment, one was attending a day centre and the fourth was receiving care on a seven-week basis, rotating between his home, a local hospital and a Cheshire Home. All three comparison group school-leavers had also obtained placements, in employment, a day centre and an adult training centre. (No attempt was made to assess independently the suitability of these placements.) Two parents in each group reported having experienced difficulty in obtaining a placement for their child. However, all four resource worker families reported having received help with this problem, from a total of seven people, in contrast to just three sources of help reported by only two comparison group parents. Therefore, in addition to the direct help they themselves gave, this particular outcome measure appears to reflect the efforts of the resource workers to put families in touch with a range of other sources of information and assistance.

149

Planning for School Leaving

As the last extract from the resource workers' records suggests, the process of arranging a post-school occupation or placement can be complex and protracted. Many parents and children may therefore need to begin making plans for this some time before the child's sixteenth birthday. To see whether the resource workers had helped with this anticipatory planning, and to assess the impact of that help, data on all those children aged 14 and over who were still at school at the end of the project were analysed. Out of a total of twenty-one such children in their sample, the resource workers gave help with planning post-school placements to seventeen children and their families. A common type of help was the giving of information and advice (to thirteen of the seventeen families):

> Suggested that the Association for Spina Bifida and Hydrocephalus would have some information about training opportunities.

> Mrs S. very worried about Lucy's future ... doesn't want her to leave school and have to stay at home and wait for a place in the adult training centre. I mentioned Department of Employment training schemes. Mrs S. will inquire what is available locally.

However, with even more of the families (fourteen out of the seventeen helped), some liaison work was also necessary, most commonly with the child's school, a careers officer, social services department, or health authority:

> Mrs J. asked me about Gemma's future after next December when she is due to leave school. I suggested we visit school next term to talk to the headteacher about the future ... Rang local further education college to find out about social training courses and was told these are held at North Hill College. Rang North Hill College – Gemma could not be considered there; suggested I rang rehabilitation centre at Department of Employment. Rang rehabilitation centre ... Had long discussion with Mrs J., teacher and headteacher about Gemma's future.

> Had interview with district officer, social services department, to discuss the lack of facilities for 16+ severely disabled youngsters like Simon J. Was advised that Mrs J. should apply to social services for day care and then an assessment could be made. Also agreed I should visit adult training centre to see why they would be unable to provide care for Simon.

To assess the impact of the help those parents whose children were currently aged 14 or more and still at school were asked during both sets of interviews whether they had discussed with anyone what would happen when their child left school. Before the start of the project, more of the comparison group parents with children of 14 and over still at school said they had already received some help with planning their child's future. By the end of the project, however, this position was reversed; two-thirds of resource worker group parents reported that they had received help as against only one-half of the comparison group. Moreover, those resource worker group parents who had received help recalled having obtained it from a larger number of professional sources (including the resource worker) than had the comparison group parents – again evidence of both the direct and indirect effects of the resource workers' intervention.

Educational Equipment and Toys

Educational Equipment and Aids

At both the beginning and the end of the project parents were asked whether their son or daughter had any types of educational equipment or special educational aids for use at home, such as TV or radio loops, speech-training equipment, tape recorders or typewriters. Parents were also asked if their child did not have, but currently needed, any of these items.

The content analysis of the resource workers' records unfortunately did not permit a separate analysis of the work they did to help families obtain such items, but there is some evidence of the effects of their intervention. Equal numbers of families (forty-one in each group) reported obtaining at least one item of equipment during the project; but those in the resource worker group obtained slightly more items between them than did the comparison group families. At the end of the project more resource worker group parents also identified between them a greater number of items which their child did not have but which they would like than did the comparison group. This suggests that, as well as helping families actually to obtain items of educational equipment, the resource workers might also have increased parents' knowledge of the range of aids which could benefit their children, so that they were more likely than the comparison group parents to report outstanding unmet needs.

Toy Libraries

One very specific source of educational and recreational equipment for children with disabilities or learning difficulties is a toy library. These

151

are located in a variety of different agencies such as hospital children's departments, special schools, family support units and voluntary organizations. However, parents may fail to make use of a local toy library because they do not know about it, or because they know too little to be able to get in touch. Before the project began, 56 per cent of the resource worker group and 65 per cent of the comparison group parents knew of a toy library in their area; but only 28 and 30 per cent respectively of these families had had any recent contact with it.

The resource workers recorded only six specific instances where they referred or introduced families to a local toy library:

> Problem of keeping Kate occupied while flat on her back after operation – suggested Mrs H. contacted toy library about this.

> Rang social services occupational therapist to ask about toy library ... Talked with Mrs M. about toy library and said that occupational therapist had offered to give her a lift there and back. Mrs M. asked if I'd arrange this.

Information about such facilities was also included in the help given to twenty-eight parents about play and leisure equipment for their child to use at home. Nevertheless, by the end of the project fewer resource workers than comparison group families reported having had recent contact with a toy library, and fewer of those who did said they had found that contact helpful. Moreover, more of the resource worker group than comparison group families ceased to have contact with a toy library during the project. It seems therefore that the resource workers' intervention had no impact on families' use of local toy libraries.

Leisure

Voluntary Organizations

Specialist voluntary organizations for disabled children and their families can provide valuable practical help, information and, above all, the opportunity to share problems and experiences with others in a similar situation.

At the start of the project 52 per cent of resource worker group and 37 per cent of comparison group parents were members of national or local voluntary organizations for disabled children and their families, most commonly the Association for Spina Bifida and Hydrocephalus (ASBAH), the Royal Society for Mentally Handicapped Children and Adults (MENCAP), the Spastics Society, locally based organization for disabled children, or a special school parent–teacher association.

According to their records, the resource workers gave information about specialist voluntary groups to thirty-seven parents:

> Asked Mrs P. if she went to MENCAP meetings – she does not belong to the society. I suggested she joined and gave her the address of local secretary.

> Phoned secretary of Rubella Association – she found the address of the local organization and promised to send literature and application form to the W.s.

More active steps were taken to help thirteen families join, or participate more fully in, a specialist voluntary association:

> Mrs C. had thought of joining ASBAH but had been to one of the [local] branch meetings and it was just a social affair. I said I thought the [next town's] branch was more active and I'd contact one of the officers. I left copies of *LINK* and *LIFT* magazines for Mrs C. to see ... Rang secretary of [neighbouring] branch, explained about Mrs C. and Lindsey. She will phone and invite her to next meeting, which is a discussion with doctors.

The resource workers also helped a few parents to form, or improve the running of, their own local groups:

> Mrs H. and her friend are interested in forming a self-help group, and I said I'd send details of Dr Barnardo's Chorley Project. Sent details of health authority course for parents of handicapped children and information on other organizations ... Took details of *Contact a Family* film to be shown locally ... Gave Mrs H. details of a course at local college – one session on self-help groups.

> Mrs. J. maintains weekly contact with mother and baby group. She hopes that now the leader has left, the group will not just become an informal discussion group. I suggested that she becomes the new leader.

> Mrs W. is running a group for parents of Down's syndrome babies but finding it difficult to get referrals from the maternity unit ... Contacted senior social worker at General Hospital. She will talk to maternity unit social worker and other social work staff about the group.

On many other occasions (as described in Chapter 4) the resource workers contacted voluntary organizations on families' behalf for information about special aids, services and facilities. However, this additional work was not really reflected in the particular outcome measure used to evaluate their intervention, families' membership of voluntary groups. In all, fifteen resource worker group and seventeen comparison group families said that they had joined one or more voluntary organizations during the project, four of the former and seven of the latter group for the first time ever. All the new members were asked whether they had been given any help to make contact with or join the group and twelve families in each group said they had.

According to this outcome measure, then, there was no evidence that the resource workers' intervention had increased the likelihood of families joining a voluntary organization. Although by the end of the project more resource worker group families did belong to such an organization, this was largely because more had already been members before the project began.

Clubs and Playschemes

The resource workers gave a total of twenty-three families help with finding youth clubs and other recreational or sports activities for their disabled child. Only one-half were just given information about such facilities; the remainder were also given practical help to make contact with a local group, or with arranging transport for the child to get to and from the club:

> Discussed hobbies for Olwen – very interested in horses. Mrs T. had never heard of Riding for the Disabled – she will check with the consultant if this would be appropriate, while I'll locate the nearest branch.

> Rang local Lions – they promised to include Liam in any future children's outings.

Before the intervention, 23 per cent of resource worker and 11 per cent of comparison group children belonged to at least one recreational club; by the end the proportions belonging had increased by roughly similar amounts, to 29 and 20 per cent respectively.

Fewer children in each group had participated in weekend or holiday playschemes before the project began – only four in the resource worker group and six in the comparison group. Help was given by the resource workers to a total of twelve families; but in addition to giving information about such schemes, the majority of families were also formally referred or helped with arranging transport for their child:

> Rang organizer of local action group to see if they could arrange transport for Glenn to their holiday playscheme – unable to help. Rang two WRVS workers – no definite decision given. Rang

secretary of local handicapped children's group – immediate offer of help, and promise to send someone to see the family and make arrangements.

Holiday day centre for deaf children planned. Mike can go, but no transport is provided. Mrs M. doesn't see how she can take Mike – she'd have to take all her children there, including the baby, and get them all ready to fetch Mike back at teatime. Offered to see if voluntary agency can help. Phoned social services and WRVS. Eventually two people found to take him three days a week.

By the end of the project the numbers of children attending a weekend or holiday playscheme had increased in both groups, but by slightly more in the resource worker group. Therefore, although the resource workers' intervention did not appear to have made any difference to the children's membership of recreational clubs, it did seem to have made a very small impact on their participation in weekend and holiday playschemes.

Holidays

Almost one-half (45 per cent) of the families they visited were given help by the resource workers with arranging family holidays (defined as four or more nights away from home). The most frequent need for help arose in meeting the cost of a holiday; the resource workers gave thirty-seven families information about sources of financial assistance, or helped them to make applications for grants:

> [Discussed with parents an application to the Family Fund for help with holiday.] They asked if they could have a large frame tent, as the one they have is too small for the wheelchair. It costs £360 ... Wrote to Family Fund ... Family received grant for £200.

> Talked with Mrs P. about holiday at Butlins – we worked out cost of holiday and agreed I should contact [local authority social worker] and Family Fund ... Rang [social worker] and agreed I should obtain money from Family Fund and have cheque made out to her. She'd send deposit and arrange payment just before family went on holiday.

Twenty-two parents were given information about, or were helped to book, holiday accommodation with facilities suitable for their disabled child:

> Gave parents a list of hotels and boarding-houses where meals provided, which will take a handicapped child.

155

Contacted 'caravan agent' of local ASBAH group. Their caravans can be hired for £25 a week. Available to other handicapped people once spina bifida families have booked, and there are some vacancies.

The resource workers also helped two families to arrange or obtain help with paying for the transport to go on holiday.

However, the impact on the frequency with which families took holidays, on their knowledge of sources of help and on their actual receipt of help was not substantial. In the resource worker group the proportion of families taking a holiday during the two years before the project, and during the two years' intervention itself, remained at 78 per cent; in the comparison group it increased slightly from 75 before to 80 per cent during the intervention. However, the proportion of resource worker group families who knew that they could get aid from statutory and voluntary sources with holidays for their disabled child did increase slightly, from 58 to 65 per cent, while remaining unchanged in the comparison group at 55 per cent.

The amount of financial and other practical aid which families reported having actually received with the cost of their holiday or with finding suitable accommodation during the two years before and during the project was also compared. Again there were virtually no changes before and after the intervention. The proportion of resource worker group families taking holidays who reported having help with costs or accommodation rose from 67 to only 69 per cent, while the proportion of comparison group holiday-takers who had help remained unchanged at 61 per cent. Most of the practical aid which was received during the project came from the Family Fund (particularly with the cost of holidays) or specialist voluntary organizations (with both the cost of holidays and finding suitable accommodation); the only difference between the two groups of families was in the slightly higher proportion (30 per cent) of resource worker group families who recalled receiving financial help from the Family Fund with holidays taken during the project as against 24 per cent of comparison group families. However, when those families who had taken a holiday during the project were asked if they had received any *other* information or advice with arranging it, only 6 per cent of comparison group parents said they had (usually from a local authority social worker) compared with a significantly higher proportion – 37 per cent – of resource worker group parents (mainly from the resource worker herself).

One way in which disabled children can be helped to become more independent is by taking holidays *without* their parents, perhaps with other relatives, or with a group of children from school or a youth club. (This does not include periods of short-term care arranged primarily to give parents a break, which is discussed in the next section of this chapter.) The resource workers assisted a total of fifteen families with arranging a holiday for their child without the rest of the family; all were helped with finding accommodation or arranging transport, and seven were also helped to obtain some financial aid towards the cost of their child's holiday:

> We talked about the possibility of Roy going off on holiday on his own next year and Mrs B. was very interested in this. I promised to send her names and addresses of holiday centres.

> Suggested social services might be able to arrange a holiday for Debbie, or she might be able to go to one of MENCAP's homes in Blackpool . . . Rang social services . . . Rang secretary of MENCAP. She will contact Mrs P. and take her to see the home . . . Debbie to go away there for a week in August.

> Mr J. thinks the cost [of child's holiday] might be prohibitive . . . Spoke to social services area officer. After checking with his senior, he gave a 'Yes, in principle' to social services meeting the £45 cost. Mrs J. can raise £30 towards cost . . . Problem of transport – no car, parents cannot get time off work, or afford cost of taking him. Spoke to Red Cross about help with transport – it would cost approximately £50, so I think this is unrealistic. Spoke to social worker for the deaf. He will organize transport one way, even if he has to do it himself. If necessary, I could do the other trip. Wrote to social services asking for £30, including £10 petrol . . . Social services allowed the money.

During the project 29 per cent of the children in the resource worker group went on at least one holiday without their families, as did 23 per cent of the comparison group children. However, more of the resource worker group children took more than one such holiday; between them they took forty-four holidays on their own compared with the twenty-six taken by the comparison group children. The majority of the holidays taken by the children in each group were with the child's school, but more resource worker group parents reported that their child had also had a holiday arranged by a voluntary organization.

These outcome measures do not show that the families visited by the resource workers were more likely to have had a holiday as a result of the intervention. However, they do suggest that slightly more of those families who had a holiday had some practical help to do so, particularly from the Family Fund; and that significantly more families received information and advice in making their holiday arrangements, mainly from the resource workers themselves. In addition, more children in the resource worker group took a greater number of holidays without their families during the project.

Respite Care

Short periods of care in a hospital, hostel, home, or with 'foster' parents on an occasional or regular basis can give parents a valuable break from the work and stress of caring for a disabled child, and enable the rest of the family to relax together. Altogether thirty families were helped by the resource workers to plan or arrange periods of respite care. All received at least some of this help in the form of information, advice, or counselling. For example, an important initial step for some families was coming to terms with their feelings about arranging short-term care for the child:

> Mrs F. feels she's letting Daniel down – and getting out of her responsibilities if Daniel goes away. I suggested she looks at it from the point of view that her husband and daughter need a break even if she doesn't; and if Daniel goes away once, it wouldn't be so difficult if he had to go away suddenly if there was ever an emergency in the family and she couldn't look after him.

The information and advice given by the resource workers was sometimes all that was necessary for parents to make their own arrangements for their child's respite care:

> Mr and Mrs L. had been thinking of starting to place Sam for short-term care. I told them about a long-stay hospital for mentally handicapped people which also operates a flexible system of short-term care ... Mrs L. approached the paediatrician about short-term care for Sam, and he has made an appointment for her to be seen by Dr Y. at the mental handicap hospital.

In other instances the advice and counselling given by the resource workers was in connection with short-term care arrangements which parents had already made themselves with a hospital or social services department:

> Raymond is to go into [hospital] while Mrs T. is in hospital having baby. I suggested it might be possible for him to go in before. Mrs T. didn't realize she could do this – was very reluctant for him to go away, but doesn't see how she'll cope for the last few weeks before the baby arrives. She'll see her GP and social services about Raymond's admission a month earlier. If any problems arise, she'll let me know.

With eleven of the thirty families, the resource workers were also actively involved themselves in arranging respite care for a child by making a referral to the local social services department, for example, or to a home run by a voluntary organization:

> Discussed the family's needs with the social services department foster scheme project organizer – it will be some time before family is actually allocated a 'foster family' . . . [Later.] The W.s now have 'foster parents' for Rosalie – a late middle-aged couple who live only 4–5 miles away, and so far the arrangement has been successful.

> Asked Mrs H. if she'd consider asking Cheshire Home if they could have Wayne for the weekend. There may be a time when he'd need short-term care – perhaps while house adaptations going on – and it would be an idea to get him used to it. Mrs H. asked me to make inquiries.

The project workers helped two families in negotiations with their local social services department about transport arrangements or paying for periods of short-term care in a voluntary organization home, and a further six families with arranging subsequent periods of respite care after a successful initial placement:

> Mrs A. would be happy for Chan to go to the Cheshire Home where they know him well, and wondered whether social services would pay for him to go in October for half-term . . . I asked social services occupational therapist if they would pay. This was willingly agreed . . . [Later.] I suggested Mrs A. should ask social services to arrange short-term care each half-term. She was worried about payment, and I said I'd contact social services about this.

> Mrs B. is happy for me to take her to collect Marvin [from the hostel] but wonders about future arrangements for transport to and from the hostel, assuming that periods of short-term care occur regularly. Rang social services – transport is only provided for families who are 'known' to the department and where the department has arranged short-stay care. This is something I'll have to ensure is a firm policy for this family from the end of this year, particularly as it seems Mrs B. will accept regular periods of temporary care for Marvin . . . [Later.] Area officer agreed social services did have a responsibility towards Marvin and will provide transport of some sort if necessary.

Before the project began, 24 per cent of resource worker group children and 29 per cent of comparison group children had had at least one period of short-term respite care. The proportions who had a period

159

of care *during* the two-year project actually fell slightly in both groups, although in each group there was a slight increase in the numbers who had regular or repeated spells of respite care.

If they had apparently not increased the overall use of respite care facilities by the families they visited, perhaps the resource workers had instead helped parents to find more acceptable or appropriate placements for their children, which might be reflected in parents' levels of satisfaction with those placements. All those parents who had used short-term facilities before and during the project were therefore asked if they were happy with the placements and the care their child received there. Before the intervention, 60 per cent of the resource worker group users and 70 per cent of the comparison group users were satisfied. However, when asked again about the short-term care their child had received during the project, a significantly higher proportion (91 per cent) of resource worker group users than comparison group users (63 per cent) expressed satisfaction.

The third outcome measure used to evaluate the resource workers' help with arranging respite care concentrated on the unmet needs which parents expressed before and after the intervention. Those whose children had had a period of short-term care were asked whether they would like this again or more often, and those whose children had not been away were asked whether they would like them to have a break of this kind. In the resource worker group the proportion expressing a need for some, or more, respite care increased very slightly, but fell slightly in the comparison group.

It appears therefore that the main impact of the resource workers' intervention lay in improving the suitability and appropriateness of respite care placements, thereby increasing parents' satisfaction with them. There is no evidence that more resource worker group children received respite care, or that their parents' unmet needs for such care were significantly reduced as a result of the resource workers' intervention.

CHAPTER 9

Outcome Measures 4: Financial Problems, Welfare Benefits and the Family Fund

Severe disablement in a child frequently has an adverse effect on families' financial circumstances. On the one hand, incomes tend to be lower (largely because the mothers of disabled children have fewer opportunities than mothers of non-disabled children to take paid work outside the home). On the other hand, extra expenditure is often incurred on a wide variety of items including, most commonly, heating, transport and clothing (Baldwin and Glendinning, 1983; Glendinning, 1983; Baldwin, 1985). Parents may consequently find it harder financially to make ends meet; for many, the day to day management of a tightly stretched budget adds to the other extra work involved in looking after their disabled child. Part of the resource workers' activities therefore included ensuring that the families they visited were receiving all the financial assistance to which they were entitled in order to help offset some of their extra expenses and compensate for their lower incomes. A substantial proportion of this financial assistance came from the two cash benefits intended specifically to help with the extra costs of disability. These are the attendance allowance, which is payable from the age of 2 at one of two rates, to people needing extra attention or supervision either by day or by night, or by day and by night; and the mobility allowance, available from the age of 5 to those unable or virtually unable to walk. In addition, parents in receipt of supplementary benefit can claim extra weekly payments and occasional lump sum payments to meet some of the extra needs arising from their child's disability. From the age of 16 the majority of severely disabled young people will be entitled to an income of their own from supplementary benefit and/or non-contributory invalidity pension (the project was carried out before the latter benefit was replaced by severe disablement allowance in 1984). Finally, the Family Fund is a source of financial help with specific items needed because of the child's disability but which are not available from statutory agencies; laundry equipment, family holidays and bedding are among the items for which the fund most frequently gives grants. The help given by the resource workers with each of these types of financial assistance, and its impact on families' take up of the various benefits and grants, will be reviewed in turn in this chapter.

Disability Benefits

Research on the take up of disability benefits by families with disabled children suggests that the attendance allowance is currently claimed by between one-half and two-thirds of those eligible, and the mobility allowance by about four-fifths (Cooke, Bradshaw and Lawton, 1983). It is possible that the take up of these benefits may be even higher among those families who are well informed enough to have applied to the Family Fund, from whom the samples for the resource worker project were drawn. Indeed at the start of the project, attendance allowance was being received by 91 per cent of resource worker group and 92 per cent of comparison group children aged 2 and over. Similarly, among the children of 5 and over in each group who were unable to walk more than a limited distance 78 and 76 per cent respectively were already receiving mobility allowance. In these circumstances the scope for the resource workers to increase the take up of these benefits was necessarily rather limited. However, this does not mean that there was no scope for intervention at all. Even among those families who were already receiving the mobility or attendance allowance before the start of the project, problems could arise in establishing their child's continuing eligibility for a benefit or, in the case of the attendance allowance, to the appropriate higher or lower rate.

The Attendance Allowance

As far as the attendance allowance was concerned, thirty-one families were given some kind of help by the resource workers with their child's allowance. Some parents just needed general information or advice:

> Mrs R. plans to get some work to do at home to supplement their income and needed reassurance that Pat's attendance allowance wouldn't be affected by this.

> Will try and find out an answer to parents' worries about whether or not Richard starting work will affect his receipt of the attendance allowance.

> Mrs B. unsure how Andrew's periods of 'rotating care' would affect his attendance allowance – will find out for her.

Two families were given more active help with applications or reapplications for the attendance allowance:

Mrs J. is reapplying for the attendance allowance. She does not mention everything and every time she has to get up to Alma in the night. We talked about this in relation to the questions which will be asked by the visiting doctor. She'll now think really hard about what she does in the light of the questions and our talk ... [Later.] Higher rate allowance awarded.

A further fourteen families were helped to apply for a review of a recent decision with which they disagreed, about their child's entitlement to the attendance allowance. (A review can be requested when an application for the allowance has been unsuccessful, or the allowance has been awarded at the lower rate only, or when an existing attendance allowance award has been reduced or terminated because of a presumed change in the child's need for attendance.) Some of the fourteen parents just needed advice about how to apply for an attendance allowance review, but others needed much more active help from the resource workers in assembling and presenting the necessary evidence to the adjudicating authorities:

We spent much time talking through the reasons for asking for a review, and how to put these to the doctor concisely and without contradiction.

Tamsin (who is deaf) has been refused the attendance allowance. Advised Mrs Y. to appeal – I will write, and she will also ask her GP for his support ... [Later.] Mrs Y. phoned – she has today received notification that she has been awarded the high-rate attendance allowance and has received backpay of £640.

Attendance allowance has been reduced to the day [lower] rate – Mrs B. does not agree that the care Lucy needs has lessened and says she wants to appeal – will I help? We drew up a daily routine of when Lucy is well and otherwise, and I said I'd get it typed for Mrs B. to check ... Asked if her GP would write a letter in support ... Letter from GP says that Lucy's condition is unchanged and that she still needs the same amount of care. I amended Mrs B.'s letter, added that Mr B. also helps and sent to Mrs B. for approval ... Sent Mrs B.'s letter with my covering letter to Attendance Allowance Board ... [Later.] Mother genuinely grateful for help I gave to get allowance raised to higher rate again. Says she'll know how to go about things if the situation arises again.

Evaluating the effects of this intervention was not straightforward because, as the last quotation indicates, some of the problems with which help was needed could occur which would not be reflected in simple measures of overall take-up before and after the project. The evaluation was therefore particularly detailed. It included comparisons between the two groups of the outcomes of any changes which had occurred in their receipt of the attendance allowance during the project; parents' satisfaction with the rate of allowance their child was currently receiving; and their recall of any help and advice which they had received during the project in connection with their child's attendance allowance.

There were in fact virtually no changes in the take-up of the attendance allowance after the project. The overall take-up rates actually fell slightly, from 91 to 89 per cent in the resource worker group and from 92 to 88 per cent in the comparison group. Of the non-claimants at the start of the project, there were seven resource worker parents and eight comparison group parents with children over 2 who said that, although they had heard of the allowance, their child was not receiving it. By the end of the project only one of these families in each of the two groups was receiving the attendance allowance. The resource worker group child was a successful first-time applicant; the comparison group child had in fact just requalified for the benefit on discharge after a lengthy spell in hospital. There were in addition three children who were under the age of 2 at the start of the project and therefore ineligible for the allowance. By the end of the project the two in the resource worker group had begun to receive the lower-rate attendance allowance; the single comparison group child was still not receiving it.

Among those families whose children had been receiving the attendance allowance at the start of the project, three in the resource worker group and four in the comparison group were no longer receiving it by the end. Five of these seven children no longer qualified because they had entered long-term hospital or local authority care during the project. The remaining two (one in each group) had had their allowances withdrawn after review by the DHSS; but only the parents of the resource worker group child had asked for a further review of this decision the outcome of which was pending at the time of the second interview.

The rate (higher or lower) at which children were receiving the attendance allowance at the start of the project was compared with the rate they were receiving at the end. The majority (about 84 per cent of each group) were still receiving the same rate as before; there was no evidence that children in the resource worker group were more likely to have moved from the lower- to the higher-rate allowance (or, conversely, less likely to have dropped from the higher to the lower rate) as a result of the intervention.

Were parents whose children were receiving the lower-rate allowance satisfied with this, or did they think their child should be receiving it at the higher rate? In the resource worker group the proportion of lower-rate recipients who were satisfied increased during the project from 71 to 80 per cent; in the comparison group it fell from 71 to 67 per cent.

All those parents whose children were still receiving the attendance allowance at the end of the project were asked if any changes or problems had arisen during the previous two years, even though they were now receiving the same rate of allowance as before. In fact only five parents (three in the resource worker and two in the comparison group) mentioned any; all had had their child's allowance reduced from the higher to lower rate and restored again following a successful review.

Finally, all those parents who had lost or successfully applied for the attendance allowance, or whose child's allowance had changed in some other way during the project (twenty-eight in each group) were asked if they had received any help or advice on the subject. Seventeen resource worker group families between them identified a total of twenty-one sources of help (most frequently the resource worker herself); only eight sources of help were named by seven comparison group families.

The impact of the resource workers' intervention is therefore difficult to assess. Against the background of an initially high take-up rate there is no evidence that the families they visited were more likely to succeed in making an initial application for the attendance allowance or in raising the rate of their child's allowance. Nor were they any more likely to prevent their child's allowance being reduced to a lower rate or discontinued. The only differences between the two groups at the end of the project were in the higher proportion of resource worker group lower-rate recipients who were satisfied with receiving the attendance allowance at this rate, and in the amount of help and advice reported by the resource worker group families.

The Mobility Allowance

Similar problems were encountered in evaluating the impact of the resource workers' intervention on families' take-up of the mobility allowance, although here their intervention was far less extensive. Only fourteen families were given help, including two who were applying for the first time and two who were appealing against a refusal of the benefit:

> Mrs J. did not realize she could apply for mobility allowance as John can walk a few steps – she will apply for this.

> Barbara can barely walk, only a few yards. Has to be carried upstairs, does not see steps and curbs, and falls. I asked if application had been made for mobility allowance – no ... Gave Mrs P. a form to apply.

The overall take-up of mobility allowance among children aged 5 and over who could only walk a limited distance fell slightly in the resource worker group, from 77 to 72 per cent; but increased slightly, from 76 to 84 per cent, in the comparison group. During the project the total number of children receiving the mobility allowance increased by eight in the resource worker group and by eighteen in the comparison group. Most of these children (seven in the resource worker group and fourteen in the comparison group) had reached the age of 5 during the project, had thus become eligible for the allowance and had successfully applied for the first time. Conversely, two children in each group who had been receiving mobility allowance at the start of the project had had it withdrawn by the end. In all four cases the child's walking ability had improved, but one family had been helped by a resource worker to appeal and was awaiting a tribunal hearing at the time of the second interview.

There were no children in either group who were almost certainly eligible for the mobility allowance (aged 5 and over and unable to walk more than a few steps) and who were not receiving it by the end of the project. It is therefore not possible to conclude that the resource workers' intervention resulted in a higher take-up of the mobility allowance among the families they visited, though in view of the initial high take-up of the allowance this conclusion is perhaps not surprising.

Supplementary Benefit

Supplementary Benefit for Families

At the time the project was carried out families who were dependent on supplementary benefit for at least part of their basic weekly income could claim additional discretionary payments to meet a very wide range of extra needs. Such payments could either be made on a weekly basis on top of the basic benefit – an exceptional circumstances addition (ECA) – or as an occasional, one-off lump sum payment – an exceptional needs payment (ENP). (The project took place before the changes in supplementary benefit legislation and terminology introduced by the 1980 Social Security (No. 1) Act.) The resource workers' intervention and its evaluation was not restricted to any ECAs or ENPs received specifically for the extra needs of the disabled child. Because of the generally greater financial pressures experienced by families with disabled children, it was anticipated that the resource workers would take a broader look at families' overall benefit entitlements.

Before the start of the project, fourteen resource worker group families and nine comparison group families had a head of household in receipt of supplementary benefit. During the two years of the project itself supplementary benefit was received by a total of twenty-five resource worker group families and twenty-two comparison group families. The resource workers themselves recorded giving help to fifteen of the families who were receiving supplementary benefit. This help included checking their basic benefit entitlement – questions about which, for reasons of simplicity, were not asked in the interviews before and after the intervention:

> Mrs J. is worried about DHSS – still hasn't received a supplementary benefit order book and is paid by weekly Giro. Thinks she isn't paid enough. Wrote to DHSS . . . Reply – book being considered and should receive one soon; allowance being received is correct.

However, in one instance correspondence with the local DHSS office about a single parent's entitlement to the higher, long-term rate of supplementary benefit resulted in her receiving an increase of £3 a week and arrears of nearly £250.

The resource workers also helped seven of the parents in receipt of supplementary benefit with applications or appeals for discretionary additions or single payments:

> Exceptional circumstances addition for Malcolm's special diet has not increased from 30p for two years. Wrote to DHSS about diet allowance; DHSS phoned about letter: Malcolm's allowance has been increased to 90p and will go up to 95p in November.

> Mrs O. has had letter from DHSS asking her to go to the office – she asked if I'd go with her. I asked her to list all the clothing she and the children possessed, and her weekly budget . . . Took Mrs O. to DHSS, asked them about a clothing allowance . . . [Later: ENP received, used to buy children's clothing.] I asked Mrs O. if she'd agree to me asking for a further grant to buy clothes for her – ENP was supposed to include a coat for her . . . Further cheque for £19 arrived.

> Mrs P. to apply for ENP – showed her list of clothing in *Disability Rights Handbook*. She took down details and will apply tomorrow . . . [Later: no visit from DHSS, so resource worker rang local DHSS office and was told that Mr and Mrs P.'s file was mislaid.] Phone call from DHSS manager, very apologetic, staff should have checked properly. File has been found, request for visit has turned up – but has been sent by Mrs P., who is not the claimant; DHSS can't do anything unless Mr P. applies . . . [Later.] Social security have visited. Once again they've refused help with clothing, but

167

have provided a bed and plenty of bedding. Mr P. said he didn't think they'd have got this without my intervention.

The impact of this intervention did not appear to be very marked, which was perhaps not surprising in view of its limited extensiveness. At each of the two sets of interviews the majority of families in each group who were currently receiving supplementary benefit said that they did not know about weekly ECAs at all. Among those who had heard of them, there was some indication that the resource workers had increased the chance of a successful claim being made. Three resource worker group families reported making four claims, three of them successful, during the project, whereas two comparison group families made two claims for ECAs, only one of which was successful.

The same pattern was true of families' knowledge of, and claims for, lump sum ENPs. The proportion of supplementary benefit recipients who knew about ENPs was the same in both groups before and after the project but again the resource worker group families seemed slightly more likely to have made successful claims for ENPs. During the project four families reported making eight claims, six of which were successful, compared to the five comparison group families, who between them claimed five ENPs, only three of which were successful.

Supplementary Benefit for Teenagers

At the age of 16 the majority of severely disabled children are eligible to claim supplementary benefit (as well as or instead of non-contributory invalidity pension – NCIP) in their own names, regardless of the financial circumstances of their parents. Eight resource worker group and eleven comparison group children reached 16 during the project. Although little comparative data was obtained on this topic during the interviews before and after the intervention, it does seem that the children in the resource worker group benefited from advice about a complex area of interlocking and overlapping benefits:

> Discussed allowances from DHSS while Roy over 16 and still at school – showed Mrs H. the *Welfare Benefits Handbook* and Disability Alliance book.

> Suggested a visit to the DHSS to obtain the whole range of forms about allowances for the blind and children in full-time education . . . Form CH7 and leaflet obtained and sent to Mrs F.

> Jessica now receives NCIP. She is going to stay on at school at least to 19, so it would be to her advantage to claim supplementary benefit – she may qualify for clothing and heating additions.

By the end of the project only one of the eleven comparison group children who had reached 16 had successfully claimed supplementary benefit, but four of the eight resource worker group children had. One of these latter four children had also applied for an exceptional circumstances addition to his weekly benefit and was waiting for the result at the time of the second interview.

Help from the Family Fund

Earlier chapters have included comparisons of the help given by the Family Fund with specific types of items; here the total amounts of help received from the fund by the families in each group are compared. Instead of using information from the interviews with parents, who may have had difficulty remembering the amounts of money they had received some years earlier, the analysis used data which are collected by the Family Fund as part of its routine statistical monitoring.

Table 9.1 *Help Received from Family Fund before and during the Project*

	Resource worker group (N = *107)*		Comparison group (N = *103)*	
	Before	During	Before	During
Percentage families helped by Family Fund	92	69	95	59
Average number of items per family	2·7	1·8	2·5	2·0
Average total grant(s) per family	£337	£202	£304	£242

Before the project began, almost all the families in each group had already received help from the Family Fund; but those in the resource worker group had received fractionally more items each, at a slightly higher average total value, than the comparison group families (Table 9.1). During the project these positions were reversed; although a higher proportion of resource worker group families received help from the fund, they received on average slightly fewer items and less money than families in the comparison group. Families in the resource worker group were more likely than those in the comparison group to have received grants towards family holidays and, to a lesser extent, for washing-machines and transport, but otherwise there was little difference in the particular items obtained by each group of families.

The Alleviation of Financial Worries

The resource workers' records provide evidence that, as well as giving information and advice about benefits of particular relevance to people caring for a severely disabled child, they also helped with more general financial difficulties and with applications for other forms of financial assistance: family income supplement (FIS); tax allowances; education welfare benefits; housing benefits; and in one case non-contributory invalidity pension for a mother who was herself disabled. Thirty-seven families were given information, advice, or help with applications or – in two instances – help with conducting an appeal in connection with these various benefits:

> Mrs K. has been advised to apply for a school clothing grant for all three children – should she put down attendance and mobility allowances as income? Told her 'yes', but it is not counted as income for this purpose. If they try and make it, I suggested she lets me know and I'll take it up with the education department.

> Showed Mr and Mrs F. *Welfare Rights Handbook* – they said they'd buy one and go through it. They're quite capable of doing so, but have never before needed to think about these things.

A further twenty-five families were given advice or help with more general financial problems or debts. No comparative data is available on the families' receipt of other benefits, so there is no way of knowing whether the help given by the resource workers resulted in a higher take-up of such benefits by the end of the project than among the comparison group. However, the evaluation of the project did include an attempt to assess the *overall* impact of both this general help and that given with the more specific sources of financial assistance. This was done by asking parents about their subjective feelings about their financial circumstances – how much they worried about money and about being able to cope financially. Before the start of the project, 79 per cent of the resource worker group and 72 per cent of the comparison group parents said they worried about money at least occasionally (and about one-third of each group said they worried about it constantly). By the end of the project there were fewer parents in each group who said they worried at least occasionally about money, but the decrease in the resource worker group was significantly greater than in the comparison group – 20 per cent as against only 12 per cent. We also looked more closely at those parents who had said at the start of the project that they worried at least occasionally about money and being able to cope financially, to see whether these problems had become more or less acute during the subsequent two years. Of those who had expressed some anxiety about money at the start of the project, a greater proportion of the resource worker than comparison group parents said they worried less than before, and a smaller proportion said they now worried more.

In conclusion, the resource worker group families apparently increased their take-up of benefits and receipt of other financial assistance only fractionally more than those in the comparison group; but the extent to which they worried about money and being able to cope financially did decrease significantly.

CHAPTER 10

Outcome Measures 5: The Impact on Families and Carers

This chapter examines three aspects of the impact of living with and looking after a severely disabled child on members of the immediate family group. First, relationships within the family will be considered, to determine whether the resource workers' intervention had any effects on relationships between the disabled child and his or her siblings, or between the parents. Secondly, an attempt will be made to assess the involvement of fathers, siblings, relatives and friends in the practical care of the disabled child, and the extent to which this involvement increased as a result of the resource workers' intervention. Finally, a number of indicators will be used to assess the quality of life of the mother (or other main carer) of the disabled child to see whether this, or her physical or psychological health, had improved at all as a result of the intervention.

Relationships within the Family

Siblings

Accounts of the impact of a disabled child on her or his siblings vary widely. For example, Kew (1975) concluded that a sample of siblings selected from the records of a social work agency were experiencing considerable problems of social and emotional adjustment. On the other hand, the mothers interviewed by Wilkin (1979) reported very few problems with their other children. In the resource worker project such problems were discussed quite extensively by the resource workers, with exactly one-half of the eighty-four families containing brothers or sisters of the disabled child (though there was no evidence that the problems were as serious as those found by Kew). Virtually all (forty-one) of these families were just given help in the form of counselling or advice:

> Eric [younger brother] tends to have aggressive behaviour mixed with tantrums and childish outbursts. Mrs L. realizes she tends to treat Eric as the older, more responsible child; also that Tania uses him as the vehicle for some of her naughtiness which her physical

limitations prevent her from expressing. Mrs L. (and Mr L. when he joined us later) agreed that they need to pay Eric more attention and reduce some of his responsibilities ... [Later.] Eric is still having temper tantrums and squabbling with Tania. Mrs L. is now more able to recognize Tania's contribution and chastises her as well as Eric. She is also now trying to reason and explain things more to Eric.

We talked at some length about Patrick [twin brother]. He has been acting and talking recently as if he too was deaf, and demanding the same sort of response from his parents as Tony. We felt it might be best to ignore it. We also talked about finding something with which Patrick was uniquely associated, and stressing this to him in an effort to make him feel special in some way.

However, six families did also need a referral to, or liaison with, another agency to help with the problems being experienced by a non-disabled sibling:

Mrs P. expressed fears that Jamie [younger brother] was not making the progress he should, and wondered if Ralph was holding him back. Asked if she'd thought of a nursery place for Jamie, and suggested she consider it and talk to husband, health visitor and social services. I will write to social services too.

Two outcome measures were used to assess the impact of the disabled child on her or his brothers and sisters before and after the intervention. First, parents were asked about the frequency with which siblings found that their own play and leisure activities were disturbed or interrupted by the disabled child. Before the intervention, just over one-third of the parents in each group said that their other children's activities were often disrupted by the disabled child. By the end of the project, however, there was a significant difference between the two groups; only 27 per cent of resource worker group parents reported frequent disruptions of siblings' activities by the disabled child as against 46 per cent of comparison group parents. When the answers of individual parents before and after the intervention were compared, a significantly higher proportion of resource worker group parents recorded a decrease in the frequency of interruptions to siblings' activities by the disabled child (31 and 17 per cent respectively).

Secondly, those parents who had other (non-disabled) children aged 5 and over were asked about the extent to which these children felt restricted or inhibited by the disabled sibling from bringing their own friends home. The proportion of comparison group parents who said their other children were fairly or very restricted fell only slightly during

173

the project (from 22 to 19 per cent) as also did the proportion reported to be not restricted at all. However, there was a significant decrease, from 31 to 10 per cent, in the proportion of resource worker group siblings reported to be very or fairly restricted, and a corresponding increase in the proportion said to be not at all restricted (from 62 to 79 per cent). Again a comparison of the answers of individual parents before and after the intervention confirmed this picture; a significantly higher proportion of resource worker group parents (32 per cent) reported a decrease in the restrictions felt by their other children as against only 13 per cent of the comparison group. These reductions in the disruptions and restrictions felt by the non-disabled children in the resource worker group indicate that the intervention had a significant positive effect.

Relationships between Parents

The extent to which the presence of a disabled child has an adverse effect on the stability and cohesiveness of her or his parents' marriage has also been the subject of some debate (Gath, 1978; Wilkin, 1979). From a purely practical point of view, at least, the day to day work involved in the child's care may limit the amount of time and energy which parents have to resolve any disagreements or to spend together in recreational activities. To what extent was this true of the marriages of the parents in the project, and is there any evidence that the resource workers helped parents to alleviate any such strains on their relationship?

Before the start of the intervention, ninety-eight of the 107 children in the resource worker group and ninety-three (out of 103) in the comparison group lived in two-parent families. During the project four marriages in each group broke down and one comparison group mother died. On the other hand, three former single parents in the resource worker group (re)married during the project, as did one in the comparison group.

Information was collected from the resource workers' records of two aspects of their intervention on this subject: the counselling and advice they gave about marital disagreements and marital problems generally, and the efforts they made to enable parents to spend more time together and go out socially. As far as the former type of help was concerned, a total of twenty-seven families were helped by the resource workers. With five of these families, the resource workers were particularly concerned about the parents' preoccupation with their disabled child and the effect this was having on their own relationship. A further eight parents were helped, for example, by referral for counselling or legal advice, in connection with an earlier or imminent marital breakdown:

Discussed Mrs B.'s total commitment to the handicapped world –
her social life revolves around other families with handicapped
children ... [Later.] Her husband seems to have related better to
her over the past few months as she has made the effort ... to
participate in a wider social environment.

Parents divorced, but Mr J. is reluctant to leave the house.
Contacted solicitor about getting an injunction against Mr J.
returning to the house. Arranged an appointment for Mrs J. to see
the solicitor.

Two questions were asked during the interviews before and after the
project to assess the impact of this intervention on the quality of parents'
relationships. The answers usually reflected the opinions of the child's
mother only. First, respondents who were currently in two-parent
families were asked to assess the impact of the disabled child on their
current marital relationship. The proportion of resource worker group
parents who thought this relationship had become closer increased
slightly during the project, while the proportion of comparison group
parents decreased slightly, but there were no other differences between
the two groups before and after the intervention.

A more definitive picture emerged from parents' answers to the
second question, about whether or not they currently had serious
disagreements with each other about the disabled child or about other
issues. (Again the answers mainly reflected the opinion of the child's
mother.) The proportions who reported no major disagreements at all
increased in both groups during the project; but the proportion of
comparison group parents reporting disagreements about both the
disabled child *and* other matters more than doubled during the project,
while remaining unchanged in the resource worker group.

Secondly, the resource workers recorded helping nineteen parents to
overcome some of the restrictions they experienced in going out together
without their children. All were given information and encouragement
to develop a social life of their own, but four were also given more active
help with finding suitable baby-sitters:

Mrs A. said her 22-year-old daughter and her husband had offered
to come and care for the children to give her parents a break. Mrs A.
was dubious about accepting their offer; it took a little persuasion
from me to agree that it would be a good idea.

I offered to try and obtain a baby-sitter through council of social
service [CSS] volunteer scheme and Mrs V. was quite enthusiastic.
They may also need help in April when they have to be away
overnight to Mr V.'s firm's dinner dance. If grandparents can't

175

help, I'll try to obtain a hostel place. Phoned CSS . . . [Later.] The CSS organizer has found a local baby-sitter, a teacher who has done remedial work, and passed on her name and phone number to Mrs V. . . . [Later.] The baby-sitting arrangement is working quite well.

When parents were asked in the interviews how often they normally went out together without their children, there were no differences in the frequency with which each group of parents went out either before or after the project. However, when they were asked to indicate on a 7-point scale to what extent they *felt* restricted in going out on their own without their children, a greater proportion of resource worker group parents felt less restricted at the end of the project, and a smaller proportion felt more restricted, than the comparison group parents.

There is therefore some evidence of the effect of the resource workers' intervention on parents' marital relationships and social life. But this evidence is not very substantial, nor wholly consistent.

Who Cares?

The evaluation of the project included an attempt to assess the contributions made to the care of the disabled child by nuclear and extended family members, friends and neighbours. Whether the intervention of the resource workers resulted in any increase in the practical or emotional support given by friends and relations was also assessed.

Fathers

The resource workers recorded only eleven instances in which the domestic division of labour and the respective responsibilities of each parent in looking after the disabled child were topics of discussion during their visits. This low level of intervention was reflected in the five outcome measures which focused on fathers' participation in the practical care of their children. Information was obtained in each interview about the frequency with which fathers helped to put the disabled child to bed; played with and kept her or him amused; took her out on his own; looked after her at home while the mother went out; and looked after any other children in the household. On none of these measures was there any indication that the resource worker group fathers had increased their levels of involvement in the care of the disabled child or her siblings; in each group the frequency with which fathers participated was almost identical before and after the intervention.

Siblings

After the disabled child's father, siblings are likely to be the next most important source of help, which might range from playing with and entertaining the disabled child to assisting with housework and shopping. Those parents who currently had other children living in the household were asked at each interview whether they regularly helped around the house or with looking after the disabled child. During the course of the project there was an increase in both groups in the amount of help given by other children in the household (probably because they were able to contribute more as they grew older). However, the increase in the proportion of children who were reported to help a lot was slightly greater in the resource worker group than in the comparison group.

Parents were also asked about the help they received from any adult children who were no longer living at home. By the time of the second interview seventeen resource worker group parents and twenty-three comparison group parents had children over 16 living away from home, of whom eight and ten respectively helped with looking after the child or children, or in other ways. From these figures it is difficult to conclude that the resource workers' intervention encouraged either younger or older siblings to help more with the care of the disabled child.

Extended Families, Friends and Neighbours

Next the contributions made by parents' own families, neighbours and friends were considered to see whether any changes in the amount of help they gave occurred during the project. There is little evidence from the resource workers' records that they actively encouraged or facilitated the development of informal family and neighbourhood support for the families they visited. Nevertheless, it does seem from parents' reports of the practical and moral support they received from families, friends and neighbours (Figure 10.1) that on the whole this increased slightly among the resource worker group families but that it consistently decreased in the comparison group.

By the end of the project therefore it appears that in the majority of families the disabled child's mother still bore the major responsibility for meeting her or his day to day needs. Although the help given to the resource worker group mothers by their other children, relatives, friends and neighbours increased during the project, this increase was only slight. Moreover, there was no evidence that the help given by the fathers in either group had increased at all. It is therefore important to see whether, rather than spreading the burdens of care more widely among nuclear and extended family members, the resource workers had achieved other ways of supporting the disabled child's main carer. The evidence on the impact of the intervention on carers' anxieties, morale and health is now examined in the final section of this chapter.

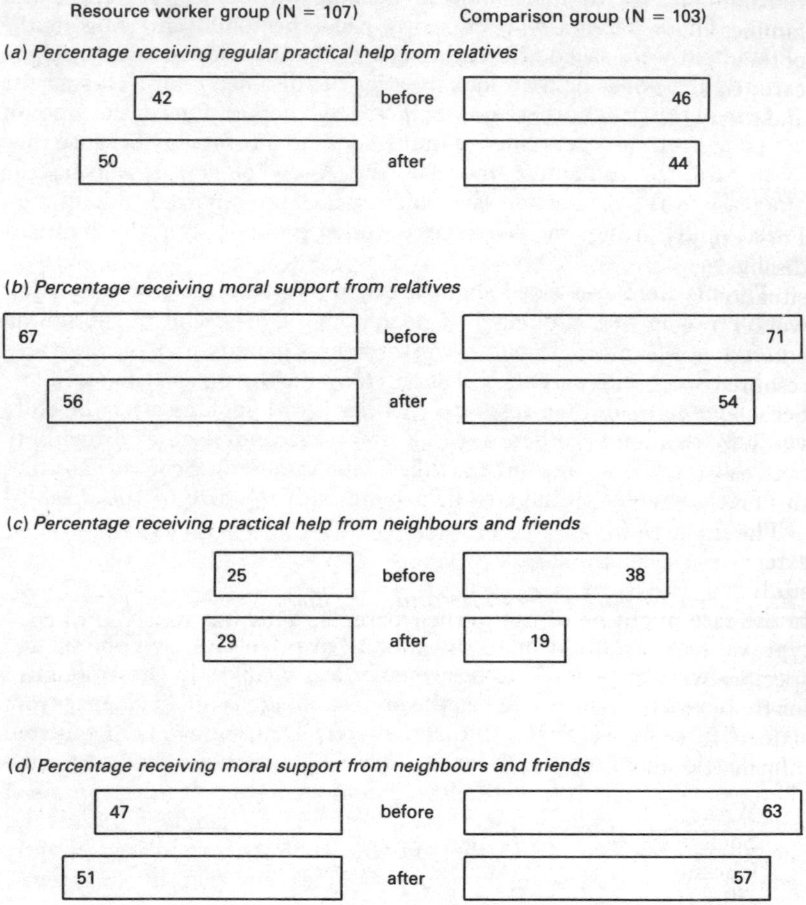

Resource worker group (N = 107)   Comparison group (N = 103)

(*a*) *Percentage receiving regular practical help from relatives*

42	before	46
50	after	44

(*b*) *Percentage receiving moral support from relatives*

67	before	71
56	after	54

(*c*) *Percentage receiving practical help from neighbours and friends*

25	before	38
29	after	19

(*d*) *Percentage receiving moral support from neighbours and friends*

47	before	63
51	after	57

Figure 10.1   Practical help and moral support received from relatives and friends.

The Impact on Carers

As the previous section has indicated, in almost all the families in both groups it was the disabled child's mother who carried most of the responsibility for her or his day to day care, and who was therefore likely to experience a substantial share of any related fatigue, anxiety, or stress. (The only exception was the single one-parent comparison group family which was headed by the disabled child's widowed father.) The remainder of this chapter therefore focuses on the mothers in two-parent families and on single parents, and examines three aspects of the quality of their lives: their anxiety about the disabled child and her or his future care; their own social lives and feeling of isolation; and their physical and mental health.

Anxieties about the Future

For very many parents, anxieties arise about who will care for their disabled child once they are no longer able to do so themselves. This situation was in fact experienced by four parents – one in the resource worker group and three in the comparison group – whose children entered residential care during the project. (A second child in the resource worker group was also taken into care during the project because of suspected non-accidental injury.) Making satisfactory provision for their child's future care may be a difficult and unwelcome task, both emotionally and practically, for many parents. However, as long as this task is deferred, the future may continue to be a source of worry.

The resource workers' records suggest that the help they gave was not extensive, largely because only a small proportion of the children in the study had reached an age where practical help and advice about their future care might be of use to their parents. This was reflected in the type of help given by the resource workers, which tended to be specifically concerned with finding appropriate residential care facilities for those children who might need them in the near future. Altogether sixteen families were given such help, more often in the form of information and advice than through a formal referral:

> Wrote to Steiner Foundation, Ravenswood Foundation, National Society for Mentally Handicapped Children, Fitzroy Foundation, Cheshire Homes, Oaklands Nursing Home, MIND and Dr Barnardo's for information for the Y. family.

> Outlined the National Society for Mentally Handicapped Children's guardianship scheme and offered to arrange for Mr and Mrs G. to see the regional director of NSMHC about it.

Evaluating the impact of this intervention involved asking mothers before and after the project whether they worried at all about the future care of their disabled child and, if so, how much. About two-thirds of each group said before the project that they worried a fair amount or a great deal. By the end of the project the proportions of both groups who said they worried had risen to just over three-quarters, with about one-half of the mothers in each group admitting that they worried more than they had done two years earlier. Those mothers with younger children were then excluded from the analysis and only the answers of those with disabled children aged 12 and over at each interview, who were likely to have the most serious worries about their son or daughter's future care, were examined. There was very little difference between the groups before the intervention, but by the end 90 per cent of these resource worker group mothers said they were worried as against 76 per cent of the comparison group. More of the resource worker than comparison group mothers also admitted to having greater anxieties about their disabled child's future care than they had done two years ago. Despite the help which they gave, there is therefore no evidence that the resource workers' intervention reduced mothers' anxieties about the future; although in the absence of any imminent crises about the child's continuing family care, the impact of such intervention may in any case have necessarily been limited and difficult to detect.

Social Life and Loneliness

The relatively restricted intervention of the resource workers in helping parents to go out together socially more often has already been described in this chapter. Here the impact on the mothers' own social lives is examined. In fact, in each group, the proportion of mothers who said they were able to go out on their own as often as once a week declined during the project; conversely, the proportions who said they hardly ever or never went out alone increased in both groups.

A complementary indicator of any changes in the social lives of the mothers was attempted by asking a question in each interview about the frequency with which they experienced feelings of loneliness as a result of having a disabled child. Just under one-half of the mothers in each group both before and after the intervention said they felt lonely at least occasionally; the only difference between the two groups appeared to be a slight increase in the proportion of resource worker group mothers who said they felt lonely most of the time. While the degree of loneliness experienced by the comparison group mothers appeared to remain about the same, then, it did seem to increase slightly among mothers in the resource worker group.

A further measure of the degree of isolation experienced by the mothers in the project was provided by a question about whom, if anyone, they could talk to if they were having problems or if things began 'to get on top of' them. Figure 10.2 shows the numbers of people who were identified by the mothers in each group before and after the intervention as people to whom they could turn for help and support of this kind. Before the project, about one-fifth of the mothers in each group were unable to name anyone at all whom they could talk to; by the end of the project this number had decreased slightly in the resource

Resource worker group (N = 107)   Comparison group (N = 103)

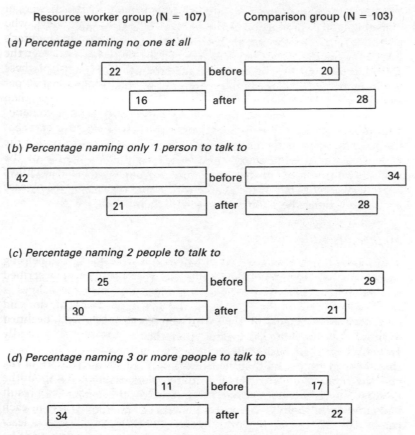

(*a*) *Percentage naming no one at all*

| 22 | before | 20 |
| 16 | after | 28 |

(*b*) *Percentage naming only 1 person to talk to*

| 42 | before | 34 |
| 21 | after | 28 |

(*c*) *Percentage naming 2 people to talk to*

| 25 | before | 29 |
| 30 | after | 21 |

(*d*) *Percentage naming 3 or more people to talk to*

| 11 | before | 17 |
| 34 | after | 22 |

Figure 10.2   Number of people to whom mothers could turn to discuss problems.

worker group but increased in the comparison group. At the other end of the scale the proportion of resource worker group mothers who were able to name at least three people to whom they could talk trebled during the project, whereas the increase in the comparison group was very much smaller. A comparison of the numbers of people named by individual mothers before and after the project revealed that by the end 57 per cent of resource worker mothers named more people than before, but only 40 per cent of comparison group mothers did so. Conversely, the comparison group mothers were almost twice as likely to name fewer people at the end of the project than the resource worker group mothers (39 and 22 per cent respectively).

Spouses, parents, other relatives, friends and neighbours were named by a high proportion of the mothers in each group, both before and after the project, as people with whom they could talk about problems or anxieties. The differences between the two groups consisted of small increases during the project in the proportion of resource worker group mothers who named other parents of disabled children, doctors, social workers and teachers at their child's school as sources of help and support – all indications of the resource workers' efforts to liaise with and improve parents' communications with such people. In addition, the resource workers themselves clearly became an additional source of support to the parents whom they visited; at the end of the project almost two-thirds of the resource worker group mothers named the resource worker as one of the people with whom they could discuss any problems if things began 'to get on top of' them.

Mothers' Health

A number of questions were asked before and after the intervention to assess whether the help given by the resource workers had made any impact on the various psychological and physiological symptoms sometimes associated with the extra work and anxiety arising from the care of a severely disabled child. First of all, mothers were simply asked whether they thought that looking after their disabled child had had any effect on their health. Before the start of the project, about one-third of each group said that their health was not affected at all; by the end the number of 'unaffected' resource worker group mothers had increased by 10 per cent, while the number in the comparison group had gone down slightly. When the answers of individual mothers were compared, 22 resource worker group mothers, who had earlier reported effects on their health, no longer thought by the end of the project that their health was affected as against only 11 comparison group mothers.

Two simple scales were used to measure more precisely the health of the disabled child's mother and the extent to which this changed during the project. Both scales focus on the borderline area of the physical and psychological symptoms associated with stress, and both have been used in other studies to measure the levels of stress experienced by mothers of disabled children.

First of all, mothers were asked whether they had experienced any of seven symptoms of a psychosomatic nature during the last two years and, if so, whether a doctor had been consulted about them. This measure was used by Pomeroy *et al.* (1978) in a survey of families with disabled children, whose mothers were found to report significantly more symptoms than the mothers of non-disabled children. The seven symptoms were headaches, sleeplessness, digestive disorders, sweating, depression, backache and 'nerves'.

In Pomeroy *et al.*'s study mothers were asked whether they had experienced any of the seven symptoms during the past month. Because the evaluation of the resource worker project was concerned with changes which might have taken place over a two-year period, the mothers in this study were also asked, at each interview, whether they had experienced any of the symptoms during the previous couple of years. The extent to which any symptoms had been experienced as severe was also assessed, by asking whether a doctor had been consulted about it.

There was a very small decrease in the average number of symptoms experienced by the comparison group mothers, and a slightly larger (but still relatively small) decrease in those experienced by the resource worker group mothers, when the two years before and during the project were compared. There were no other differences between the two groups, either in the average number of symptoms experienced during the four weeks immediately preceding each interview or in the number of symptoms during either time period which had been referred to a doctor for consultation. A further analysis, of changes in the number of symptoms experienced by each individual mother, also revealed no differences between the two groups in the proportions reporting more or fewer symptoms after the intervention than they had done before.

The other scale used to assess changes in maternal health was the malaise inventory, which has been used in a number of other studies (see Philp and Duckworth, 1982, ch. 3) to measure the levels of stress experienced by the mothers of disabled children. The inventory consists of twenty-four questions about a range of physical and emotional symptoms, each of which is considered to have some psychological or psychosomatic component. It is completed by the respondent herself and the total number of symptoms which she says she experiences are added together to form a score ranging from 0 to 24.

Comparison of the scores of the mothers in each group before and after the intervention showed that the average score of the resource worker group mothers decreased by 1·6 (from 8·5 to 6·9), and that of the comparison group mothers by only 0·8 (from 7·7 to 6·9). When the scores of each individual mother before and after the project were compared, more of the comparison group mothers' scores had increased, and by a larger amount, than had those of the resource worker group mothers. The mothers in the resource worker group therefore appear to have experienced a slight reduction in – or at least, experienced no increase in – their levels of stress during the project.

Finally, mothers were asked whether they took sleeping tablets, anti-depressants, or tranquillizers and, if so, how often. The proportion of mothers in each group who said they never took such medication increased during the project; and among those who did report taking one or more of these drugs, there were no differences between the groups in the frequency with which they were taken.

According to the parents' comments which were reported in Chapter 4, the resource workers' intervention had apparently had a significant impact on their morale, and by equipping them with information and knowledge had increased their capacity to cope. Yet according to the standardized and pre-validated scales described here, the impact of the intervention on their experience of stress and stress-related symptoms was only small. One of the reasons for this is that 'stress' is a multifaceted concept which can describe different phenomena. Its measurement is therefore notoriously difficult (Bradshaw and Lawton, 1978b; Bradshaw, 1980; Philp and Duckworth, 1982). Other possible reasons for this discrepancy, and other issues raised in the interpretation of the outcome measures used to evaluate the project, are discussed in Chapter 11.

CHAPTER 11

Conclusions: Issues for Evaluation

The Intervention and its Outcomes

The resource worker project was designed and evaluated against a background of universal popularity for policies of 'community care'. From that background have emerged the figures on whom the implementation of such policies is increasingly to depend, the so-called 'informal' carers – those neighbours, friends and, most commonly, close relatives who provide most of the physical and social care needed by disabled or dependent people. Some politicians, policy-makers and professionals have argued for a radical shift in the respective responsibilities and roles of informal carers and formal welfare services, with the latter playing a subsidiary and 'enabling' role to the former. Others have argued for an increased input of formal service provision to informal carers, particularly inputs whose effectiveness and efficiency is improved by a degree of specialization within generic social services organizations. The major factor which has prompted these debates, and indeed the development of 'community care' policies as a whole, has been the increasingly stringent restriction on public expenditure. This restriction has at the same time led to mounting political and public pressures for thorough and critical assessments of social work and social welfare intervention in order to make explicit their impact and demonstrate their effectiveness.

The resource worker project itself was prompted by the widespread concern of politicians, voluntary organizations, independent committees of inquiry and the research community about one particular group of informal carers: families looking after a severely disabled child. There was increasing evidence that such families had apparently failed to benefit from many of the important policy developments and service innovations of the 1970s. On the whole they seemed to lack adequate practical and emotional support, and were widely reported to feel isolated and neglected by the mainstream welfare services. Furthermore, the continuing fragmentation of service provision for disabled children and their families presented problems for parents in learning about, and gaining access to and using, those services and facilities which were available.

The project was intended to remedy these two central difficulties through the intervention, over a two-year period, of specialist social workers (the 'resource workers'), who would be responsible for maintaining regular (though not necessarily frequent) contact with families; for identifying unmet needs; and for planning and co-ordinating the delivery of appropriate services to meet those needs. At the same time the content of the resource workers' intervention was to be documented and analysed and its effectiveness evaluated.

These goals were successfully achieved. Five qualified social workers, all with appropriate specialist experience, were recruited to work part time (15 hours a week) with groups of between nineteen and twenty-three families drawn from the register of applicants to the Family Fund. The resource workers worked independently for the project but received initial briefings and ongoing information and professional support from an established voluntary child care agency. Their intervention showed that, on the whole, the total sample of 107 families did not appear to have contact with any single, easily identifiable source of support. The content of the resource workers' intervention, which has been fully documented in Chapter 4 and in Chapters 6–10, showed how extensive was the scope for giving help in the form of information, advice and counselling. In respect of every type of problem raised by parents during the course of the intervention these were the most frequent forms of help given by the resource workers. The intervention also clearly demonstrated the families' needs for assistance with understanding and negotiating a range of services fragmented into different organizations and professional groups. Referring families to the appropriate professional or agency, co-ordinating the involvement of more than one service agency and acting as an advocate on a family's behalf when delays or other problems arose were also common forms of intervention.

The data on the levels and content of the resource workers' intervention were taken from the records they kept during the project, and from interviews carried out before and after it. From these sources a detailed picture was generated of the frequency with which the resource workers encountered various types of problems; the different skills which they employed to deal with the problems; and the range of agencies and other professionals whom the resource workers brought in to help solve the problems. These data, together with the information provided for the resource workers before and during the intervention (Appendix A), give a comprehensive account of the range of problems likely to be experienced by families with a disabled child and an indication of the training needs of specialist social workers who might work with them.

Although all the families in the study had children whose disabilities had been very severe at the time of their application to the Family Fund, the causes of these disabilities were very varied, as were the children's ages. Therefore, not surprisingly, there were substantial variations in the current needs of the families, which resulted in varying amounts of input from the resource workers. For example, the number of home visits by the resource workers to each family ranged from three to twenty-nine, with an average of thirteen over the two-year period. There was a significant association between the number of visits and an assessment by the resource workers of how much they had achieved in their work with each family. Particularly substantial inputs were made to those families with older children (aged 11 or over): they received a significantly higher number of visits, and the resource workers were also more likely to consider they had achieved a greater amount with them. Variations in inputs by the resource workers were also reflected in some of the assessments made by parents of the outcomes of the project. Families who had had a higher number of visits were more likely to report having received a greater amount of help overall. They were also more likely to feel that the project had made a substantial impact on their lives.

Apart from these two summary outcome measures, the remaining outcome measures fall into two broad groups: first, the opinions of the parents who were visited by the resource workers about the impact and appropriateness of the intervention; and secondly, detailed comparisons of the intervention families and a further 'control' group (the comparison group) of 103 similar families who had not received any specialist intervention. This latter group of outcome measures focused on the families' social and economic circumstances, their use of services, their unmet felt needs and their subjective experiences of the care of their disabled child before and after the intervention.

The outcome measures indicate that the intervention generally appears to have been successful. According to the first group of measures, almost all the parents visited by the resource workers said that the intervention had made some difference to their lives; for just over one-half, it had made 'a very great difference'. Two-thirds of the parents said that for them the greatest value of the intervention had been having somebody to talk to, or to whom they could turn for help if they needed it. One-third said thay had most valued the information, advice and practical help they received. Hardly any parents said at the end of the project that they had outstanding needs which the resource workers had not dealt with. An overwhelming majority endorsed the service, both immediately afterwards and some two years later, as the most appropriate way of giving help to families looking after a disabled child; and preferable to the equivalent cost of the service (about £4 a week per family at 1985 prices) in the form of a regular cash grant.

When the circumstances, needs and feelings of the project and comparison groups before and after the intervention were examined, similar positive outcomes were on the whole observed, although here the analysis was slightly more complex. For example, it was not sufficient

187

just to try and detect 'improvements' which occurred in the resource worker group, but not in the comparison group. There was also the possibility that the circumstances of families in the comparison group might deteriorate while those in the resource worker group were maintained, that deteriorations might occur in both groups but to a greater extent in the comparison group, that improvements might occur in both groups but to a greater extent in the resource worker group, or that an initial relative disadvantage suffered by the resource worker group might no longer exist by the end of the intervention.

For example, Chapter 6 showed that although the resource workers had apparently (and perhaps not surprisingly) had little impact on the medical and paramedical care of the disabled children, they had made a significant impact on several of the practical day to day problems arising from their disabilities. More resource worker families than comparison group families obtained bathing aids, alterations to their bathrooms, toileting aids and protective bedding for their incontinent children. There were significant decreases in the degree to which the resource worker group families felt the care of their incontinent child to be onerous and in the overall burdens of personal care (washing, dressing, incontinence, daytime supervision and night-time attendance) felt by the parents of the older children. More items of laundry equipment were obtained by the resource worker group families, as were telephones which were needed because of the child's medical condition. Significantly more resource worker group families obtained help during the project to meet their disabled child's needs for extra, or special, items of clothing and bedding; more reported having received information and advice about the Motability scheme; and there was a significant increase in the proportion of resource worker group families claiming exemption from payment of vehicle excise duty on a car used for their disabled child. Finally, as a result of the help given with transport problems to those parents who had difficulty taking their disabled child on public transport, there was an increase in the proportion of carers who said they felt no more than occasionally restricted in going out during the daytime, while the proportion of unrestricted comparison group carers declined.

The impact of the help given by the resource workers with families' housing and other major environmental problems was examined in Chapter 7. The overall proportion of families who were satisfied with and considered their homes suitable for their disabled child decreased in the comparison group, but remained the same in the resource worker group. Conversely, of those families who had considered their houses to be unsuitable at the start of the project, significantly more resource worker than comparison group families had apparently made their houses suitable by the end. Sometimes this suitability was achieved by moving house. Of those families with initial housing problems, twice as many resource worker group families as comparison group families had moved by the end of the project. Resource worker group movers were also more likely to be satisfied with their new houses.

Other families tried to make their homes more suitable by carrying out adaptations. Again slightly more housing adaptations were carried out during – or planned for after the end of – the project among the resource worker group families. In addition, a significantly higher proportion of resource worker group families intended to, or had already carried out, alterations to their gardens by the end of the project. A slightly higher proportion of resource worker group families also reported having received some financial assistance from the authorities with the costs of these adaptations.

Chapter 8 examined the impact of the resource workers' intervention in connection with educational issues, recreation and the use of respite care facilities. Despite extensive inputs by the resource workers, and some well-documented clear successes, there was no evidence that overall the resource workers had raised the level of parents' satisfaction with their children's education or increased the frequency of their home–school contacts. However, at the end of the project the parents of both school leavers and those approaching school-leaving age reported having received more help with planning and finding post-school placements than did similar comparison group parents. A significantly greater number of resource worker group families also received information and advice with arranging family holidays; and more resource worker group children took more holidays alone without their families during the project. Although there was no evidence that the resource workers' intervention had increased the frequency with which families used respite care facilities for their children, parents' satisfaction with such facilities did increase to a significant degree.

The resource workers' intervention in connection with financial problems and cash benefits was limited to a large extent, as Chapter 9 showed, by already high take-up levels of attendance and mobility allowances. However, the resource workers do seem to have helped parents ensure that they were receiving the correct allowances. The proportion of lower-rate attendance allowance recipients in the resource worker group who were satisfied with this rate of the allowance increased, whereas more comparison group recipients became dissatisfied.

Slightly more claims for supplementary benefit weekly additions and single payments were made by resource worker group families during the project, and such claims were also more likely to be successful. In addition, slightly more claims for supplementary benefit were made by resource worker group 16 year-olds, and slightly more resource worker group families received help from the Family Fund during the project (though the average amount of their grants was lower than in the comparison group). The overall impact of these changes was that, by the end of the project, there had been a significant decrease in the proportion of resource worker group parents who said they had worries about money and financial matters.

Finally, the impact of the resource workers' intervention in connection with family and personal matters was examined in Chapter 10. A big improvement seems to have occurred in the quality of life of the siblings in the resource worker group. Significantly more resource worker group parents reported a reduction in the extent to which siblings' activities were disrupted by the disabled child, and a significantly higher proportion of resource worker group parents reported a reduction in the restrictions experienced by siblings in bringing their own friends home. On each of these outcome measures there was also a significant drop in the proportion of resource worker group siblings reported to feel *frequently* disrupted or inhibited.

Parental relationships also appeared to have been beneficially affected to some extent as a consequence of the intervention. The proportion of comparison group parents who reported having major disagreements about both the disabled child and other issues more than doubled during the project but remained the same in the resource worker group, and more resource worker than comparison group parents said by the end of the project that they felt less restricted in going out socially without their children.

There was no indication that the resource workers had enabled the work of looking after the disabled child to be shared more evenly between parents or with other children in the family. However, there were some increases in the moral and practical help received from relatives and friends, in contrast to a consistent slight decrease in the comparison group.

As far as the morale of the disabled children's main carers, their mothers, was concerned, there was a decrease during the project in the number of resource worker group mothers (but an increase in the number of comparison group mothers) who thought their health was adversely affected by the care of the disabled child. There was also a slightly greater reduction in the resource worker group mothers' scores on the malaise inventory (a measurement of physical and emotional stress). A final indication of the personal support which carers had derived from the resource workers' intervention was that the number of resource worker group mothers who said there was no one they felt they could talk to if they were having problems decreased, while the number of comparison group mothers with no one to talk to went up. In addition to relatives, friends, and other professionals, two-thirds of the resource worker group mothers at the end of the project also named the resource worker as someone to whom they could turn if they had problems.

This summary has presented some of the major findings of the evaluation. The resource workers' intervention was clearly appreciated by parents, in particular, because of the information and practical help they received, and because of the support they obtained from having someone to whom they felt they could turn for help. Indeed at the end of the project more mothers said that they would talk to the resource worker than to their husband about problems concerning the disabled child.

The comparative outcome measures also showed some clearly significant differences between the two groups of families, and very many more smaller changes for the better in the resource worker group. There were very few instances in which the circumstances of the comparison group apparently improved more than those of the resource worker group, though there were several in which the outcomes for the two groups were more or less identical. The *consistency* of the many small improvements in the resource worker group is important, and is a more salient indication of the positive impact of the intervention than any single statistically significant outcome measure.

The intervention was therefore clearly successful, and achieved what had been the main aims of the project. It provided families with the kind of regular support they valued and had previously lacked; and it made a consistently positive impact on their circumstances and experience of looking after a severely disabled child.

There were, however, some noticeable disparities between the inputs to the project and its measured outcomes – where, for instance, the resource workers had given a large proportion of the families help with, or particularly intensive work had been done on, a particular problem but where no more than small changes in the circumstances of the resource worker group were detected after the end of the intervention. For example, although many of the families received information, had referrals made or advocacy carried out in connection with a wide range of different educational, daily living and mobility aids, their acquisition of such aids by the end of the project was not always substantially greater than in the comparison group.

Negative or inconsistent research findings are often as important as those which are unambiguously and conclusively positive. In this instance there was some concern about the apparent disparities between, on the one hand, the well-documented inputs of the resource workers, and the unequivocally positive attitudes of the parents towards the intervention; and, on the other hand, the small differences between the two groups of families according to some of the comparative outcome measures. Some of these disparities reflected very real constraints on the scope and impact of the resource workers' activities which were imposed by the setting, organization and duration of the project. It had been anticipated that these constraints might have some effect on the results, and they were discussed in interviews carried out with the resource workers after the intervention had ended. However, consideration also had to be given to the possibility that other effects of the intervention had occurred but had somehow remained hidden and undetected. This meant reviewing carefully the overall research strategy, the choice of outcome measures and the methods used to collect the data for those measures. Apart from perhaps throwing further light on the interpretation of the resource worker project, this exercise also had a more important heuristic purpose; to indicate some of the more general problems which might arise in the evaluation of intervention programmes with long-term informal carers.

Interpretation: the Research Context

As Sheldon (1983, p. 487) has put it: 'All scientific data require interpretation; only rarely will a self-evident conclusion leap off the page. This is especially true of the kind of data gathered in natural settings, which are at best a compromise between rigour and relevance.'

The Organization and Setting of the Intervention

There were two particular aspects of the way the resource workers' intervention was organized which may have constrained its scope and extensiveness and thus limited the size of any changes in families' circumstances *vis-à-vis* the comparison group. First, there was the amount of time available to the resource workers which, as Chapter 4 described, was limited both during the project and by the project's fixed duration of two years.

The resource workers themselves thought that had they had more time *during* the two-year project to enable them to work more intensively, they could in fact have achieved more with altogether 80 per cent of the families. The overall duration of the intervention may also have limited the outcomes, so that had the resource workers worked for a longer period of time, more changes would have become apparent. There are several reasons for suspecting this to be the case. In the context of the long-term care of a severely disabled child the resource workers' intervention was relatively brief. This, as the resource workers themselves recognized, to some extent affected the aims and focus of their work, and meant that some of their intervention was devoted to equipping parents with the knowledge and skills they might need to deal with future as well as current problems. However, anticipating and trying to prevent future difficulties was not the type of intervention which was likely to result in immediately tangible outcomes. The limited duration of the intervention probably also affected the extensiveness of some of the outcomes. As the case studies appended to Chapter 7 illustrated, a proportion of practical difficulties necessitated very intensive inputs by the resource workers. However, the solutions to these problems were often delayed by bureaucratic complications or public spending restrictions until well after the intervention had ended. The resource workers themselves certainly considered that had they worked for a period of *longer* than two years, they could have achieved more with 85 per cent of the families they visited. Therefore, while it might be expected that the largest effects of an intervention would be detected during or immediately after that intervention, the impact of any intervention which deals with anticipated or particularly protracted problems will be impossible to detect.

The second aspect of the project's organization which may have adversely affected the outcomes of the resource workers' intervention was their independent status. Certainly, when the issue was discussed with the resource workers (Chapter 4), they considered that this independence had brought positive advantages: it had increased their acceptability to families, and it had enhanced their own freedom of action. Both these factors may well have contributed to the very positive opinions expressed by parents at the end of the project. Nevertheless, the fact remains that their independent status may have limited some other, more tangible, achievements. The resource workers were relatively powerless without any formal communication channels or authority to negotiate with statutory or voluntary organizations. They also had no access whatever to any material resources or services of their own or of an employing agency. Every piece of equipment, service, or facility which they wanted to help a family obtain had to be acquired through a process of formal referral, negotiation, liaison and, where necessary, advocacy. It is possible therefore that the resource workers were able to obtain fewer material resources for the families they visited than they would have done had they been employed by an established, service-providing statutory or voluntary organization. This process of obtaining material resources may also have added to the length of time it took to obtain items, thereby also leaving some needs unmet by the end of the intervention. It may be therefore that the outcomes of an intervention programme based in an established statutory or voluntary agency would involve the more widespread acquisition of material resources and use of services, although in the current economic climate this seems unlikely. Indeed it may well be that in such circumstances there is simply a limit on the amount of resources and services which any group of people with long-term dependencies can obtain from statutory or voluntary sources, however specialized their social workers or however skilful their advocates. Ultimately, overriding economic constraints may go some considerable way towards explaining the apparent failure of *either* group of families to improve some aspects of their material circumstances.

Economic factors, however, are by no means the only ones to have affected the outcomes of the intervention. The way in which any intervention is evaluated is likely to affect the eventual results, and it is to these issues that we now turn.

The Evaluation Strategy and Methods

Certain aspects of the evaluation strategy and methods of data collection may also have led to some disparity between the inputs of the resource workers and the comparative outcome measures. For example, there were a number of problems inherent in the use of a quasi-experimental research design as the basis of the evaluation (Chapter 3). First of all, because the families' circumstances, experiences and feelings before and after the intervention were to be compared, this meant that the comparative outcome measures had to be devised in advance of the intervention itself. Certain assumptions therefore had to be made about the likely focus of the resource workers' intervention. These assumptions were reflected in the choice of comparative outcome measures. In the event certain aspects of the resource workers' intervention may have been insufficiently evaluated, and too much emphasis given to other aspects. For example, in view of the comments of parents after the end of the project, it might have been appropriate to have devoted more outcome measures to trying to detect changes in morale, coping skills and the acquisition of information, and fewer to changes in material circumstances. Anticipating appropriate outcome measures does seem to be an inherent problem with this type of research design. The problem may be reduced by paying close attention to the stated aims and objectives of those who will be carrying out the intervention; but even so, in the context of social work intervention, these objectives are likely to be modified by the opinions, needs and resources of individual clients.

A second difficulty which arose as a result of the quasi-experimental research design was that it was impossible to obtain information on the help received by the comparison group families during the two-year project which was comparable in detail to the information obtained from the resource workers' records about their intervention. The design had assumed that both groups of families would continue during the project to receive whatever services they already had; what was being evaluated was the impact of the *additional* help given by the resource workers. However, the similarity between the two groups in some of the outcome measures raised an interesting question: had the comparison group families managed to obtain services, aids, or benefits entirely unassisted, or had the help given from their existing services been as effective as that given by the resource workers?

There was unfortunately no way of answering this question conclusively, even if it had been anticipated. It would have been very difficult to have collected from either the comparison group families or the various people involved with them information during the project on their respective activities without risking a substantial 'Hawthorne' effect – the inadvertent and artificial enhancement of research subjects' performance, simply by reason of research scrutiny (Homans, 1950; Cook and Campbell, 1979). There would also have been limits to the amount and reliability of information which could have been collected retrospectively from the comparison group families at the end of the two-year period. Such information would have had to rely heavily on the accurate memory of parents, and also would almost certainly have underestimated the amount of liaison and co-ordinating work which had been done by professionals on their behalf.

Nevertheless, even without these data, there is reason to suspect that the lack of observable differences between the two groups on some of the outcome measures was not the result of the comparison group families' own unaided efforts, or because they had received help similar to that provided by the resource workers. In the first place, there was evidence (Chapter 3) that before the project both groups of families were lacking the kind of support and help which the resource workers' intervention was intended to provide. Secondly, there was hardly any evidence from the comparative outcome measures that the circumstances of the comparison group families had improved substantially during the project. In most instances in which the outcomes were similar for both groups it was because *neither* group had apparently 'improved' since before the intervention, not because both had 'improved'.

A third disadvantage of the quasi-experimental design was that it relied very heavily for many of the comparative outcome measures on parents' memories of what had happened during the previous two years. Parents were asked to remember their contacts with a wide range of professionals and organizations, their acquisition of aids and their use of services. They were also asked to assess changes which had taken place in their child's condition during that time; in their own experiences of problems; and in the quality of family relationships. This heavy reliance on accurate recall could well have led parents to underestimate the changes which had occurred, the more so since the continuing pressures of looking after a severely disabled child may have obscured the memories of parents in both groups about changes in their circumstances and experiences which had taken place early on in the two-year period. It is here that one explanation for the lack of substantial changes in both groups of families, and the disparity between this and the inputs of the resource workers, may lie.

A further explanation undoubtedly lies in the predominant methods of intervention used by the resource workers. In relation to virtually every type of problem dealt with the most common forms of help they gave were the provision of information and advice, discussion and counselling. (It was suggested earlier in this chapter that the limited duration of the project may have additionally encouraged the prevalence of this type of intervention.) Yet while clearly appreciated by parents, information and advice were not always immediately acted upon; and discussion and counselling did not necessarily lead straight away to changes in circumstances or experiences which could be measured and contrasted with the comparison group. Similarly, the liaison and co-ordination activities of the resource workers did not always mean that families obtained more aids or services than they would otherwise have done, though they may have obtained them more quickly and with less difficulty. Process factors such as these, though clearly of some importance, would have been difficult to measure in the resource worker group and even harder in the comparison group.

There is, finally, a problem of measuring the impact of intervention which is diffuse and wide ranging. The children and families who were visited by the resource workers had between them a large number of different needs, which in turn prompted intervention from the resource workers on many different topics. Some families received help with some problems, while others received help of a different kind with a completely different set of problems. The impact of intervention on any one problem, when measured across the group as a whole, was therefore not necessarily likely to be very large. The only way to avoid this problem would be to draw samples consisting of matched pairs of subjects, to isolate only those who received help with a particular problem and compare their outcomes with those of their matched control equivalents.

Clearly, the methodological issues raised by the resource worker project have a much wider significance. The implications for other evaluative research of this kind are discussed in the final section of this chapter.

The Development of Evaluative Research

It was pointed out in Chapter 1 that as economic constraints have increasingly affected the scope of social work activities, so the pressures on social workers and social service providers to evaluate and demonstrate their effectiveness have grown. The response to these pressures has been the development of more structured social work experiments, which have in turn been successful in demonstrating constructive changes and positive outcomes (Reid and Hanrahan, 1981). Clearly, the more specifically the goals of any intervention are defined and the more precisely they are operationalized within an experimental research framework, the easier it should be to discern whether that intervention has had any effects. However, this type of short-term, task-centred contractual intervention appears inappropriate to the task facing those who seek to improve support and services for informal carers. Here the intervention is unlikely to be concerned with changing specific deviant behaviours or undesirable interactional patterns. It is instead more likely to be concerned with sustaining and improving carers' capacity to cope with the long-term and increasingly onerous dependency of a disabled person by providing the appropriate practical, social and emotional support. This intervention is, as the resource worker project demonstrated, likely to involve a very wide range of activities and goals. If the intervention is diverse, so too must be the outcome measures – and the effects of the intervention may be correspondingly harder to detect.

In addition, some of the more substantial effects of such intervention may lie in precisely those areas which are most difficult to detect and measure; the improvement of morale, the development of confidence, the increase of resourcefulness through the provision of information and the easing of access to services. Conversely, more conventional and easily measured indicators of effectiveness and success – changes in carers' use of services, take-up of benefits, material circumstances and physical ill-health, for example – may be far less appropriate for use in evaluating this type of intervention.

It is clear from the evaluation of the resource worker project that the intervention was greatly appreciated by parents. Central to the project was the hypothesis that parents looking after a child with severe disabilities felt isolated and unsupported. According to their views as service 'consumers', the resource workers' intervention reduced that isolation and gave much-appreciated information and support. These are not tangible outcomes, yet they are crucial to assessing the success of the intervention.

Positive outcomes such as these are clearly necessary to any conclusion that the intervention was effective. The development and measurement of criteria of effectiveness is, however, not an easy task. Intervention programmes and other schemes explicitly designed to provide support to informal carers are only just beginning, and their evaluation is even less well advanced. The resource worker project has made an early contribution to the process of service development and evaluation. Despite the research problems which clearly exist, this process of development and evaluation must continue if we are to be confident that resources are being used in a way which is most appropriate for meeting the needs of long-term 'informal' carers. The ways in which these resources are currently being used – and might be used in the future – are, finally, the subject of Chapter 12.

CHAPTER 12

Implementation: Issues for Policy

Recent Policy Developments

Since the establishment and evaluation of the resource worker project a number of important initiatives have been carried out with the aim of improving services for disabled children and their families. Following the recommendations of the Court Committee (1976) and the subsequent government circular (LAC(78)2), many district health authorities have established multi-disciplinary district handicap teams (DHTs) to provide diagnostic assessment and treatment services for disabled children and advice and support for their parents (Court Committee, 1976, para. 14.22). Simultaneously, the National Development Group for the Mentally Handicapped proposed the development of multi-disciplinary community mental handicap teams (CMHTs) as the best way of improving domiciliary support to families with mentally handicapped relatives and avoiding admission to long-term hospital care (National Development Group for the Mentally Handicapped, 1977). The help provided by these latter teams was not, however, intended to be universally available to all mentally handicapped people and their families within a given catchment area, but was to provide 'the more specialised support and assessment services needed by some mentally handicapped people and their families' (Development Team for the Mentally Handicapped, 1982, para. 42).

The development of DHTs and CMHTs has apparently been neither universal nor consistent. A 1982 survey of the health districts in England and Wales found that some districts had a DHT and others a CMHT, while some had neither and others had both. There were also discernible differences in the policies and functions of the two types of team. In particular, a larger proportion of CMHTs (but by no means all) had policies of assigning a key worker to be a point of first contact for parents and responsible for the carrying through of treatment plans. However, as far as mentally handicapped children were concerned, the survey concluded that 'the existence of two models for multidisciplinary teamwork . . . has caused great confusion' (Plank, 1982, p. 29).

Disappointment, rather than confusion, has marked the implementation of the recommendations contained in the report of the Warnock Committee (1978) on children with special educational needs. Subsequent legislation has concentrated on the assessment of each child's educational needs and, to a lesser extent, the integration of children with disabilities into the mainstream school system. Nowhere has there been official encouragement for the development of the kind of 'named person' role so strongly advocated by the committee to 'provide a point of contact ... [and] introduce parents to the right services' (ibid., p. 157).

Other policy developments have nevertheless taken place. Within social services departments specialist fieldwork practitioner posts are becoming more common, particularly in the fields of adoption and fostering, intermediate treatment and services for mentally handicapped people. Some traditional voluntary organizations are developing an innovative range of specialized services for disabled children and their families, but these are unfortunately limited to a few specific localities (Shearer, 1978). In other areas voluntary and statutory agencies are together providing a range of services, often based around parents' support groups and respite care facilities (Pugh and Russell, 1977; DHSS, 1984). However, innovative services such as these are far from universally available. Even where they are available, their aims, priorities and organization may be such that the needs (for regular contact, information, advice, the identification of unmet needs and the co-ordination of services) which prompted the establishment of the resource worker project are still not being met. In short, while some important developments in policies and services for disabled children and their families have taken place, the total range of service provision still appears by and large to be fragmented, variable in scope, implemented in different ways and available in some areas but not others.

Perhaps the major recent policy development, however, affecting adults with disabilities and their families as well as children, has been the increasing visibility of and explicit reliance upon relatives and friends to provide day to day physical and social care. The main thrust behind this trend has been a growing official awareness of the increasing numbers of elderly and very elderly people, and anxiety about how they will be cared for in the next few decades. Concern about the needs of 'informal' carers has therefore tended to focus on the needs of those friends and relatives who are looking after physically or mentally infirm elderly people. There is a very real danger that in this preoccupation with the care of older people, the needs of those looking after other, less numerous groups of disabled or dependent people will be overlooked. As far as disabled children and their families are concerned, there are still many outstanding needs to be attended to by social work and social welfare services, many of which were highlighted by the resource worker project.

The Resource Worker Project and Policy: the Development of the Key Worker Role

The most important conclusions which can be drawn from the resource worker project concern the specific role which can be played by a specialist worker in providing support and delivering services to families looking after a severely disabled child. Integral to this role is a commitment to maintaining regular contact with families at home through routine (but not necessarily frequent) visiting. This on its own was undoubtedly a source of support for the parents in the resource worker project, for it meant that there was at last someone to whom they could turn for help with any problem concerning their disabled child – and this they valued immensely. However, this feeling of support was not the only benefit to be derived from the regular domiciliary visits. Routine contact also enabled the resource workers to monitor developments in the child and changes in the families' circumstances. They did not have to depend upon parents' telephoning or writing to ask for help in order to know that help was needed. This meant that they were able to take on and share with parents some of the responsibility for anticipating and identifying a range of unmet needs. As one of the resource workers pointed out during an interview after the project had ended, without regular contact:

> you're relying on people coming to you and saying that *they* recognize that they need information or something. If giving information is part of the structure of a relationship, then there are two people who can recognize the need for information.

This is in marked contrast to the more common situation in which the responsibility for identifying needs, initiating contact with a formal agency or professional and expressing those needs in appropriate terms lies exclusively with parents. One of the consequences of this sharing of responsibility between parents and a professional with a commitment to maintaining regular contact is that requests for services or applications for help of various kinds, when they are made, are more likely to be made to the appropriate person or agency, using the correct procedures and supported by the relevant information.

A second major feature of the role played by the resource workers was that it encompassed a concern with a very wide range of issues and problems experienced by disabled children and their families. Although the resource workers thought of themselves and were seen by the families as social workers first and foremost, their activities were certainly not confined to casework intervention and the provision of social welfare services. Instead they acted as a point of first contact, a 'single door' through which all kinds of problems and queries could be

201

channelled. The capacity to step outside the confines of a traditional professional role, with responsibility for allocating the services supplied by a single welfare agency, and become involved in the whole spectrum of problems experienced by families looking after a disabled child is perhaps the central element in the role of a 'key worker'. In this instance, as Chapter 4 illustrated, the resource workers' involvement encompassed a very broad range of medical, social, educational, practical, financial, recreational and emotional issues.

How the resource workers responded to these issues, also documented in Chapter 4, gives an indication of the range of activities involved in the key worker role. The most common activity was the provision of information and advice to parents. It was suggested in Chapter 11 that the frequency of this type of activity may have been increased by the limited duration of the intervention; parents were given information to equip them for future situations as well as for dealing with current problems. However, as we have just seen, routine information and advice-giving was also facilitated by – indeed was an integral element in – the pattern of regular visits to families. Again the broad range of topics on which information and advice was given (or, where necessary, obtained from other sources for families) was a significant dimension of the resource workers' role as key workers.

A further major activity which is clearly integral to the role of a key worker is that of co-ordination and liaison with other services and professionals. Against the background of service fragmentation which prompted the establishment of the project, it is not surprising that these activities formed such a major part of the resource workers' inputs. Again these co-ordination and liaison activities covered a very wide range of different statutory and voluntary organizations, professionals and service administrators (Chapter 4).

Specifically this broad range of liaison and co-ordinating functions can be subdivided into four main groups. First, there is the work of making initial referrals for a particular service or piece of equipment, or helping families to make applications themselves for services or benefits. Being in a position to identify and anticipate unmet needs leads naturally to the alerting of relevant professionals or agencies with the appropriate resources to meet those needs. This was also to have been one of the main functions of the 'named person' recommended by the Warnock Committee (1978).

A second aspect of a key worker's liaison activities involves the establishment or improvement of communication channels between parents and other professionals such as doctors, teachers and therapists. A third aspect is the co-ordination of several different agencies and professionals who might be simultaneously or consecutively involved in arranging, ordering, designing, constructing and delivering a single item of help or service to a particular child or family. This type of co-ordination was a particularly important feature of the resource workers' intervention when families needed help with the design, execution and funding of adaptations to their houses or alterations to their gardens.

The fourth type of liaison activity deals with the problems which can arise when poor inter- or intra-agency communications or inefficient bureaucratic procedures cause inexplicable or inordinate delays. In these instances a certain amount of advocacy on a family's behalf may be needed.

The commitment to regular visiting by the resource workers and their activities as key workers were complemented by two further features of the project which appear to have been crucial to its success. One was the specialist knowledge and specialized caseloads of the resource workers. Their existing specialist experience was further enhanced, first, by the briefings and information which they received both before and during the intervention, and second, by the fact that that knowledge was put to regular daily use, and not forgotten for long periods of time while the problems of other groups of clients in a generic caseload were dealt with.

Equally important was the clear assignation of responsibility to desig-nated workers for supporting and helping families looking after a severely disabled child. With more heterogeneous caseloads, there is a substantial risk that less obvious or urgent needs will be overlooked or overwhelmed by the competing demands of other, more crisis-oriented social work functions. Only with the specific allocation of specialized responsibility could a commitment to providing the type of long-term support needed by this group of informal carers adequately be obtained.

Finally, it must be stressed that the type of service given by the resource workers can apparently be provided at relatively low cost. The salary and administrative costs of the intervention averaged around £4 a week (at 1985 price levels). Additional indirect costs may have been borne by the statutory and voluntary organizations whose services were disproportionately obtained by families in the resource worker group. However, on the other hand, there is considerable potential in the 'single door' aspect of a key worker's role for counselling and advising families on the most appropriate ways of meeting their needs and avoiding referrals to service-providing agencies for inappropriate forms of help. Ultimately these two factors may balance each other out.

The evaluation of the resource worker project has documented in detail the types of activities involved in providing help to one particular group of informal carers. However, there is every reason to believe that the needs of families looking after a severely disabled child, and the ways in which these needs might be met, are not dissimilar from those of informal carers looking after disabled or dependent people of other ages (Bayley, 1973; Levin, Sinclair and Gorbach, 1986). Frequently such carers will need to be in contact with many different professionals and departments, either simultaneously or during the duration of their time as carers: hospitals, community and primary health services; social services departments' domiciliary, day care, transport and occupational therapy services; the Department of Health and Social Security, for cash benefits; and specialist voluntary welfare agencies. The specialized key worker role may well be a highly appropriate one to adopt in developing support for other groups of informal carers. How this might be done is discussed in the final section of this chapter.

The Key Worker Role and Future Policy

Without some kind of wholesale reorganization of the present systems of health and welfare services, there will be a continuing potential for some one person to act as a key worker: to help carers to identify and specify their needs; and to liaise with and co-ordinate the appropriate services to meet these needs. There are a number of options as to who that key worker might be, and within which organizational structure she or he might most appropriately be located.

There were cogent arguments (Chapter 3) behind the recruitment of professionally qualified and experienced social workers as resource workers for the project. That choice was vindicated by the project's results. The resource workers were able to offer families personal support, co-ordinate services and tackle a wide range of other problems in a number of different ways. The project has therefore demonstrated the scope offered by this particular professional base for the development of the key worker role. Whether other types of professional training and experience – medicine, education, nursing, or psychology, for example – would offer an equally appropriate basis must remain an open question, which only further evaluative research would be able to answer. A tentative answer can, however, be suggested to the question of whether the service provided by the resource workers could effectively be played by trained volunteers. The resource workers themselves thought that, given sufficient appropriate training and support, some of the work they had been doing could have been done by volunteers. However, they thought that they themselves had only been able to tackle some issues effectively because of their professional training, and the expertise and status which this lent them. Indeed volunteers may experience considerable difficulties in establishing their credibility and acceptability to families, and their legitimacy with other agencies. This latter factor would in turn be likely to have a substantial detrimental impact on the effectiveness of a volunteer's activities as a co-ordinating key worker.

Assuming for the time being therefore that there is considerable potential for developing a key worker role from the basis of social work training and experience, how might that key worker activity best be organized? Four alternative scenarios will be briefly considered in turn.

First, there is the option of a key worker operating from within the health services. For children, or for people with mental handicaps, the assigning of a key work role to the social work members of district handicap teams and community mental handicap teams would be an obvious development. (This to some extent already happens in the latter type of team.) A similar role in supporting carers of elderly infirm people could be played by social workers attached to community geriatric or psychogeriatric teams, where they exist.

However, we have already seen that the existence and coverage of such teams is far from universal. Moreover, especially so far as disabled children are concerned, hospital-based teams may not be very readily accessible, especially once children have no further needs for treatment or medical surveillance.

A second alternative is for the role of a key worker to be played by social workers employed by local or national voluntary organizations. To some extent the latter situation already exists; some national voluntary organizations for specific groups of disabled people and their families do employ locally based specialized social workers. This would seem an ideal basis and allow an even greater degree of specialization than was practised in the resource worker project, where the children suffered from a very wide range of disabling conditions. However, in order for the liaison and co-ordinating activities of key workers from this type of organizational base to be fully effective, their position would have to be clearly recognized and legitimated by all the relevant statutory agencies. Even so, the experience of the resource worker project suggests that some additional time and effort could be involved in negotiating with statutory agencies from an extra-statutory base. This might well ultimately lessen the key worker's effectiveness.

This problem could perhaps largely be overcome by a formal arrangement between statutory authorities and locally based voluntary organizations about the provision of services to disabled people and their families. There is a well-established precedent for this type of arrangement in the widespread provision of meals-on-wheels by voluntary organizations acting as agents of local social services departments. Similar types of agreement (though based on different financial arrangements) exist between some social services departments and established voluntary organizations, like Dr Barnardo's, who provide a comprehensive range of services for all the disabled children and their families in a given local area.

Finally, there is what might be termed the 'in-house' option – the assigning of key worker responsibilities to specialist case workers within each local authority social services department. This option would overcome the problems of geographical coverage, access and legitimacy *vis-à-vis* other statutory bodies which may occur with other organizational bases, although the resource workers suggested that key workers from statutory social services departments may be less acceptable to some families, at least initially. The additional advantage of this model (and perhaps to a lesser extent of the health services based option) is that it should be relatively easy to establish channels whereby the day to day practice and experience of the specialist key workers fed into more strategic functions of service development and planning.

However, there comes a point at which a discussion such as this moves beyond the recommendations and proposals which can legitimately be derived from the conclusions of an experimental project and enters into the realms of relatively well-informed speculation. Only by a continuing commitment from service administrators and professional workers to innovation, implementation and evaluation can policies and practices designed to support the informal carers of children and adults with disabilities be developed and improved further.

Appendix A   Briefing the Resource Workers

Publications

The following sources of information were circulated to the resource workers throughout the project.

Publications from Voluntary Organizations

Pamphlets and newsletters from: Association for Spina Bifida and Hydrocephalus; National Society for Mentally Handicapped Children and Adults; Spastics Society; Cystic Fibrosis Research Trust; Royal Association for Disability and Rehabilitation; Disabled Living Foundation; and Equipment for the Disabled.

Welfare Benefits

Information from: Child Poverty Action Group – *Welfare Benefits Handbook*; Disability Alliance – *Disability Rights Guide* ; and DHSS – leaflets and application forms.

Professional Journals and Magazines

Articles in: *British Journal of Social Work*; *Community Care*; *Social Work Today*; and *Child: Care, Health and Development*.

Talks and Visits

Talks from Other Professionals

During the meetings which the resource workers held regularly throughout the intervention with their social work consultants from the Yorkshire regional division of Dr Barnardo's discussions were introduced by visiting professional speakers on the following topics: the organization of child psychology services and access routes to assessment, treatment and training facilities; behaviour modification programmes at school and home; the development of community and volunteer involvement in informal care; the development and role of parents' self-help groups; opportunities and facilities for disabled school leavers; Motability car leasing and purchase schemes; rehabilitation engineering movement advisory panels (REMAP); and attendance and mobility allowance review and appeal procedures.

Visits to Specialist Organizations

Again in conjunction with the social work consultants from the Yorkshire regional division of Dr Barnardo's visits were arranged to the following organizations: Disabled Living Foundation; Spastics Society headquarters occupational therapy department and aids exhibition, and a residential assessment centre; Association for Spina Bifida and Hydrocephalus headquarters, and fieldwork liaison, aids and employment advisory staff; Wolfson Centre, London; and Hester Adrian Research Centre, Manchester.

Checklist of Services and Facilities

During the preliminary briefing of the resource workers they were supplied with the following checklist and asked to ensure that they were familiar with the range of services and facilities with which they would be likely to have contact during the project.

Social Services Department

Headquarters and relevant divisional offices; occupational therapists or social workers for the disabled; social workers for blind and deaf people; day nursery facilities for disabled children; respite care and permanent care facilities; and schemes involving home helps, family aides, or volunteers with disabled children and their families.

Health Authorities

Hospital facilities: child development centres and the specialist services available – physiotherapy, speech therapy, audiology and psychological services – and how to gain access to these professional services (e.g. via school or GP); hospital policies on admissions for short-term relief and permanent residential care; and nearest artificial limb and appliance centre.

Community medical services' supply of equipment for nursing and incontinence: laundry service; disposable nappies; protective and disposable bedding; hoists; commodes; and other home nursing supplies.

School-based medical services: are some kinds of incontinence or nursing equipment provided through schools? The role of school medical service in referring to specialist medical personnel; and reimbursement of fares and provision of transport to hospital.

Education Services

Special schools and their parent–teacher associations; policies on the integration of disabled children in ordinary nursery, primary and secondary schools; role of school in referral to other agencies and professionals (e.g. educational psychologist), and obtaining medical and other services; and education welfare officers or social workers attached to special schools.

Other Local Authority Departments

Housing department – availability of specially built housing and local district council housing departments' policies on adaptation of existing housing. Environmental health, for special refuse collection of disposable incontinence equipment. Environmental health/architect's department, for improvement grants.

Voluntary Agencies

Any local housing associations which provide purpose-built accommodation for disabled people; toy libraries; voluntary organizations for handicapped children and their families: headquarters addresses and how to contact local branches; volunteer schemes run by councils of voluntary service or volunteer bureaux; and other facilities and resources available for disabled children through local council of voluntary service.

Miscellaneous

Holiday facilities for disabled children and their families; holiday playschemes for disabled children; and short-term care and permanent residential facilities run by voluntary organizations.

Financial Benefits

DHSS local offices; attendance allowance, mobility allowance, invalid care allowance and non-contributory invalidity pension; and supplementary benefit entitlement, weekly additions and single payments.

Appendix B A Note on Statistical Testing

In this report tests of statistical significance have been used on many of the outcome measures which assess the impact of the resource workers' intervention. Any differences which are observed between the resource worker and comparison groups might have occurred by chance. Tests of statistical significance help to assess the likelihood of this: if a test shows it to be unlikely that any particular difference was the result of a chance occurrence, this increases the degree of confidence with which that difference can be attributed to the effect of the resource workers' intervention. By convention the term 'significant' is used in the text where a test has indicated that a difference could have occurred by chance on less than one out of twenty occasions, or less than five times in 100.

However, a degree of caution should be exercised in the interpretation of these tests. Tests of statistical significance are applicable, strictly, for making inferences from a randomly selected sample about the population from which it has been drawn. For example, if a relationship or difference is observed in a sample, a test of significance will indicate the degree of confidence with which we can expect the same relationship or difference to be found in the population from which the sample was drawn.

In the resource worker study, however, the sample was not entirely random. From within a defined population (certain categories of Family Fund applicants from ten different local authority areas) the sample was selected at random, but was stratified *within* each area according to the disabled child's age. (Full details of the procedure used in drawing the sample for the study are contained in Chapter 3.) It is not possible to estimate the sampling error or bias resulting from this sampling procedure. No inferences can therefore be made about the population of families from which the sample was drawn.

Tests of statistical significance have, however, been used to estimate the probability that any differences observed in the outcome measures might have been the result of chance factors. Differences were observed both between the two groups of families after the intervention and within each group before and after the intervention. In technical terms significance tests have been used to check the validity of the classifications used in the analysis as the independent variable; that is, the division of the sample into resource worker and comparison groups. The significance tests therefore indicate whether the classification produces a difference between the two groups which is unlikely to have occurred with a random allocation.

References

Algie, J. (1980), 'Priorities in personal social services', in M. Brown and S. Baldwin (eds), *The Yearbook of Social Policy in Britain 1978* (London: Routledge & Kegan Paul), pp. 179–205.

Armstrong, G., Race, D., and Race, D. (1979), *The Role and Function of the Social Services Department in the Total System of Provision for the Mentally Handicapped*, Evaluation Research Group Report No. 5 (Sheffield: Evaluation Research Group, University of Sheffield).

Bailey, N. T. J. (1959), *Statistical Methods in Biology* (London: English Universities Press).

Baldwin, S. (1985), *The Costs of Caring* (London: Routledge & Kegan Paul).

Baldwin, S., and Glendinning, C. (1983), 'Employment, women and their disabled children', in J. Finch and D. Groves (eds), *A Labour of Love: Women, Work and Caring* (London: Routledge & Kegan Paul), pp. 53–71.

Bayley, M. (1973), *Mental Handicap and Community Care* (London: Routledge & Kegan Paul).

Booth, T., Martin, D., and Melotte, C. (eds) (1980), *Specialisation* (Birmingham: British Association of Social Workers).

Borsay, A. (1982), 'An uneasy alliance: the relationship between occupational therapists and housing officials', *Housing Review*, vol. 31, no. 5, pp. 175–7.

Bradshaw, J. (1980), *The Family Fund: An Initiative in Social Policy* (London: Routledge & Kegan Paul).

Bradshaw, J., and Lawton, D. (1978a), 'Some characteristics of children with severe disabilities', *Journal of Biosocial Science*, vol. 10, no. 1, pp. 107–20.

Bradshaw, J., and Lawton, D. (1978b), 'Tracing the causes of stress in families with handicapped children', *British Journal of Social Work*, vol. 8, no. 2, pp. 181–98.

Bradshaw, J., and Lawton, D. (1985), '75,000 severely disabled children', *Developmental Medicine and Child Neurology*, vol. 27, no. 1, pp. 25–32.

Bradshaw, J. R., Glendinning, C. and Baldwin, S. M. (1977), 'Services that miss their mark and leave families in need', *Health and Social Services Journal*, April, pp. 664–5.

Browne, E. T. (1982), *Mental Handicap: The Role for Social Workers*, Social Services Monographs: Research in Practice (Sheffield: Joint Unit for Social Services Research, University of Sheffield).

Burden, R. L. (1978), 'An approach to the evaluation of early intervention projects with mothers of severely handicapped children: the attitude dimension', *Child: Care, Health and Development*, vol. 4, no. 3, pp. 171–81.

Caro, Francis G. (1981), 'Demonstrating community-based long-term care in the United States: an evaluation research perspective', in E. M. Goldberg and N. Connelly (eds), *Evaluative Research in Social Care* (London: Heinemann), pp. 151–76.

Central Council for Education and Training in Social Work (CCETSW) (1974), *People with Handicaps Need Better Trained Workers*, CCETSW Paper No. 5 (London: CCETSW).

211

Challis, D., and Davies, B. (1980), 'A new approach to community care for the elderly', *British Journal of Social Work*, vol. 10, no. 1, pp. 1–18.

Challis, D., Luckett, R., and Chessum, R. (1983), 'A new life at home', *Community Care*, no. 455, 24 March, pp. 21–3.

Chartered Institute of Public Finance and Accountancy (1974–5, 1975–6), *Personal Social Services Statistics (Actuals)*, (London: CIPFA/Society of County Treasurers).

Cook, T. D., and Campbell, D. T. (1979), *Quasi-Experimentation* (Chicago: Rand McNally).

Cooke, K., Bradshaw, J., and Lawton, D. (1983), 'Take-up of benefits by families with disabled children', *Child: Care, Health and Development*, vol. 9, no. 3, pp. 145–56.

Court Committee (1976), *Fit for the Future: Report of the Committee on Child Health Services*, Cmnd 6684 (London: HMSO).

Central Statistical Office (1980), *Social Trends 1980* (London: HMSO).

Davies, B., and Challis, D. (1981), 'A production–relations evaluation of the meeting of needs in the community care projects', in E. M. Goldberg and N. Connelly (eds), *Evaluative Research in Social Care* (London: Heinemann), pp. 177–98.

Denzin, N. (1970), *The Research Act in Sociology* (London: Butterworth).

Department of Health and Social Security (DHSS) (1969), *Report of the Committee of Enquiry into Allegations of Ill-Treatment of Patients and Other Irregularities at the Ely Hospital, Cardiff*, Cmnd 3975 (London: HMSO).

DHSS (1971), *Report of the Farleigh Hospital Committee of Enquiry*, Cmnd 4557 (London: HMSO).

DHSS (1976), *Report on the Sunningdale Seminar on Disablement* (London: DHSS).

DHSS (1983a), *Supporting the Informal Carers: Project Paper and Report of a Seminar at Oxford*, Social Work Service Development Group (London: DHSS).

DHSS (1983b), *Supporting the Informal Carers: Report of a Day Conference, 2 November 1983*, Social Work Service Development Group (London: DHSS).

DHSS (1983c), *Supporting the Informal Carers: Information*, Social Work Service Development Group (London: DHSS).

DHSS (1984), *Services for Handicapped Children: Schemes and Developments in England*, Social Work Service Development Group (London: DHSS).

Development Team for the Mentally Handicapped (1982), *Third Report, 1979–81* (London: HMSO).

DoE/DHSS/Welsh Office (1978), *Joint Circular: Adaptations of Housing for People Who Are Physically Handicapped*, Department of the Environment (59/78), Department of Health and Social Security (LAC(78)14), Welsh Office (104/78) (London: HMSO).

Equal Opportunities Commission (EOC) (1982), *Caring for the Elderly and Handicapped: Community Care Policies and Women's Lives* (Manchester: EOC).

Family Policy Studies Centre (1984), *The Forgotten Army: Family Care and Elderly People*, Briefing Paper No. 1 (London: FPSC).

Fox, A. M. (1974), *They Get this Training but They Don't Really Know How*

You Feel . . . (Horsham: National Fund for Research into Crippling Diseases).

Gath, A. (1978), *Down's Syndrome and the Family* (London: Academic Press).

Gibbons, J. (1981), 'An evaluation of the effectiveness of social work intervention using task-centred methods after deliberate self-poisoning', in E. M. Goldberg and N. Connelly (eds), *Evaluative Research in Social Care* (London: Heinemann), pp. 23–44.

Glendinning, C. (1983), *Unshared Care: Parents and their Disabled Children* (London: Routledge & Kegan Paul).

Glendinning, C. (1984), 'The resource worker project: evaluating a specialist social work service for severely disabled children and their families', *British Journal of Social Work*, vol. 14, no. 2, pp. 103–15.

Goffman, E. (1974), *Asylums* (Harmondsworth: Penguin).

Goldberg, E. M. (1970), *Helping the Aged* (London: Allen & Unwin).

Goldberg, E. M. (1984), 'Evaluation studies: past experience and possible future directions', *Research, Policy and Planning*, vol. 2, no. 1, pp. 1–6.

Goldberg, E. M., and Connelly, N. (eds) (1981), *Evaluative Research in Social Care* (London: Heinemann).

Goldberg, E. M., and Connelly, N. (1982), *The Effectiveness of Social Care for the Elderly* (London: Heinemann).

Hadley, R., Webb, A., and Farrell, C. (1975), *Across the Generations* (London: Allen & Unwin).

Hall, P. (1976), *Reforming the Welfare* (London: Heinemann).

Harris, A. I., Cox, E. and Smith, C. R. W. (1971/2), *Handicapped and Impaired in Great Britain* (London: OPCS/HMSO).

Hart, D., and Fassam, M. (1979), 'The role of the handicap specialist in Haringey Social Services Department', Research Report, Thomas Coram Research Unit, University of London.

Hegarty, S., and Pocklington, K. (1981), *Educating Pupils with Special Needs in the Ordinary School* (Windsor: NFER/Nelson).

Hill, M. (1980), 'Specialisation in field social work: a research perspective', in T. Booth, D. Martin and C. Melotte (eds), *Specialisation* (Birmingham: British Association of Social Workers), pp. 9–16.

HMSO (1957), *Report of the Royal Commission on Mental Illness and Mental Deficiency*, Cmnd 169 (London: HMSO).

HMSO (1966), *Health and Welfare: The Development of Community Care. Revision to 1975–76 of Plans for the Health and Welfare Services of the Local Authorities in England and Wales*, Cmnd 3022 (London: HMSO).

HMSO (1971), *Better Services for the Mentally Handicapped*, Cmnd 4683 (London: HMSO).

HMSO (1976), *Public Expenditure to 1979–80*, Cmnd 6393 (London: HMSO).

HMSO (1981), *Growing Older* (London: HMSO).

Homans, G. (1950), *The Human Group* (New York: Harcourt, Brace & World).

Imber, V. (1977), *A Classification of the English Personal Social Services Authorities*, DHSS Statistical and Research Report series, No. 16 (London: HMSO).

Jones, K. (1960), *Mental Health and Social Policy 1845–1959* (London: Routledge & Kegan Paul).

Jones, K., Brown, J., and Bradshaw, J. (1978), *Issues in Social Policy*, 1st edn (London: Routledge & Kegan Paul).

Keeble, U. (1979), *Aids and Adaptations* (London: Bedford Square Press).

Keeble, U. (1981), 'The disabled person's aids and adaptations', in D. Guthrie (ed.), *Disability: Legislation and Practice* (London: Macmillan), pp. 180–223.

Kew, S. (1975), *Handicap and Family Crisis* (London: Pitman).

Kiernan, C. (1982), 'Research, demonstration and dissemination project on social work involvement with the handicapped: final report', Research Report, Thomas Coram Research Unit, University of London.

Levin, E., Sinclair, I., and Gorbach, P. (1986), *Family Services and Confusion in Old Age* (London: Allen & Unwin).

McKay, A., Goldberg, E. M. and Fruin, D. J. (1973), 'Consumers and a social services department', *Social Work Today*, vol. 4, no. 16, pp. 486–91.

Mayer, J. E., and Timms, N. (1970), *The Client Speaks* (London: Routledge & Kegan Paul).

Meyer, H. J., Borgatta, E. F., and Jones, W. C. (1965), *Girls at Vocational High: An Experimental Study in Social Work Intervention* (New York: Russell Sage).

Moroney, R. M. (1976), *The Family and the State: Considerations for Social Policy* (London: Longman).

Morris, P. (1969), *Put Away* (London: Routledge & Kegan Paul).

National Development Group for the Mentally Handicapped (1977), *Mentally Handicapped Childen: A Plan for Action*, Pamphlet No. 2 (London: NDGMH).

National Institute for Social Work (NISW) (1982), *Social Workers, their Role and Tasks: Report of the Barclay Working Party* (London: Bedford Square Press).

Oliver, M. (1983), *Social Work with Disabled People* (London: Macmillan).

OPCS (1979), *General Household Survey 1977* (London: HMSO).

Oswin, M. (1971), *The Empty Hours* (London: Allen Lane).

Philp, M., and Duckworth, D. (1982), *Children with Disabilities and their Families: A Review of Research* (Windsor: NFER / Nelson).

Pincus, A., and Minahan, A. (1973), *Social Work Practice: Model and Method* (Itasca, Ill: Peacock).

Plank, M. (1982), *Teams for Mentally Handicapped People*, CMH Enquiry Paper No. 10 (London: Campaign for Mentally Handicapped People).

Pomeroy, D., Fewtrell, J., Butler, N., and Gill, R. (1978), *Handicapped Children: Their Homes and Lifestyles*, Housing Development Directorate Occasional Paper No. 4/78 (London: Department of the Environment).

Pugh, G. (1981), *Parents as Partners* (London: National Children's Bureau).

Pugh, G., and Russell, P. (1977), *Shared Care* (London: National Children's Bureau).

Rees, S. (1978), *Social Work Face to Face* (London: Edward Arnold).

Reid, W. J., and Hanrahan, P. (1981), 'The effectiveness of social work: recent evidence', in E. M. Goldberg and N. Connelly (eds), *Evaluative Research in Social Care* (London: Heinemann), pp. 9–20.

Reid, W. J., and Shyne, A. W. (1969), *Brief and Extended Casework* (New York: Columbia University Press).

Robinson, T. (1978), *In Worlds Apart* (London: Bedford Square Press).

Rutter, M., Graham, P., and Yule, W. (1970), *A Neuro-Psychiatric Study in Childhood* (London: Heinemann).

Sainsbury, E. (1975), *Social Work with Families* (London: Routledge & Kegan Paul).

Sainsbury, E., Nixon, S., and Phillips, D. (1982), *Social Work in Focus* (London: Routledge & Kegan Paul).

Seebohm Committee (1968), *Report of the Committee on Local Authority and Allied Personal Social Services*, Cmnd 3703 (London: HMSO).

Shearer, A. (1978), *A Community Service for Mentally Handicapped Children*, Barnardo Social Work Papers No. 4 (Barkingside: Dr Barnardo's).

Sheldon, B. (1983), 'The use of single case experimental designs in the evaluation of social work', *British Journal of Social Work*, vol. 13, no. 5, pp. 477–500.

Smith, G. (1980), *Social Need: Policy, Practice and Research* (London: Routledge & Kegan Paul).

Snowdon Working Party (1976), *Integrating the Disabled* (Horsham: National Fund for Research into Crippling Diseases).

Stevenson, J. (1980), 'Policy implications of the Seebohm Report', in M. Brown and S. Baldwin (eds), *The Yearbook of Social Policy in Britain 1978* (London: Routledge & Kegan Paul), pp. 151–78.

Stevenson, O. (1981), *Specialisation in Social Service Teams* (London: Allen & Unwin).

Stevenson, O., Parsloe, P., and Hill, M. (DHSS) (1978), *Social Services Teams: The Practitioner's View* (London: HMSO).

Townsend, P. (1962), *The Last Refuge* (London: Routledge & Kegan Paul).

Walker, A. (ed.) (1982), *Community Care: The Family, the State and Social Policy* (Oxford: Blackwell/Robertson).

Warnock Committee (1978), *Special Educational Needs: Report of the Committee of Enquiry into the Education of Handicapped Children and Young People*, Cmnd 7212 (London: HMSO).

Weale, J., and Bradshaw, J. (1980), 'Prevalence and characteristics of disabled children: findings from the 1974 General Household Survey', *Journal of Epidemiology and Community Health*, vol. 34, no. 2, pp. 11–18.

Webb, A., and Wistow, G. (1982), 'The personal social services: incrementalism, expediency or systematic social planning?', in A. Walker (ed.), *Public Expenditure and Social Policy* (London: Heinemann), pp. 137 64.

Wilkin, D. (1979), *Caring for the Mentally Handicapped Child* (London: Croom Helm).

Younghusband, E. (1978), *Social Work in Britain 1950–1975* (London: Allen & Unwin), Vol. 2.

Younghusband, E., Birchall, D., Davie, R., and Kellmer Pringle, M. (eds) (1970), *Living with Handicap* (London: National Children's Bureau).

Index

Numbers in italic refer to figures

Algie, J. 7, 17
Armstrong, G. 14
artificial limb and appliance centre
    (ALAC) Table 4.2, 58, 115
Association for Spina Bifida and
    Hydrocephalus (ASBAH) 61, 152
    social worker 68
attendance allowance 15, *4.6*, Table 4.6,
    161, 162–5, 189
    reviews 54, 164, 165
autism Table 3.2

Baldwin, S. 12, 13, 161
Barclay Committee of Inquiry 4, 6–7, 17
bathing problems *4.4*, 51, 95–7, 107, 188
    aids 95–7, 188
Bayley, M. 71, 204
bedding
    extra needs 52, 108, 110–11, *6.2*, 161,
    188
    protective 101–3, *6.1*, 188
blindness Table 3.2, Table 4.1, Table 4.3
Borgatta, E. F. *see* Meyer, J.
Borsay, A. 128
Bradshaw, J. 12, 13, 14, 28, 30, 33, 36,
    162, 184
Browne, E. T. 14, 17
Burden, R. L. 30

Campbell, D. T. *see* Cook, T. D
careers advice 47, *4.2*, 148–51
    officer 47, Table 4.4
Caro, Francis G. 19
car seats 49, 119
Central Council for Education and
    Training in Social Work (CCETSW)
    6, 17
cerebral palsy Table 3.2
    see also Spastics Society
Challis, D. 9, 19
Chartered Institute of Public Finance
    Accountancy (CIPFA) 28
Cheshire Home 149
Chessum, R. *see* Challis, D.
Chronically Sick and Disabled Persons Act
    7, 15
clothing – extra needs 52, 108, 110, 111,
    6.2, 161, 188

community care 1–5, 9, 185, 200
    and disabled children 1, 12, 14–18, 185
    and elderly 2, 3, 200
    and mentally handicapped 1–3, 199
    and social work 4–5, 9, 204–6
    Kent Community Care Scheme 9
    see also informal carers
community health services
    medical officer Table 4.2
    nursing services 15
    see also health visitor, incontinence
Community Mental Handicap Team 199
Connelly, N. 4
Cook, T. D. 195
Cooke, K. 162
Court Committee of Inquiry 14, 17, 18,
    199
Curtis Committee 2

Davies, B. 9, 19
deafness Table 3.2, Table 4.1, Table 4.3
Disability Alliance 62
Disabled Living Foundation 61–2
disablement resettlement officer 15
District Handicap Team 199
Down's syndrome Table 3.2
Dr Barnardo's 24–5, 65, 67, 69, 87, 205
dressing problems *4.4*, 95, 97–8, 107, 188
Duckworth, D. *see* Philp, M.

education services 14, *4.2*, 45–7, Table
    4.7, 142–5
    aids *4.7*, 151–2, 191
    benefits 54, *4.6*, Table 4.6, 170
    contact with schools 45, Table 4.4, 59,
    62, *4.7*, 66, 142–3, 145–8, 189
    welfare officer Table 4.1, Table 4.4, 69
Equal Opportunities Commission (EOC)
    3

family care 41–2, 172, 176–8, 187, 190,
    195, 200
Family Fund
    applications to 28, 31, 49, 52, 109, 110,
    111, 120, 125, 156, 157, 161, 169,
    Table 9.1
    establishment of 12
    research on 12–13

resource workers' background in 24
family income supplement (FIS) 54, *4.6*,
170
Farrell, C. *see* Hadley, R.
Fassam, M. *see* Hart, D.
feeding problems *4.4*, 51, 95, 97, 98
aids 98
footwear
extra needs *4.4*, 52, 108, 110–11, *6.2*
Fox, A. M. 13
Fruin, D. *see* McKay, A.

gardens
alterations to 52, *4.5*, 54, 123, 124, 132,
133, 189
Gath, A. 174
General Household Survey (GHS) 32–3,
36, Table 3.3, Table 3.4
general practitioner 34, Table 4.2
Gibbons, J. 27
Glendinning, C. 12, 13, 17, 161
Goffman, E. 3
Goldberg, E. M. 4, 8, 9, 25, 27, 71
Gorbach, P. *see* Levin, E
Graham, P. *see* Rutter, M.

Hadley, R. 71
Hall, P. 6, 8
Hanrahan, P. 8, 197
Harris, A. I. 12
Hart, D. 17
health centres *see* general practitioner
health visitor 12, 13, 15, 34, Table 4.1, 42,
Table 4.2, 58, 89
heating
extra needs 111, 114, 161
Hegarty, S. 14
Hill, M. 6, 7, 17
holidays
for child alone 47, *4.3*, *4.7*, Table 4.7,
156–8, 189
for family 47, *4.3*, *4.7*, 142, 155–6, 161,
169, 189
play schemes *4.3*, 49, 154–5
Homans, G. 195
hospital
admissions 47, 92–3
consultant Table 4.2, 58, 92
outpatient visits 43, 94–5
school 47
social worker Table 4.1, Table 4.3, 58,
69, 92
transport to 43, 49, *4.1*, Table 4.2, 92–5
housing 52–4

adaptations 35, *4.5*, 59–60, *4.7*, Table
4.5, Table 4.7, *5.3*, *5.6*, 96, 123–4,
127–31, 188–9
benefits 54, *4.6*, Table 4.6, 170
moving house *4.5*, Table 4.5, *5.6*,
125–7, 188–9
hydrocephalus *see* spina bifida

Imber, V. 28
incontinence 15, *4.4*, 51, 58, 95, 107, 108,
109, 188
aids Table 4.7, 101–5
training 99–100
informal carers 4, 5, 9, 185, 203–4, 206
of the elderly 5, 9, 200
of disabled children 14, 16–17, 185,
203–4
support for 4–5, 9, 11, 204
see also community care
invalid care allowance (ICA) 54

Jones, W. C. *see* Meyer, J.

Keeble, U. 17, 128
Kew, S. 172
key worker role
and resource workers 10, 19–21, 201–4
for all disabled children 199, 201–6
Kiernan, C. 142

laundry problems *4.4*, 51, *4.7*, 108–10
equipment 109, 161 188
Lawton, D. 28, 30, 33, 162, 184
Levin, E. 5, 204
local authority
architect's department 60, Table 4.5,
127, 128
chief executive's department 60, Table
4.5
environmental health department 60,
Table 4.5, 127, 128
housing department 60, Table 4.5, 125,
127, 128, 131
planning department 60, Table 4.5, 127
Luckett, R. *see* Challis, D.

malaise inventory 30, 183, 190
marital problems 56, *4.7*, 174–6, 190
maternal health 172, 178, 182–4, 190–1
Mayer, J. E. 71
McKay, A. 71
MENCAP (Royal Society for Mentally
Handicapped Children and Adults)
61
see also mental handicap

mental handicap 42, Table 4.3, 123
and community care 1–3, 199
Development Team for 199, 205
see also MENCAP
Meyer, J. 27
Minahan, A. *see* Pincus, A.
mobility allowance 15, *4.6*, Table 4.6, 161,
162, 165–6, 189
appeals 54, 165–6
mobility problems 43, *4.1*. *4.3*, 49, *4.7*,
92–4, 108, 114–18, 119, 120–1, 123,
143, 145, 159, 161, 188
aids 43, 51, *4.7*, Table 4.7, 114–18,
191
Moroney, R. M. 3
Morris, P. 3
Motability 119, 188

NAIDEX 62
night time care 106–7, 161, 188
Nixon, S. *see* Sainsbury, E.
non contributory invalidity pension
(NCIP) 54, *4.6*, 161, 168, 170

occupational therapist 15, 17, Table 4.2,
Table 4.3, 89, 115
Oliver, M. 71
orange parking badge 119, 120
Oswin, M. 3

Parsloe, P. 6, 7, 17
Perthes disease 68
Phillips, D. *see* Sainsbury, E.
Philp, M. 30, 183, 184
physiotherapist 15, Table 4.2
Pincus, A. 19
Pinker, R. 6–7
Plank, M. 199
Pocklington, K. *see* Hegarty, S.
Pomeroy, D. 13–14, 30, 182, 183
probation officer 39
psychologist 14, 15, Table 4.1, Table 4.2,
58, Table 4.4
Pugh, G. 200

RADAR (Royal Association for Disability
and Rehabilitation) 62
reading problems 91–2
Rees, S. 71
Reid, W. J. 8, 27, 197
REMAP (Rehabilitation Engineering
Movement Advisory Panels) 62
residential care 2–3, 9, *4.2*, 47, Table 4.3,
59, Table 4.7, *4.7*, 65, 179, 199

resource workers
advice giving 39, 42, 47, 51, 56, 73, 84,
85, 86, 186, 202
advocacy 42, 57, 62, 76–7, 191, 193
counselling 42, 56, *5.5*, *5.6*, 81–2, 186
interviews with 30–1, 64–6
liaison by 42, 47, 73, *5.5*, *5.6*, 193
records kept by 30, 37, 42, 128, 186
recruitment of 22–5, 186
referrals by 42, 52, *4.5*, 69, 128, 191,
193
respite care 5, *4.2*, 47, Table 4.3, 59, 65,
Table 4.7, *4.7*, 142, 158–60, 189, 200
Robinson, T. 71
Royal Commission on Civil Liability and
Compensation for Personal Injury 14
Russell, P. *see* Pugh, G.
Rutter, M. 30

Sainsbury, E. 71
schools *see* education services
Seebohm Committee 5, 6, 7, 16
Shearer, A. 200
Sheldon, B. 192
Shyne, A. W. 27
siblings 56, *4.7*, 172–4, 176–7, 190
Sinclair, I. *see* Levin, E.
Snowdon Working Party 6
social services
evaluation of 1, 7–11, 13–14, 185, 196–8
future development of 9, 204–6
organisation of 1, 4–7, 16–17, 185, 200,
204
priorities within 4–5, 9, 185, 203
resources within 3, 9
supply of adaptations 127, 128, 131
supply of aids 17, 35
see also social workers
social workers
families' contacts with 12–14, 15, 34–5,
Table 3.5, 37–9, Table 4.1, 42, 89
priorities among 16–17
specialisation among 1, 5–7, 16–17, 200,
203
see also social services
Social Work Service Development Group
5, 9
Spastics Society 61, 152
see also cerebral palsy
speech therapist 15, 51, Table 4.2, 91
spina bifida Table 3.2
see also Association for Spina Bifida and
Hydrocephalus
Stevenson, J. 8

Stevenson, O. 6, 7, 17
Sunningdale seminar on disablement 18
supplementary benefit 54, *4.6*, Table 4.6,
    61, 161, 189
  for disabled teenagers 168–9
  for families 166–8

telephone installations 111–13, 188
Timms, N. *see* Mayer, J. E.
toileting problems 95, 99, 100
  aids 100–1, 188
Townsend, P. 3
toy libraries 151–2

voluntary organisations Table 4.1, 49,
    61–2, Table 4.7, *4.7*, 89, 128, 129,
    152–4, 159, 185

see also Association for Spina Bifida and
    Hydrocephalus, Disabled Living
    Foundation, MENCAP, NAIDEX,
    RADAR, REMAP, Spastics Society

Walker, A. 4
Warnock Committee 14, 17, 18, 199,
    202
Weale, J. 33, 36
Webb, A. 8, 71
wheelchairs *see* mobility problems
Wilkin, D. 172, 174
Wistow, G. 8

Younghusband, E. 13, 86
Yule, W. *see* Rutter, M.